by *Jane Bowles*

Two Serious Ladies (novel) (1943)
In the Summer House (play) (1954)
Plain Pleasures (stories) (1966)
The Collected Works of Jane Bowles (1966)
Feminine Wiles (1976)
My Sister's Hand in Mine (1978)

by *Millicent Dillon*

Baby Perpetua and Other Stories (1971)
The One In the Back Is Medea (novel) (1973)
*A Little Original Sin: The Life and Work of
    Jane Bowles* (1981)

OUT IN THE WORLD

SELECTED LETTERS OF JANE BOWLES
1935–1970

EDITED BY MILLICENT DILLON

BLACK SPARROW PRESS • SANTA ROSA • 1990

OUT IN THE WORLD: The Selected Letters of Jane Bowles, 1935-1970.
Copyright © 1985 by Paul Frederic Bowles.

INTRODUCTION AND NOTES.
Copyright © 1985 by Millicent Dillon.

The cover portrait was painted by Maurice Grosser in 1947 and is reproduced here with the permission of the artist.

LIBRARY OF CONGRESS CATALOGING IN PUBLICATION DATA

Bowles, Jane Auer, 1917-1973.
    Out in the world.
    1. Bowles, Jane Auer, 1917-1973—Correspondence.
2. Authors, American—20th century—Correspondence.
I. Dillon, Millicent. II. Title.
PS3503.0837Z48   1985   818'.5209 (B)   84-24470
ISBN 0-87685-626-1
ISBN 0-87685-625-3 (pbk.)

Second Printing

Introduction

Tennessee Williams considered Jane Bowles to be the most underrated writer in American literature. To John Ashbery she was "one of the finest modern writers of fiction, in any language."

Her body of work is small: one novel, *Two Serious Ladies*, one play, *In the Summer House*, and six short stories, all completed by the time she was in her early thirties. Thereafter, in notebook after notebook she attempted to bring other works to completion but always stopped—or was stopped. (The story of her struggle to write is described in *A Little Original Sin: The Life and Work of Jane Bowles*.

This volume contains one hundred and thirty-three letters spanning the years 1935 to 1970. They begin with Jane Bowles's late teenage years in Greenwich Village, her marriage to the writer-composer Paul Bowles, and the writing of *Two Serious Ladies* in Mexico in the early Forties. Subsequent letters detail her decision to go to Morocco (where Paul Bowles had gone in 1947), her arrival in Tangier, and her beginning struggle with her writer's block, coincident with her passion for the Arab women she met. The letters continue from Paris and New York and once again from Tangier, through the onset of her terrible illness—she suffered a severe stroke at age forty—through her battle for recovery, to the words eked out before her final silence in a convent hospital in Malaga in 1973.

A major proportion of the letters are written to her husband. Another large group are addressed to her friend Libby Holman. (A number of letters to Holman, previously unpublished in whole or in part, were released by the Holman estate for use in this volume.) A number of the letters are "agonizers," a term Jane Bowles used to describe her attempts to speak about her obsessions. They are the explicit record of her anguish about what has to be done, what has not been done, and what may never be done.

Out in the World is the name of a novel Jane Bowles began in the late Forties and never completed. She envisioned in the work, she told her husband, a departure from the style of *Two Serious Ladies*. *Out in the World* would be classical—nineteenth century—in style and in structure. Partway into the narrative she wrote in a notebook, "This is a book about travesties, and about two different generations. Emmy Moore represents the one and Andrew McLain the other." (Emmy Moore is a childless middle-aged woman who, at the urging of her husband Paul, goes to a hotel in a New England town to write. There she keeps slipping into evasions, drinking and flirtations with women. Andrew McLain is a shy secretive young man, who falls in love with a young soldier, Tommy, and is forced to examine the evasions of his own childhood.)

The word "travesty," defined as burlesque imitation or parody, carries with it the implication of disclosure of that which has been hidden. The disclosure Jane Bowles never brought to finality in her novel is accomplished in these letters. They are exercises in literary precision, as she told Paul, and they are exercises in emotional accuracy as well. In the search for this precision she felt compelled to examine all decisions, whether large or small, in terms of their consequences. To Jane Bowles all choices were ultimately moral choices.

The sequence of the letters reflects accurately the change in her style of existence: from the early sense of certainty in her powers of wit and charm, to the puzzlement about what happened to that certainty after her affair with Helvetia Perkins, to her wonderment as to her place and future course as a writer. The letters to Paul after her trip to Taprobane (Sri Lanka) with him and Ahmed Yacoubi divulge her terror and the sense of what is slipping away from her. The letters immediately after the stroke show her trying to discover and reveal what has happened to her.

(In a composition for a speech therapist in New York, not included in this book, she explained that she could not write: "If it is a failure of the will—then my will is sick—it is not lazyness . . . but there is such a thing as a failure of the will which is agony for the person who suffers from it. I did not suffer a stroke for nothing at my age—age—and I have gone far away down the path of no return . . .")

In her letters from Tangier from 1960 on, when she had recovered to a certain extent from her stroke, she tried not to reveal the fears of her own imminent decline. But from 1966 on, when the ultimate decline began, she had little else to speak of. The final letters, written in the convent hospital in Malaga, as she was losing all capacity to see and hear and speak, reveal her effort to write a single word, now the equivalent of what once was the effort to write an entire narrative.

*   *   *

Jane Bowles's letters written *before* her stroke have been corrected for inconsequential and erratic errors of spelling and punctuation. Written at top speed, often by hand, the letters prove what she said to Paul, that she didn't care about spelling or punctuation. The letters written after her stroke are printed here as they were written, since from then on her errors became a source of great concern to her.

It was Jane Bowles's custom never to date a letter, though occasionally she might begin with "Monday" or "the fourth," so the dating of all letters is an estimation based on the context of known events in her life. The exceptions to this uncertainty are the letters from the Holman collection, since the envelopes were retained and the posting date is in most instances legible.

*   *   *

I want to thank the following for permission to reprint letters here: Jack Clareman and the estate of Libby Holman, Ruth Fainlight, Isabelle Gerofi, Katharine Hamill, Natasha von Hoershelman, the estate of Spivy LeVoe, Miriam Levy, George McMillan, Gordon Sager, Lawrence Stewart, Virgil Thomson, the Humanities Research Center at the University of Texas at Austin, the Hedgerow Theater, the Mugar Memorial Library at Boston University, the Beinicke Library and Music Library at Yale University, and the Katherine Cowen De Baillou Collection at the University of Georgia Libraries, Special Collection.

I want to thank Alison Wilson for assistance with the typing of the manuscript.

I wish to acknowledge, once again, my debt to Paul Bowles for his kind assistance and cooperation.

I have chosen to insert brief passages from Jane Bowles's novel, *Out in the World*, at various places in this volume. Fragments of an incomplete novel, they illuminate and are illuminated by the life in these letters.

Millicent Dillon

7

Contents

Out in the World

The Selected Letters of Jane Bowles

1935–1970

From Out in the World
(Andrew's story)

He was sitting in an upstairs parlor that had served as his nursery throughout his childhood. His cousin Julia Hammet came into the room talking and laughing. His throat was cold. He would have left had he not been told to remain. He was going to eat with her . . . He was ashamed of his food but it was the only food he could eat. His food was sweet and natural to him but like his naked body it was shameful. No other child should see it: He knew they wanted to attack his food, perhaps to throw it on the floor and stamp on it. Any child's food looked like the food of any other child but his food was like the food of a foreign child — humiliating freakish food and at the same time sweet and natural to him, the only food he could eat . . .

In 1935, at the age of eighteen, Jane Auer was living in the Hyde Park Hotel in New York with her mother, Claire Stajer Auer. Sidney Auer, Jane's father, had died in 1930. From 1932 until 1934 Jane had been in a sanatorium in Leysin, Switzerland, for treatment of tuberculosis in the bone of her knee. On her return to New York she was operated on and her right leg permanently stiffened.

In New York she began a novel in French, Le Phaéton Hypocrite, *but spent most of her time exploring Greenwich Village.*

The first letter is to George McMillan, a young man who was working in a Village club as doorman, bouncer, and cashier. The incident that precipitated the letter was Jane's running away from home after a fight with her mother. She had been found in Greenwich Village by her Aunt Constance and brought back to her mother's apartment.

1

Jane Bowles to George McMillan
The Hyde Park Hotel [Letterhead]
Twenty-five East Seventy-Seventh Street
New York
[1935]

Dear George,

Here's what happened when I arrived home. (Connie was lying about taking me to her place but I didn't raise a kick. I knew I'd be with Mother sooner or later anyway.)

Mother was potting around the kitchen (anticlimax) and Aunt Flo was wrapped up in Uncle Carl's bathrobe. Whenever there's grief around, women always accumulate blankets, men's overcoats, hot water bottles, woolen scarfs.

They whisked me into the bedroom while Mother finished gnawing at her roast beef bone. Connie said, "Get undressed, dear."

13

She was at the burping stage and felt very ill as she had told us once or twice in the car.

I remained dressed—they were four against one anyway. Then Mother came in, in the awful black kimono she had on the night you were here. She said, "What's this?"

I took an arrogant stand. I had a "Who are these people" look on my face and "I must get back down to the party."

Then Connie started in: Now Claire, you know I don't feel well and I've been looking for Jane for four hours and I was cold and—

Mother: Well, what has Jane to say for herself?

Jane: Nothing. I don't know why I'm here.

Connie: Now Jane, you know that's not true! You wanted to come back. She told me she couldn't hurt you, Claire!

Hysterics on my part here—I don't know quite what I said but I know I almost killed the poor woman and started cursing myself because I couldn't hurt her.

Then she kissed me and they all sat down and said what a wonderful girl I was and what a fine young man you were—and that if I still wanted to marry you twenty-five years from now I could—that Mother wouldn't think of standing in the way of my happiness—and that I was a grand normal girl—and that this Lesbian business was just an adolescent phase (adolescence being from seven to thirty-three in our family) and that if only I didn't have such an analytic mind I certainly would throw it off—and if I really were a Lesbian they'd get up a fund for me and send me down to the Village in my own private bus (I suggested that they might organize picnics for all us girls every two weeks), but I really wasn't one so they couldn't let me go to my ruin!

Aunt Flo suggested 130 more men to straighten me out—Aunt Connie 135. The same remedy seems to go for you and the Les's— like 3 in 1 Oil, or bleeding in the Middle Ages.

In two weeks I shall leave for college—Rollins down South (Florida).

They have beautiful low white buildings. "We have the best equipped dorms in the U.S.A.," says Pres. Holt, "and we hope to suck enough of the rich students' blood so as to be able to install a radio in every room, which will look very well in our catalogue."

It is a modern college and you can specialize in anything you please—conferences they have instead of lectures.

I have been writing this letter for three days. Mother always comes in when I get started. George, pardon the tone of all this but I'm trying to counterbalance all the emotion and drama that's

14

been hanging between us so that we could hardly see each other.

You may come to see me! And tell Lupe anything you like. She hasn't called me since the night you were here.

Love to you—

Jane

Miriam Fligelman had been a childhood friend of Jane's in Woodmere, New York. Miriam had visited Jane in 1935 on her honeymoon trip, following her marriage to Irving Levy.

2

Jane Bowles to Miriam Fligelman Levy
[New York City, New York]
[1936]

My Dear Miriam

Trust me—I'm not going to say anything trite such as "Better late than never" or "Excuse the delay, but I've been so busy."

My problem is much bigger and deeper.

I find myself staring at my writing materials from the couch as though they were "Nazis."

I get nauseous at the thought of putting a pen to paper for any purpose, literary or otherwise. This incapability of mine to "act" is spreading. I stare at my corset for hours now before I put it on.

I am perfectly serious and solemn about the whole thing.

I feel particularly badly about not having written you because I remember the emphatic way in which I agreed that we must not—absolutely must not—lose contact this time and that I would certainly write. Either I don't know myself or I'm a confounded skillful liar.

I thought about you for such a long time after you left—your face that looks just like little Miriam's in a magnifying glass—now—your subdued voice and the Russian toque which you were somehow destined to wear.

The silliness of your being married first—you with your inky hands and your ten thousand books and your skinniness—you were so thin you looked like a drawing instead of a person.

To think you would deceive me too—and develop into a real human being.

I'm sitting in my living room with an old purple cover over me. The sun is in the room and the walls (remember they are yellow) glow. Little strips of sky shine thru the Venetian blinds like blue birds' wings and the mirror that stretches between the two windows takes on a green reflection like a pond.

All this is very soothing to a convalescent. I am recovering from a carefully nurtured grippe. It seems as though it just won't linger any longer—too bad.

Soon I shall be back in bed reading. As I look down my life I see one picture: "me in bed reading." The only difference is that the heap under the bedclothes grew larger.

As you see you will get no news from me today. I prefer irrelevant detail. I never will write you any news probably—unless I marry—and then I shall probably insert a sentence or two about it between a description of a rice pudding and a thumb-nail sketch of Miss Foulke.[1] I depend on you for facts, Walter Winchell, and plenty of them because I love reading them.

You have noticed my slipshod sentences and my repetition of words and my hundreds of prepositional phrases and my bad handwriting. It is because I am still nothing but a precocious child—and am I even precocious?

You have my sincerest love Miriam dearest—write me.

Jane

Tell Irving, "I like his looks." Don't by any means show him this. I am in one of my less lucid moments.

The following letter was written in January 1937 from Deal Beach, New Jersey, where Jane and her mother had spent several summers. Apparently Jane had gone there to be alone and write, challenged to do so by her friend Genevieve Phillips.

[1] A former English teacher.

3

Jane Bowles to "Spivy" LeVoe[2]
Deal Beach, New Jersey
[January 29, 1937]

Dear Spivy—

I am all alone in a great big bed, twenty feet wide. Send me homeless Italian family at once. Man and wife retired at ten thirty. She sat all day twirling a long strand of hair round and round her second finger. Had a glassy look in her eye. At dinner they played foot games underneath the table. Neither of them seems to know who I am.

The "apartment-by-the-sea" is very cold, very quiet, and very sad. I know that the janitor has been lying dead in the basement for weeks under ten feet of water. In the field at our left are the corpses of twenty million crickets. They died on Labor Day. There is also a picnic basket with a dead water rat in it. Sorry to report that the ocean is not pink. The house is rocking in the wind. We sail at any minute I'm sure. Did you know that in New Jersey the wind has a pale lavender nose and a big fat pigtail tied with a whip? Well, it doesn't—really. I'm expecting the Morro Castle ghosts in a half an hour. They sank right outside my window.

I am distressed because Mother is taking me to Havana in three weeks—almost definitely. I'll either be eaten by sharks on the way or I'll marry a Latin and all my children will be born with earrings. I don't want to go to Havana, Spivy. I wonder if you've had your coffee yet. I'm starving. I ate meat balls that tasted like German bullets for dinner.

Drop me a note and I'll have them forward it to New York if I suddenly get weak or hungry and come home. I'll try my best not to because Genevieve would be furious—why I don't know. I won't come home—really.

Love to you, Miss Spivy

Jane

---

2 Owner of a New York nightclub.

Note for LaTouche:[3]
How do you do—LaTouche

P.S.   Give my regards to the Malfis and write me a sad, sad letter if you write at all. It doesn't matter really—just a whim.

I kees you!

Rudolf

4

Jane Bowles to Miriam Levy
Hotel Meurice [Letterhead]
145 West 58th Street,
New York City, New York
[February, 1937]

My Dear Miriam—

Just received the letter and am sitting down in my fur coat answering it. Will probably get "La Grippe." For Heaven's sake don't name any babies Jane—ever—unless you're a sadist. I'm very jittery about this. I simply can't connect you with a baby. Why only a minute ago we were going to school. Life suddenly seems as short as a pistol shot. After this will you please address me as a "Maiden Aunt" or something. My God, I'm not anywhere near getting married. I know I've been a beast again about writing but I guess I always shall be. You ought to know by now that that does not mean I've forgotten you but simply that I hardly know how to spell.

I am having a very lovely time here with many mad people—artists and pseudo-artists but very night-clubby. As usual I am surrounded by musical people, I who dislike everything but "Swing."

I am very very blue at the moment. I wasn't when I started this letter—my moods are getting almost pathological.

It's so cold and the winter's so long and there seems nothing to

[3] John LaTouche, who later wrote the lyrics for *Cabin in the Sky*, *Beggar's Holiday*, and *The Golden Apple*, as well as a number of other Broadway productions.

experience that I haven't experienced before. I'm tired of loving and being loved. I'm sick of my own voice and I hate books. I'm not even hungry.

I hope you have the most beautiful baby in the world, and I wish you lots of luck.

I shall now go and drink myself to death for a few hours and what is more I shall have no hangover, for which all my friends loathe me.

Please write me some more news. I'll write you a real letter soon, this is just a hurry note.

All my Love

Jane

In the winter of 1937 Jane met Paul Bowles through John LaTouche. Shortly afterwards she went to Mexico with Paul and Kristians Tonny, a Dutch painter, and Tonny's wife, Marie Claire. Jane ended the trip abruptly and went on to Arizona and then California before returning to New York.

5

Jane Bowles to Miriam Levy
Hotel Meurice [Letterhead]
145 West 58th Street
New York City, New York
[June, 1937]

My darling darling friend

I have been in Mexico I have been in Arizona I have been in California. I did not know you had a baby—it's beautiful. I am in the middle of a novel—and Big dramas all around me. I'm not sure whether I'll come out on top there are so many things against me. Believe me Miriam I would have written you if I had known. I was very ill in Mexico. I can't write you now—I was on my way out when I got your letter and I was so horrified at what you must think was carelessness on my part that I had to sit down and write. Darling the baby *is* beautiful but is it a boy or a girl — I must know — and the name? I am so glad you were persistent and wrote me. I lost all my addresses in the desert somewhere. I should love to visit you. Will you write me and tell me whether you are really serious or not and how soon or how late I can come? We have all year of course — there is no hurry.

Please believe me I appreciate your loyalty.

Love

Jane — your vagrant friend.

6

Jane Bowles to Virgil Thomson
Asbury Park, New Jersey
[August 31, 1937]

Friday

Dear Virgil —

Il n'y a pas de plume dans ma grande maison. I want to thank you mille fois de m'avoir invitée au prevue. Nous aimons tellement ta musique. I hope you were not sad that Paul and I did not wait at the bar. Il faisait chaud — on n'avait pas d'argent — la valise pesait — Paul dormait debout — but I worried a lot about it once we were in Jamaica. Maybe you would have come with us and maybe you wanted to talk.

I hope you were a good Massachusetts man and that you will come and spend some time with us on your return. And you can bring your Maggie [Marion Dunham]. I send her a big kiss. Do not tell anyone but I have written three chapters of a bad first novel — anyway c'est de la merde — régulière. Je travaille tous les jours cinq ou six heures.

Lots of Love —

Janie

20

In February 1937 Jane married Paul Bowles. Immediately after the wedding they set out on a honeymoon trip to Central America and France.

7

Jane Bowles to Virgil Thomson
[Postcard]
San Jose, Costa Rica
[March 23, 1938]

We are doing what Pavlik used to do to Gertrude, so she said: J'ai rêvé à vous cette nuit.[4] We discuss them in the morning when they occur. [Paul's handwriting]

Scarcely any Indian blood here — my darling Virgil. I shall write you all about Costa Rica. [Jane's handwriting]

Love,

Jane

8

Jane Bowles to Virgil Thomson
[Postcard]
Guatemala
[April 21, 1938]

Dearest Virgil —

Think of you once daily at least — Lake — Indians — a couple of more volcanoes. I want to go to *Trinidad*. I like ports best — they're full of negroes and camelote. The inside of the country is always

---

[4] According to Paul Bowles: "Gertrude Stein told me that Pavel Tchelitchew used to tell her, 'J'ai rêvé à vous cette nuit.' She thought it absurd."

Saint Peter's University Library
Jersey City, New Jersey 07306

high true and beautiful. I don't know when we'll arrive in Paris—
the end of May or the end of June.

So much love to you—

Jane.

9

Jane Bowles to Virgil Thomson
[Èze-Village, France]
[1938]

Dear Virgil,

That was an awfully nice writeup you gave Paul, and such a
beautiful picture of him on top. You know how much I would like
to see you and how sweet and how clever I always thought you
were. Baby there ain't nobody here at all but do they love each
other. Some hautes Dykes from Cagnes sur Mer, on the corner of
the Avenida Delicias and Las Palmas and otherwise row upon row
of pederasts. C'est même pas bon, pour passer le temps.
Quand-même un peu. The climate is really beautiful and good for
lunatics. J'aime ma maison et j'apprends à faire des gateaux et des
puddings. Aussi je suis de temps en temps à la récherche d'une idée.
Je t'assure qu'il ny en a pas qui volent autour, ici. Plenty of liquor
but don't want it. Perhaps I shall see you soon but I doubt it. I'm
so glad that you are a critic.

So much love

Jane

*In September 1938 Jane and Paul returned to the U.S.
for Paul to work on music for the Mercury Theater. By
the spring of 1939 they had rented an old farmhouse on
Woodrow Road in Staten Island. There Jane worked on*
Two Serious Ladies *and Paul on his opera* Denmark Vesey.

10

Jane Bowles to Mary Oliver[5]
[1116 Woodrow Road]
[Staten Island, New York]
[Summer, 1939]

Dear Mary Oliver,

I would be so delighted to have you and your German maid come to Staten Island (S.I.). First I shall explain about money and then I shall go on. Paul earns at the moment twenty-two dollars a week on W.P.A. (music project) and that is what we live on. I'm perfectly willing to take a chance on our all eating on that if you are. There are many exceedingly cheap foods such as rice, potatoes and faroja—faroja is a strange Brazilian flour which you brown in butter and salt. You receive it by mail from a Mr. Silver in Brooklyn. There are also the excellent Brazilian black beans which when cooked with a lump or two of fatty meat and a great deal of garlic make an exceedingly tasty dish. Two people or rather four people are not twice as expensive to feed as two, strangely enough. And if you ever do get a little money while you are here I might tell you that around eight dollars will feed two people for a week. Paul will probably stop getting his checks suddenly anyway and then we will all be in the soup, which doesn't frighten me. The only people who must eat are Paul and the cats. Paul is extremely desperate and neurotic if he doesn't. I have explained all this to you because I want you to know what you are getting into. We would all have a place to live as the rent has been paid until November the fifteenth. I daresay we might get some friends such as Harry Dunham who has paid half of the rent to keep it with us another month or two. As for room during the week there are two extra beds. On many weekends Harry Dunham comes down with his fiancée, therefore one bed is occupied. I have two very fine mattresses which we bought in Nice and three thick sofa cushions all of which could be made into an adequate bed which I would be glad to sleep on when there were extras. A German man slept on them last summer on the roof for weeks so it would be no hardship for whoever gets them. I myself have a huge inner spring mattress on a straw mat which sleeps at least three and many extra

[5] Mary Oliver—a friend of Paul's who had helped him in Paris in 1929.

ladies have slept with me on weekends. Paul has one too but he refuses to share it with anyone. You can see that there is enough room presenting no problem at all during the week and really none on the weekend as weekends are always very complicated or terribly simple and rainy and lonely.

We have now dispensed with the purely physical aspects of your visit if there is to be one. Paul is terribly worried that you might not like the house. He wants you to know it is like a little cottage in Glenora. We have no servant and very few rugs. At any rate you can see no other house from our grounds. We are surrounded by fields rather dry. I do not think it's depressing. There are fruit trees and a rotten vegetable garden. Harry Dunham just arrived, and he is a wonderful person to have around. We go into New York City once a week. One can get there for around forty-five cents so you could if you liked see your friends when you wanted to. And for people with cars it is no effort at all to drive out here nor does it take much time at all. The only thing that worries me is that you might be bored as Paul is working on his opera and I on my book, but he says you love to read. In the evenings we can play games and drink champagne. I am not working every minute of the time but I must finish it while we still have a roof over our heads and I am always tempted to chat and lazy around. If you do not think it will be too awful we would really love to have you. I myself am always completely happy when there are three people in the house and four people will be a real *nest*.

Please let us know if you will come. Elsie Houston, a singer, is here at the moment for a few days. If you do come and she is still here I am sure you will like her. I am looking forward to meeting you. Paul will write you details of how to come. If you can phone long distance from where you are our number is Tottenville 8-1392. It would be the same price as phoning New York City perhaps a dime more.

Yours,

Jane (Bowles)

24

11

Jane Bowles to Charles Henri Ford
[1116 Woodrow Road]
[Staten Island, New York]
[Fall, 1939]

Dear Charles,

I am so glad you and Pavlick [Tchelitchew] are settled in your barn. I went to New York yesterday and I ended up on Columbus Avenue. I started to sweat. No means of locomotion seemed plausible. I will not live in New York. I think we shall try and find a house nearer the other end of [the] island so as to be able to get in very easily. Mary Oliver will probably take an apartment in New York and the three of us will live between the two places. I think it is very necessary to be able to get out of New York the minute you want to. More important than getting into it. We will only have this place until November first and we shall try and get our things moved a little ahead of our time and then come to your party if you'll let us with free minds. Mary has many friends whom she hasn't seen in a long time near Norwalk and it is possible that we shall be able to get a night's lodging with one or the other of them. Living the way we do it is delightful to be invited to a party a long way off. I am asking your permission for Mary to come although it is hardly necessary as she is the nicest lady in the whole world. You must tell Pavlick that she is the friend of Dilkousha [Princesse de Rohan] and Katousha. I was rather upset about what you wrote concerning Robeson and the other *Denmark*. I shall take matters into my own hands and phone Juanita Hall immediately because Paul is a slow person. Juanita said earlier in the summer that she would introduce Paul to him as she thought Paul Robeson would be excited about the opera. He was then abroad. I am going to call Juanita this evening. Of course the opera isn't finished. Paul hasn't worked this week because we got into debt. Since the arrival of Mrs. Oliver our life has been quite exciting and there are a lot of changes in the house. I hope Paul will work next week. He wrote another beautiful song in *Denmark* and if you were sweet you and Parker Tyler both, you would weep when you heard it. I will let you know if anything happens as a result of my call to Juanita. Good luck to you both and please write again. I always like your poems. I hope you will like my book. I hope to get it finished this month if too many upsetting things don't happen.

Jane Bowles

In 1940 Jane and Paul and a friend, Robert Faulkner, went to Mexico. In Taxco Jane met Helvetia Perkins, a forty-five year old divorcee. By the end of 1941 Jane had finished writing Two Serious Ladies.

12

Jane Bowles to Virgil Thomson
Taxco, Mexico
[Late December, 1941]

My dear Virgil,

I hope that you are well and happy and that you are in New York. Mr. Saroyan is not here. Mother writes that you were under the impression that he was but Paul *is* working on a script of his. I have finished my novel — it seems like a long time but I spent two months in a very bad humor rewriting and drinking and finally threw half of it away and wrote half a new novel — which is an experience I should not like to go through again. After a while it was fun but the beginning was dreadful. I intend to come to New York in a month or so and try to publish. Do you have any ideas about the "state of publishing" as a result of the war? Is it hopeless or with little hope? If you know of anyone who does things about books will you smile at them for me if you still love me? Because I have no idea where to begin. I shall write Touche too. He was very nice actually to read the mess I handed to him last year and not to call me on it. I heard a piece of yours, a vocal piece, with Copland this summer and I liked it. I have your copy of *The State of Music* which I shall bring with me when I return. It's been nicer than you'll know having it here in Taxco so forgive me for taking it. Do you still have that nice "Mimi"? I hope so. If you have time could you possibly find out the price of a room and bath at the Chelsea — if possible without salon — and write me a note about it?

I'm riding up with a friend called Mrs. Perkins and I *hope* that I can persuade Paul to come too, but he doesn't fancy coming unless he has a job. I do hope I shall be able to see Maurice [Grosser] on this trip and a little of you. We are going to stay at the Chelsea with or without Paul. I shan't write about the parrot as I'm sure Paul has written you *plenty*. I am bringing a fluffy kitten, however.

Love and Kisses—

Jane

13

Jane Bowles to Virgil Thomson
Hotel Carlton [Letterhead]
[Mexico City]
[January, 1942]

Friday, 9th

Dearest Virgil—

Just to inform you that Paul and I are always thinking of you. Thank you so much for your letter about Chelsea rates and your nice attitude about my book. I daresay there is little point in hoping to publish anything right now. That is why I am in no great hurry to return to the States. However I believe we shall be arriving in the beginning of March—in that way we avoid the long hard winter. One thing is certain and that is my decision *not* to stay in Mexico throughout the duration of the war, which naturally has occurred to all of us in view of the unpleasantness in the States. I read a long article about you in *The Nation*. I enjoyed most the quotations. Who is that man?

Paul's attitude is peculiar. He seems lighter-hearted altho' constantly ill. We have both been reading Henry James' novel *Portrait of a Lady* and we have both loved it. I have also been reading C. G. Jung's *Psychological Types* and I am astonished about the past and fairly ashamed at a lack of information which is common to so many of my friends and most of all to me. I shall try in the future not to be so pompous.

I know that you are fond of a letter full of news but I'm not sure whether or not you really mean it.

Paul and Antonio [Alvárez] (a very good Mexican artist whom Paul has undoubtedly written to you about) left this morning for Vera Cruz, a tropical port, where Helvetia and I shall join them in a few days. From there we are going to Tehuantepec, which is a distant isthmus inhabited by a special type of Indian. We will all be there for a few days and then we will promptly return to Taxco. Perhaps we will spend another week down at the seashore (Acapulco) and then in the beginning of Feb. leave for New York, travelling slowly and stopping off at various places in the South if they look inviting.

A little card or a note from you is always so welcome to me. This letter springs from real tenderness because I dreamed of you all last night. You can reach me at "Lista de Correos" in Taxco. I shall be back there in another two weeks. Give my love to Maurice if he is still in N.Y. I would like to know just how depressing New York is.

Much Love

Jane

14

Jane Bowles to Virgil Thomson
[Taxco, Mexico]
[Early March, 1942]

My dear Virgil—

I haven't forwarded your letter to Paul because I am expecting him here in Taxco any day. I was glad to read that life is pleasant. Naturally we get nothing but "gloomies" down here—and their reports have been discouraging. I'm finishing reading a book. I wrote two little . . .⁶ but I won't tell you what they are. We are leaving here on the 30 of March, gas willing. I hear it has already been rationed on the Atlantic seaboard. At any rate it will be about two

---

⁶ Two songs, "Farther From the Heart" and "Song of the Old Woman," which Paul set to music.

or three weeks from that date before we arrive in N.Y. because we are stopping off on the way. I hope you will not be in Kansas.

Much Love

Jane

15

Jane Bowles to Virgil Thomson
Hotel De Soto [Letterhead]
Savannah, Ga.
[April, 1942]

Dear Virgil—

Just to advise you that I have sent some of Paul's luggage to myself in care of you at the Chelsea. If they bother you about it just tell them to leave it in the cellar.

Paul stayed on after me (in Mexico) because he was to hear about his trip to S.A. within a few weeks. He has heard, he writes me, and apparently the government is no longer appropriating funds for music so that question (the South American trip) has at last been settled. It has been hanging over our heads.

It now remains to be seen whether I cut my trip short and return to Meji or whether Paul comes up here very shortly. This depends largely on tourist visas—the draft, etc. These things I'd like to talk to you about. If you will be around.

Much Love

Jane

Two Serious Ladies *was published in New York in 1943. The reviews were generally disheartening. From 1943 until 1946 Jane lived most of the the time with Helvetia Perkins either on Helvetia's farm in East Montpelier, Vermont, or in an apartment in New York. She completed the first act of* In the Summer House *and a story, "Plain Pleasures."*

16

Jane Bowles to Virgil Thomson
[New York City]
[1946]

Dearest Virgil,

I hope you will enjoy being in Paris and that you will come to dinner next year. I'm sorry Paul's off the paper[7] in a way and thank you very much for getting him on. It was lovely while it lasted, for me anyway because I didn't have to worry about Paul's worrying. I wonder what will happen now. Insecurity and a lot of travelling I suppose, which I concede is more fun (for boys anyway). I kiss you and thank you again.

Bon Voyage

Jane

In early 1947 Jane went with Libby Holman on a trip to Cuba. On her return she met Helvetia Perkins in Florida.

17

Jane Bowles to Libby Holman
[Florida]
[March 27, 1947]

Dearest Libby,

Thank you for your wire. Florence [Codman] is a mine of misinformation and I hope that Paul has not been listening to her reports and ignoring my wires and letters. I sent Paul one "agonizer" by night letter and one by mail the day after I arrived. He must

[7] The *New York Herald Tribune*, for which Paul had been doing music reviews.

certainly have them both by now, ossir.[8] Must I wreck this letter by telling you what I told him? We are starting off tomorrow morning, willy nilly. I wired Bubble [nickname for Paul] that we would arrive within five days if there was anything imminent, which is the driving time from here, but that we might take a week longer if there wasn't. We thought we might stop at Marine Land, Savannah, etc. on the way up, if we feel like it. I have of course received no answer yet from Paul and I'm working myself up into a rage already. I shall certainly leave tomorrow and call him from somewhere along the road, but I may die of apoplexy in the booth, I shall be so angry by then. There is no way of contacting anyone from here because of all the radios and the juke boxes. A very cheap crowd.

I think that it is wonderful Doug met you at the plane and I wonder how you carried it off. I could not stop crying the day that I arrived. I felt very ashamed of this because you upon your return had so much more to face than I. I hated the last night in Havana but I have never in my life been so happy as I was in Varadero. (Even though I didn't take many advantages.) Those blue walls were really beautiful. The dog screamed in his box all the way over and we had to sit in quarantine until two-thirty in the afternoon.

I have a new shoulder pad plan which I would like to discuss with you when I return. I have to buy about five thousand snappers and find a dressmaker. It is a plan that you may find useful for your own shirts, bathrobes, brunch coats, etc. The left pad on my blue long sleeved button-down-the-front dress came loose last night. I got a little excited but I controlled myself and sewed it right back on. Helvetia has a good choice of spools, all the basic colors, and not the fantasies that you and I carried around. The orange cat is nice, a little young of course to be really interesting but it is nice to have him because we have that box. I imagine we shall have to buy another cat box for the books and sugar. I am trying to make a shell collection for Paul and if I can get some Cuban money here I'll bring it back to you. It's interesting because it's so darned old. How is Topper [Christopher Reynolds, Libby's son] and are you driving him up to Putney? As you probably will before my return, I shall give you Cory's[9] address in case you want to stop there for meal . . . I'm sure they would love to see you.

[8] Ossir—a word used frequently in Jane's mother's family (of Hungarian origin?). It implies the denial of what's just been said.

[9] Editor's pseudonym, a new lover of Jane's. Address omitted.

Have you gotten word one out about the trip? I can't even tell Helvetia what side of Cuba Varadero is *on*. I told her about Amelia finally because I was so desperate for a story. She thought it was interesting. Call Paul if you can and find out whether or not he answered my wire.

I think it is wonderful of Larry to have cabled you. Janice is booking us into Marine Land and trying to get the dog and the cat in too. He thinks he can manage all right. If he can't I'll wire Larry to get in touch with his uncle. I miss you terribly.

Much much love,

Jane

Give my love to Clarissa please and Shirley [Stowe].

I know Doug will be better for having stayed with you. After all — I AM — in spite of having just attacked Helvetia and both animals with an axe.

In July 1947 Paul went to Morocco, which he had visited in the early thirties, with the intention of writing a novel. He had been offered a contract by Doubleday after the successful publication of a short story in Partisan Review. *Jane stayed in the U.S. at Treetops, the country estate of Libby Holman, where she worked on a second novel.*

18

Jane Bowles to Paul Bowles
[Treetops, Merriebrooke Lane]
[Stamford, Connecticut]
[Early August, 1947]

Dearest Bupple,

I am happy to have an address at last, and I hope for your sake that you will decide not to go to Spain. I don't think you will like it there as well as you do in Morocco and certainly I think Portugal would bore you in short order. I do not say this to be mean because actually I should prefer you in Portugal, letters there are very quick flying over and I imagine it is healthy. I should hate it however if you left a place you liked (just because you do always prefer to move on) and ended up with a lot more money spent, in a place that you didn't find nearly as much fun. But perhaps you mean only to take a flying trip through Spain and then return to Morocco, if you leave at all.

It has been hard enough for me to get on with my novel *here* because of four or five tremendous stumbling blocks—none of them however due to the circumstance of my environment. (My novel is entirely in this laborious style.)

The more I get into it, which isn't very far in pages but quite a bit further in thinking and consecutive work the more frightened I become at the isolated position I feel myself in vis-à-vis of all the writers whom I consider to be of any serious mind. Because I think there is no point in using the word talent any longer. Certainly Carson McCullers is as *talented* as Sartre or Simone de Beauvoir but she is not really a serious writer. I am serious but I am isolated and my experience is probably of no interest at this point to anyone. I am enclosing this article entitled "New Heroes" by Simone de Beauvoir, which I have cut out of *Town and Country*, at least a section of it. Read the sides that are marked pages 121 and 123. It is enough for you to get the meaning, since you know the group so well, and their thinking; read particularly what I have underlined. It is what I have been thinking at the bottom of my mind all this time and God knows it is difficult to write the way I do and yet think their way. This problem you will never have to face because you have always been a truly isolated person so that whatever you write will be good because it will be true which is not so in my case because my kind of isolation I think is an accident, and not inevitable. I could go on and on with this and explain to you better what I mean but there is not space for such a discussion. Not only is your isolation a positive and true one but when you do write from it you immediately receive recognition because what you write is in true relation to yourself which is always recognizable to the world outside. With me who knows? When you are capable only of a serious and ponderous approach to writing as I am—I should say solemn perhaps—it is almost more than one can bear to be continually doubting one's sincerity which is tantamount to doubting one's product. As I move along into this writing I think the part I mind the most is this doubt about my entire

33

experience. This is far more important than feeling "out" of it and "isolated," I suppose, but it also accentuates that guilt a thousand times. It is hard to explain this to you and in a sense it is probably really at bottom what this novel will be about if I can ever get it done! Another souris [*tsuris: Yiddish for troubles*] (or is that spelled Tzoris?) I realize now, after these two months at Libby's, that really *Two Serious Ladies* never *was* a novel, so we are both facing the same doubt exactly, although I cannot imagine your not being able to write one. Helvetia is making her way into this novel which is inevitable since I have thought so much about her for the past seven years. I am also in it in the person of her son, Edgar. This is good because I am usually trying to be too removed from my own experience in writing which can be tricked in a short story very well but not in a novel. It is *bad* because it is simply not much fun. It is upsetting and I get confused. You know what a state of confusion Helvetia has put me into anyway so that I am a far more uncertain person today than I was at twenty-three, so you can imagine how difficult it is for me to hammer a novel out of anything she has prompted me to think. Because it is really not Helvetia whom I mind writing about; I have transformed the situation sufficiently so that I am not too certain every second that she is this character but it is difficult, very difficult to put into words all the things she has caused me to brood about which are I think foreign to my nature but which now obsess me. There are *other* elements in the novel, natch.

I am working and I am diligent and faithful about it but I feel it's such a Herculean task that I shall not finish for years! On the other hand it may, if I can just get over having myself in a book, it may go quickly. But I think it is better to prepare for the worst than the best.

My slowness is appalling and the number of hours when I simply lie on the bed without reading or thinking would shock you. If I can get 150 pages typed, corrected and in to a publisher this fall I shall consider myself very lucky. It is natural that I have had to keep dropping material all along the way. I have never been for two months in one place before without being completely uprooted either physically or emotionally. In any case the work I did in Cuba and the spasmodic work I did in New York is all I can really count on using, together with the work I have done this summer. All those other notebooks don't count and it is time you stopped thinking of them because it simply makes me nervous. I shan't chuck them however because there may be material—in fact I'm sure there is—among them for a short story or two. Even the work in Cuba is out of kilter with what I am doing now but during the four weeks that I had down there or five maybe, when I worked, I at least established the atmosphere, but God knows the characters have changed or at least grown considerably—so that the Cuban part has to be retouched. As for the work I did in N.Y. after I returned it was pretty spasmodic and interrupted but I can use some of it. There isn't much I'm sure—but it is not completely of a different texture like the *Pre-Cuban* work. To give you an idea of my slow pace—I have done about thirty-three typewritten pages in the same number of days. One day I do *three* pages but then the next I do nothing—possibly—and this is working *all day* and after dinner! I mean going at it and stopping for a while and then going at it again. Of course I do a great deal of thinking which takes me forever because my mind is apt to wander—every twenty minutes if I have reached an impasse or a complicated thought and then I am apt to dream the whole morning about some flirtation. It is always nice to slip out and escape into the pool at a bad moment but actually I have been conscientious about staying in my room almost all of the time. I don't write much and I don't read but I am at least in my room. And in a few months I will know once and for all whether I can write this novel or whether I have to give up writing anything. I have thus far been saved by an idea or a little run of dialogue at the last minute when I was about to despair.

I flew down with Libby (for a weekend) to Louisa Carpenter's and Sister [Eugenia] Bankhead's. The plane—Louisa's mother's it is—was wonderful and I loved every minute of the flight. I drank heavily on the weekend, played poker and did no work.

Louisa C. is the most sexually attractive woman in the whole world but I am alas not alone in thinking this. We went crabbing and we saw two litters of baby pigs—eleven little piglets in each— or maybe nineteen. Also Sister's two *black Pekes*!! Naturally I was "aux anges" with them.[10] They are really pitch black. Can you imagine it? When we flew back we dropped Libby at La Guardia and then in less than ten minutes we were here. I am forwarding this check because I don't know what to do with it. I had hoped I would have an address from you sooner. My mother is coming this Sunday, the ninth, and staying in New York until the nine-teenth, so I shall be in New York ten days. Write me here however as Libby will be coming in and out of New York every other day and bringing my mail—if it's important. Then on the 19th or 20th

---

[10] Jane's Pekingese Donald had been killed by a car.

I will be back here anyway. Naturally I hate this break but I hope to get *some* work done while I'm there. I shall write about sailing to Africa later in the summer. Certainly I shouldn't before a much more substantial amount is done on the novel but I'm not certain I should wait until the bitter end. I cannot decide about this right now anymore than I can about when and if to see Helvetia. I shall certainly not go to Africa before late fall—when you will perhaps return. If not you must let me know *what* to do about the apartment.[11] It will be terribly easy to sublet from Sept. or Oct. on I imagine. I know it is hard to keep paying that money out but Oliver [Smith] has not been able to find anyone who is interested. It would be nice to find a house there, wouldn't it? In Africa, I mean. I am of course delighted that Gordon [Sager] likes it better than he did. I read Brion Gysin's piece in *Town and Country*?? That strange story, about the Japanese house that was lifted up intact with all the people in it and put down again on some crazy British Isle, is in it. You have undoubtedly heard him tell it—the story—it's one of his myths. It's all not very amusing. My swimming stroke is improving. I am reading *Sons and Lovers* as well as Kierkegaard. I wish you were here. I am by myself more than I have ever been since childhood. I am worried about Helvetia getting me down but otherwise O.K. except when the work is stale. I suppose both you and G. [Gordon] have *written* novels already. I still think that it was a good idea for me not to go to Africa, don't you? Because with outer complications as well as inner ones I don't think I could have got anything done. But then perhaps you are so disgusted with my slow pace that you don't think what I do matters at this point. I do think I might come to Africa before I have entirely *finished* the book but I shall not think of that until November as I said when you will have either returned or not. I shall not move before then unless something awful happens which would make it impossible for me to work here. I must document myself on hurricanes too before long. I hope to have better news on my progress the next time I write, but I want you should always know the worse so that you will have no false idea of me. I loved G.'s postal card. Give him a kiss for me and tell him that Libby is *very much* taken with him in every way.

I am sending you your literary correspondence so that you will be encouraged by your *prowess* in this field. Don't be worried about

[11] Paul's apartment was on the top floor of the house at 28 West 10th Street in Manhattan. Helvetia Perkins and Jane had an apartment on one floor, and Oliver Smith on another.

my losing your mail either. I am very conscientious about it and open only those business letters which I think might require immediate attention. As for packing your passport away—I thought it was mine—I looked to see whose picture was in it and I dimly remember my own face and not yours. As Libby said when I told her, "How psychosomatic can you get." Otherwise I am extremely reliable. The Hilltop theatre has been writing you and I shall send them a card explaining that until now you have been in Africa without an address so that they won't think you rude. They invited you to see the show, etc. Also sign the enclosed check (unless you will be back in time to deposit it yourself) and send it to me so that I may deposit it or it will be lost entirely. Perhaps they will honor it in Africa and you can give a party. I hope you and Gordon will stick close together.

Perhaps Florence would rent your apt. from the middle of Sept. to the middle of Oct. and by then you will know what your plans are—but I don't know how interested she'd be. You will surely have no trouble however from then on. She will move into mine Oct. 23 because it's lower down and she naturally prefers that, unless H. changes her mind about next winter which I seriously doubt.

I hope the books you sent me will arrive soon and your story. Please write.

Much Love

Jane

P.S. I shall write Gordon later. The Delkas Music Co. 625 South Grand Avenue has sent you your proofs to be corrected with *Blue Pencil* only at your earliest convenience. Shall I forward them? I shall try to find a picture of you to give to Pearl Kazin for [*Harper's*] Bazaar. (I'll ask her about the big one but I'm so afraid they'll *lose* it.) Your story appears in October. There is a letter from [Edouard] Roditi—otherwise nothing interesting. I did not of course read it. Shall I forward all vaguely interesting mail? I think I had better read it first—if not personal—because it's expensive to send air-mail as you know.

Love

Jane

P.P.S. You also have a profit of two cents (.02) from some sheet music you sold. I won't look through my files now to locate the document. Peggy Bate sent you the *Age of Reason* in English, the first book in Sartre's trilogy. I am keeping it for you.

The Fan[12] is my constant friend and I *love* it.

19

Jane Bowles to Paul Bowles
[Treetops, Merriebrooke Lane]
[Stamford, Connecticut]
[Late August, 1947]

Dear Bubble,

Perhaps you are back from Spain and will receive this letter when it arrives. It is disturbing, I find, to write to someone when there is no certainty of their receiving the letter for weeks or months, but I trust you will not stay in Spain that long. On the other hand this may arrive after you have left Tangier, for a second time, and gone off into the desert or on to Fez. I don't imagine you are going to be staying long anywhere, somehow, particularly with no house. I am sorry Gordon left you, naturally, because the whole thing now sounds incredibly gloomy to me. Not that it is gay here either, or anywhere.

Libby is in and out like the wind because she has found an "interest" in New York, for which I am extremely grateful. She was getting terribly despondent and cried herself to sleep every night which I could hear but do nothing about. I am out here a good deal with Topper and Clarisse and Grandma [Libby's mother] which I like, although I am apt to idle away ten or eleven hours easily. Still with all that time one is bound to get some work done. I wrote you that I was going to spend ten days in New York with Mama which I did. It was a terrible holocaust, worse than I expected, because I did not do one lick of work for ten days. I slept in a different bed every night, including I.B.'s (of film research fame). You know whom I mean; I.B. was pretty annoyed to find me in her place the next morning, I think, which upset me for a good three days.

[12] A present from Paul.

38

I spent one pleasant afternoon at the little zoo on 59th Street and thought of you all the time. There was a little baby monkey you would have loved. It was so terribly hot that I drank at the public fountain all the time, a thing which I haven't done for a long while. Not since I was ten years old, or younger. I saw several lunatics sitting around waiting for night to fall and I was sure glad it was only four in the afternoon. I have got back on my work again with unbelievable difficulty and continue crawling along. I am so slow it is almost as though I were going backwards. In a sense I am a little less discouraged than in my last letter but I don't dare even say that because by tomorrow I may be in despair. Tonight I read a story by Katherine Anne Porter called "Pale Horse, Pale Rider." It has completely ruined my evening because it [is] so sad and depressing and moving—and yet I am not sure I like it. If I feel terribly sad and terribly moved by something it is very puzzling not to be able to say I like it. I keep forgetting what writing is supposed to be anyway. I cannot however think of anything that I have really liked that has made me sad or depressed, no matter how depressing or sad it really was. Perhaps you can write me what I mean.

On the day after tomorrow I am taking a train to Pittsfield where Helvetia and Maurice [Grosser] (he is visiting her) are meeting me. I shall be with her for about five days and then I'm coming back here. We have to see each other I suppose to settle certain things, but it is naturally "inquiétant." I'll bet she's written more than I have this summer. I used to read Valéry when I was younger and I loved it but I'm sure I couldn't now. Florence I think is going to take your apartment until October the 23rd. I wired her that she could have it. (I suggested it to her because she wanted to get into mine on the tenth of Sept. but it is rented until the 23rd of Oct., so I suggested yours to her until she could move downstairs.) That will give you a breathing spell and certainly by the end of Oct. we will know whether or not you are returning or staying over there. If you stay I know you could rent the apt. at a profit because things are still impossible in New York, space I mean, and I think even with the additional rent for steam heat which Oliver wrote you about you can come out gaining. Naturally winter rentals are far easier than summer ones, in fact there is no comparison. Of course if you come back we, rather I, won't rent it from Oct. 23rd on, but you will know soon what you intend doing. As for me, I can't stay here at Libby's forever but probably through the fall. I hope that after I do about twenty more pages of this novel, I shall have completed a section, at least psychologically and then I will write a short story and try to sell it to [Mary Louise] Aswell [of *Harper's Bazaar*]. I shall need more money eventually, when I leave here, and although I know you would send me some I don't want to ask you to because there is no reason why I shouldn't earn a little, since I am doing no housekeeping whatsoever. If you come back before the twenty-third and Florence is in your apartment we can certainly find a place to stay for a week or so, here or at Helvetia's. I never went to any New Canaan which was merely Oliver's idea of a good joke. He meant Great Barrington, which is actually Salisbury, where the woman who owns the Inn lives. I went there for a weekend almost two months ago. In any case even if I did go somewhere if it were for more than a few days I would certainly leave a forwarding address! In your letters you sound as though it were *I* not you who were disappearing into the wildernesses and the inaccessibles, which is typical of you. Virgil told me that X—a man whom we both know, and who is serious, but I can't remember his name— told him that up at Knopf's they all deny ever having *heard* of me or published my book.

I am plump and in extremely good health though not at all satisfied. I miss you very much indeed and wonder how we are ever going to meet again with all these distances. I feel quite homeless and yet I think in spite of everything maybe it is better I didn't go to Africa. I am not too worried or sad as long as I keep hearing from you because I know that all at once you will be coming here or I shall simply be going there. I might prefer Paris, however, except for the expense. Oliver and I were both horribly worried by the Cadiz explosion, but I gathered from your letter which arrived on the following day that you were most likely not there. I saw Bobby Lewis who almost flirted with me, I think. He was very cute looking and did not talk about his "wecords" once. He and Libby have made up their friendship. I sometimes feed and diaper the baby at midnight, and I have grown to love him very much—the little one.

I mention renting the apartment, if you don't come back, because surely it will be too expensive to keep just for me even if I have a little money. Maybe I could go to Europe with Florence in December and get over to Africa from there if nothing happens before then. Oliver says he's working on jobs for you, (ossir) so I'm sure everything will be fine (ossir). In any case you must do what you see fit to do. Maybe if you came back we could go down to our beloved Mexico. I am being vague and half cocked about plans because I'm trying to fool myself out of an "agonizer." I can feel this letter slipping into one.

I shall see little Puppet [Helvetia Perkins' Pekingese] anyway in a few days. The fan is my dearest possession and it has been with me every second. I have actually kissed it, which you can believe. It is right here now with its soft harmless little paddles. Do you want me to forward your mail? At least some of it and shall it be airmail, expense and all? I hope the packet of books arrives soon. I am enjoying my *Sickness unto Death* throughout the summer. Please write to me. It is much easier for you to write than for me, because I always feel that unless I present a problem in a letter I have not really written one.

Much love

Teresa[13]

P.S. Oliver is perfectly willing to move his things out so that Florence can rent the entire floor if she wants to—otherwise she will merely pay your share, but I'll let you know definitely in a couple of days—if she takes it or not—with or without Ollie in the studio. *Please* be careful of your health. I say I would prefer Paris to Africa but *only* if I had finished my book. I think it would upset me more—and I would prefer it out of masochism maybe.

I have just received your letter about the Perrins' etc. and enjoyed it thoroughly. How I wish I *were* with you, because I find that kind of thing inspiring and not upsetting. I'm sure I could work in Spain in a little hotel better than here, and I do have moments of terrific remorse. Or even in a Tangier hotel. Still it is best not to brood about all of this and I must try to work whether the decision was right or wrong. I'm sure you are way ahead of me already and it makes me nervous, but you will always be faster than I am so it shouldn't. I am glad you are finally working because there is really no time to lose for anybody. It is wonderful to hear from you often, in fact it is very important that I do. Libby is wonderful but I shall never be quite satisfied or easy about being a guest for so long. She said she would tell me if she wanted me to get out and I do think that the place is good for the fall if we don't get together before December. I have no set ideas about anything since you never

[13] Jane's name in a game she played with Paul about a parrot.

41

mention even remotely your intentions. Keep in touch with Oliver in any case since he may have suggestions for you. I wish that I could write you something amusing but I have no adventures to tell you about. Certainly you would be bored hearing about Iris and Cory and Louisa and Sister Bankhead. You know it is always the same old grind with me or "bringue" as they say in French. Of course I think I shall simply never be interested in any one who is Latin or Arab or Semitic. I am more and more crazy about the Scotch and the Irish and think seriously of paying a visit to those countries and getting it over with. It takes days to get a letter from here to the post office after one has written it. I keep asking Johnny to let me know when he is going to town but often he forgets and I am stuck until the next day. You must write me if you know the works of Katherine Anne Porter, and the sequel of the Perrin[14] story at Ronda. I would love to be in Ronda, perhaps you could find a house there. The train trip sounds dreadful, however.

Much love again

T.

You said in your letter the train was "pitching and lurching" so you must want to bar Spain to me forever!—or at least Ronda.

20

Jane Bowles to Paul Bowles
[Treetops, Merriebrooke Lane]
[Stamford, Connecticut]
[September, 1947]

My dear Bubble

I should write this single space but then I would have no room for my grammar corrections. Libby is asleep so I am using Mrs. Swazie's typewriter, mine being locked into Libby's sitting room.

[14] Paul kept "running into the Perrins, mother and son, everywhere in Morocco and Spain."

I am living sort of half on the third floor and half on the second, but I will explain that later. In some other letter—it's not interesting. It is terribly hard for me to type on this machine because I have to use twice as much pressure as I do on my own, and you can see for yourself what it has done to the edge of the paper. I loathe it and would sooner be using Erika, who I thought was the last straw. It is too hot however to use a fountain pen. I can't imagine that Africa can be much worse than it's been this summer on the Atlantic seaboard. I was in New York during the worst of the heat spell and it was unbelievable. I can't remember now whether I wrote you since seeing my mother or not. I must have. As you remember I spent ten days with her and completely stopped working which I think you might have done too considering the heat and the way I was living. Then I came back here and spent a week or ten days, during which time I did get back on my work again after a few days of adjustment and then I went off again to see H. I would have preferred not to see her until October because then I could have worked here for a month, but perhaps it is just as well that I got all the interruptions in at once. I was with her a little under two weeks and we got a great many things settled. There were some things that were indispensable, such as discussions about my apartment and other details. She offered to keep my room for me if someone else paid for the other half of the apartment but I refused because she said that she did not think she would be in New York very much and I saw no reason for her keeping a room all winter mainly for me. D'abord she would in no time feel that she was being used and the psychological dramas would begin all over again. I said that there was no reason why I had to be in New York at all if you weren't there and that she should only take the room for herself if she really wanted it. I can stay in the studio if you *are* here and if not I would only be in New York to visit Oliver and his couch is perfectly good. Helvetia and I are much better seeing each other away from Tenth Street anyway. She would like at this point to have a room to go to there for when she does come to New York, however, and God knows she may decide to take half the apartment after all on her own hook but nothing need be done about it yet. I was satisfied with my visit to her and I know that I can be with her this winter somewhere if you do not come back and if I don't get to Africa. Oliver says your money situation is very bad which naturally it would be. He seems to think he'll be free in January to go somewhere but that doesn't mean he'd take me necessarily and I don't suppose you or

I can afford a ticket or will be able to by then. Well, we will see. I shall come to my novel in a second. I wish that you would tell me what you want me to do about the apt. You complain about paying for it, but as I told you Oliver is now willing to get out of it—but how *can* I sublet it if you do not mention for what length of time you want me to do so. Do you want me to rent it for six months, two months or a year? I have a feeling you would like everything to happen without your taking a hand in it so that it would be impossible for you to come back, perhaps. I assure you I don't like you to have to pay out the seventy-five a month anymore than you do but it is difficult to do anything about it unless you decide that you are going to stay over there and want to risk not having any place to stay here. I can sublet it on a two month lease with option to renew but then the people will leave the minute they get a permanent place. Just as Florence decided after I wrote you that she would not take it because someone wired her that she could have a place for a year. Of course she was unusually lucky and one could take a chance on people staying on from month to month without too much risk perhaps. I think you *can* lease it that way but I am not certain and there is the disadvantage of their moving the minute they get a permanent lease. I am not sure that the shortest lease would not be two months either, but perhaps with the unusual apartment situation even a month is considered. I am renewing my lease on Helvetia's suggestion since there is no possibility of getting stuck with the apartment for the next three years at least and since it will on the contrary be profitable to sublet. She may want to pay for it for two months when the present tenants leave and then she would sublet again if she went South in Jan. or Feb. I am going to speak to Oliver next weekend as well who might be interested in taking one of those rooms down on my floor over, if he is flush this winter and you sublet your floor. The other room could be rented separately and I wondered if by any chance your floor was rented at a large enough profit if you would be interested in hanging on to a room on my floor; Helvetia I am sure would rent it from you for part of the time, and at any other time it would certainly be easy to rent with Oliver in the back room because the layout is perfect for sharing whereas your apartment is impossible. I don't imagine you will want to do this but Oliver may take one of the rooms anyway and then I'll rent the other to either a stranger or Helvetia. I think too he'd be willing to get out of his half and rent it to you if you got back while yours was still rented. This is only a possibility but it might mean that you would at least not be out on the street when your apt. was sublet. As for me, upstairs or downstairs I probably will never have a real room of my own again. I am not writing an agonizer but trying [to] tell you that there *might* be an alternative if you had to come back suddenly and for this reason are hesitating about subletting. I am not at all sure however that he will be willing to pay nearly 80 dollars a month instead of twenty-five! On the other hand if he paints on my floor in the back room and rents the front to a stranger he may make enough profit to overcome the difference. Theoretically the lease is mine but of course since I don't have any money with which to pay for the apartment Oliver would get the profit money for it. I may even suggest transferring the lease to him, in fact I think I will. It is important only to keep it in the family a little longer while space continues to be so unbelievably tight.

About your apartment you must write me what to do and *if you want to sublet even if Oliver DOESN'T* go into such an arrangement or refuses to give the back room on my floor over to you when you do come back. In other words are you willing to take a chance on no place to stay except a hotel and if so for how long should I sublet it? On the shortest possible lease or not. That would mean of course that I would have to be around to *re*lease it at the end of two months unless I could get people who promised to take it on if I wanted them to, for another two months. Second item to consider is the fact that you left of course without considering all this and unless I can get a friend to take it *everything* in the closets will have to be packed away. I am willing to do this as best I can but I will take no responsibility about doing it wrong. Are there grips there wherein I can pack your clothes or not? Third item is that John LaTouche is apparently desperate for a place but neither Oliver nor I are willing to take the responsibility of renting to him without your sanction. You know his character and habits of neatness so you cannot blame me for hesitating. I won't even advise you on it but I left word for him to call me here at Libby's and I expect to hear tonight how much he'd want to pay and if he'd be willing to take it on a short basis or a long one. Naturally I wouldn't have to pack everything away for Touche and if you are interested cable me that he can have it. Of course you know all the histories it might involve. There is Jean Stafford who wants an apartment for a year.

About my work it is a month now (when I include some bad days in between my seeing Helvetia and Mother when I didn't work because of various preparations for moving around and the general anxiety of it) since I have done anything. As I say I did not *choose* to see either one of them at this point but Mother could not change her dates and Helvetia is tied up with well diggers and carpenters from now until the end of October when our tenants leave and we had to talk about things at some point which you will appreciate. I am desperate however at all this time passing and have done little more on my novel than you have in spite of not moving around. I am terribly discouraged and of course the fact that you get these letters from publishers complimenting you on stories is no help to my morale as far as a *career* is concerned. I have never once received a letter from anyone about "Plain Pleasures" or the first act of my play or my little *Cross-Section* stories ["A Guatemalan Idyll" and "A Day in the Open"] and *Partisan Review* would laugh and probably does at my work. This does not concern me deeply but I realize that I have no career really whether I work or not and never have had one. You have more of a one after writing a few short stories than I have after writing an entire novel. All this while, I have been slap-happy, not realizing that publishers did write anybody but now I see how completely unnoticed my work has been professionally. Arthur Weinstein told Virgil that at Knopf's they pretend never to have heard of me so I'm sure they will not publish my next novel. I am quite discouraged about all that and must say that if it were not for you and Edwin Denby, I would feel utterly lost. However none of that bothers me except to make me frightened about never making any kind of reputation which means no money and I refuse to have my non-existent career referred to any longer. I feel silly about it. I don't feel like being in New York at all and would like to go and live somewhere in a small town. I am eager to get back on my novel in spite of all this but that is probably because I haven't been writing it for a while and possibly when I begin again I will feel an inner discouragement and boredom compared to which any hurt pride is poppycock. I wish too that you would not refer to *your* work as your "little novel" [*The Sheltering Sky*] which you did in your letter as I'm sure it will be very powerful and twice as excellent as mine, as well as more successful, and so are Dostoievsky and Sartre. Oliver says your story is wonderful and I am certainly eager to see it. I don't mind how much better or worse you write than I do as long as you don't insist that I'm the writer and not you. We can both be, after all and it's silly for you to go on this way just because you are afraid to discourage me. I suppose I was irritated and appalled because you referred to your work as your little novel just as Helvetia would do! She has written more than either of us this summer but also she has had more time. Well I hope all the novels will be good novels and published. I must now however write a short story in order to get some money. Perhaps I can. You will have to pay for your apartment for Sept. and part of October as I simply cannot pick up now and go into town to rent it. Whenever I do it will be a holocaust anyway and I would like to write the story and get back on the novel first. It is still hot in New York, Oliver is on the road or will be next week and I could simply not be there alone. You have not asked me to do this of course but I feel responsible for it, naturally, although I wished you'd made some provisions for such an eventuality before leaving—with your clothes I mean, and your perfumes. When I do go in I shall probably have to find someone to stay with me because I hate letting strangers in when I am alone particularly on that top floor which scares me to death anyway. I am going to telephone Dione [Lewis] and see if she will perhaps join me there when I do go in and stay with me while I sublet which should help a lot but I have no idea whether or not she will do this. Touche I have spoken to since I wrote you about him a page or so ago and he is interested in having an apartment for six or eight months. I told him I'd have to write you about it first. He has to move Tuesday and hopes to have a place by then but is going to call me on Monday if he hasn't. I won't know what to say to him about it frankly and he was very irritable with me over the phone already for not knowing what you wanted to do. Naturally I wouldn't rent it to him for six or eight months without hearing from you but I may *have* to let him in there for a few weeks. He seems to think he'll get a place, however. I am weary of thinking of it all and I had hoped that in your letters you would have something definite to say about it. Naturally I would be more than delighted not to have to bother but then on the other hand I feel I should if it is making you terribly strapped—holding on to it. Your concert is not being given this year as you know so you probably have no reason to come back except to see me and find a job which I guess you can do from there. Helvetia refuses to go to Africa and my going will depend mainly on Oliver and your finances I guess, plus my novel if it still exists by then which it either will or won't. At the moment I don't give a hoot where I am but would prefer a place like Gloucester which I visited with H. and loved. I liked certain towns in Maine very much as well. I would of course like to see you right now but you have been so generous with your letters that I have not felt separated from you nor have I thus far had cause for anxiety except when Cadiz blew up. I do hope you will understand if I wait until October to go in about the apartment. I am desperate to do some work and being there with all the packing and seeing people etc. will be death on any work at all. If Dione will join me I will not dread it so much. She may even want to take it herself and perhaps it would be just the thing because I could always tell her to leave when she stopped paying. The last time I spoke to her she had an income that Bergner was giving her but God knows what has happened by now. She wanted to take my apartment with me and said she could afford 110 dollars rent but no more. If it goes to strangers it will be of course more difficult. You must write me what to do and if you would be interested once yours was sublet in sharing mine with Oliver if *he* wants to. It would cost you 75 a month *but* when you weren't there you could sublet your part because the two rooms even have separate entrances. I might leave my present tenants in it in fact, in the front room, I mean, on condition that they would get out when you came back. Perhaps this is all too complicated but I have tried to mention all possibilities to you just because I feel this once that it might be of some interest to you and necessary to your decision. Don't forget to mention to me what kind of sublet you want me to make if any and bear in mind that the short term ones are more difficult but possible and require someone to be around every two months when the lease gives out. Even if I don't have it rented October fifteenth of next month if I do rent it shortly thereafter you will get most of your money back on the October rent I hope, because surely I can rent it at a profit. But I do hope you understand my asking for as much grace in time before going into the subletting horror as I can get. It will take a while before you answer this anyway and before I receive it; I am asking this only because all is not lost as a result of Mother's visit and the Helvetia interlude but I must get another stretch of work in. I shall have to go to New York towards the middle of October anyway and then I will do something about it if you want me to. You have never asked me to in your letters but what else could you mean by mentioning that your life would be cheap there if you didn't have to spend the seventy-five a month? Naturally I understand and I worry about you but I will do nothing unless you write me a letter as clear as this one is (ossir) and as conscientious because surely you must know what a terrible day this has given me. I have been at this for many hours and it has been so very hot too. I have

48

put in a call to Dione so that I might know whether she'd join me in New York and I am calling Maggie to find out if *she* has any tuyaux about friends looking for a place. All the crickets and bugs are singing outside. I daresay O. may want to go to Africa and maybe he'd take me, quién sabe. Are there any Scotch or Irish there because I *must* have a bit of romantic adventure with all that singing and guitar playing going on. I am thinking of Spain now of course but we would probably hop over. Still it sounds very gloomy somehow and rather like trying to live in a dream. But then so is Gloucester a dream because most of the cod fish balls don't really come from there any more but from Canada and the Groton factories there are of minor importance compared to the new Canadian ones. In fact fish are being pulled in by huge nets attached to derricks and the old time fisherman is a thing of the past except for a sportsman. Would my ladies at the Salisbury Inn enjoy Tangier? They are not very imaginative but could they get over by boat and quote to me again the prices in your next letter. I spent a night in Great Barrington as Oliver calls it, on my way down from Helvetia's. There is a jealousy situation there between two people who have yet never been lovers. Not so very unusual I suppose. But it is a nuisance. We had cocktails with two business women who were friends of my ladies and on vacation at the Inn. One of them heads the design department at the Cannon Towel factory. Her name is Dorrit. I suppose the other lady, the jealous one, would never consent to go to Africa if I were going and actually they would both *bore* you and O. to extinction. If I don't go I hope maybe H. will take me to Mexico or Maine or Canada. She has added more rooms to her house and is altogether being quite wonderful. I think she will invite us all up there. Maurice has been with her half the summer, sharing in her grocery bills. I enclose ad from the *Saturday Review of Literature*. I am quite fat and not a pleasure to myself at all. But you would love my face. You must not be testy because I didn't mention the city where the Elkan publishers were—was that Elkan-Vogel? In any case perhaps it wasn't that name at all but the MS is arriving under separate cover and it *is* Los Angeles. How was I to know you didn't even know what city your music was being published in? I find you unfair sometimes particularly as you leave in a cloud of dust and never give me instructions. I didn't dare forward the manuscript without your permission. I shall go through your mail presently after I have fed the baby and diapered it although it is past midnight and I have been at this since morning. It is small wonder that I cannot write

49

as often as you do. Libby is mostly in New York. Gian-Carlo [Menotti] wants to give my play to his producers. Nick Ray is a huge success in Hollywood but there has been not a peep out of him in reply to Oliver's letter about my play. I suppose he is having his revenge now on Oliver's rudeness, and the general disinterest we showed him. The minute I told Oliver that Gian-Carlo was going to take the play to his producers Oliver said he preferred to do it himself although he gave in very quickly—but I can't understand why he would not have done it before this. Gian-Carlo of course would like to direct it but I am not going to worry about that yet. I intend to spend next weekend there if it's O.K. with them and with Oliver. We naturally have a great deal to talk about concerning the winter, apartments, Africa etc. Apparently he looks very poorly, gaunt and ill.

Now that I have gotten this off my mind I shall be able to work tomorrow after a few business letters, one to [Harry] Nessler.[15] I just returned from my trip with Helvetia and so things have piled up. We visited Florence in Maine and the telegram about the apartment she could rent for a year arrived while we [were] there. I'm very sorry because I thought I wouldn't have to start worrying about your situation until November, and that you would have decided by then what to do. I hope you don't think I *want* you to sublet. I merely want to help you if you want me to in a month or so because I feel very sorry that you lose that money. But if you want to let it slide and take a chance on friends getting in there when they do, I'd be delighted. I called East Hampton and discovered that Dione is in New York. Perhaps she will come and live with me there while I sublet *or* if by any chance she had any money maybe between us if I make some we could hang on to it, if you were willing to contribute a little too. It would not be then like losing it to strangers who wouldn't move when you got back. She is living at the moment with Verne. Naturally I would prefer that to anything and I am sure Dione will keep me company there if it comes to that but the money I don't know about yet. Don't trouble your head about the complicated section of this letter concerning my *own* apartment and sharing it with Ollie because if you don't understand it right off you never will and I don't know if he'll do it anyway. Just concentrate on your own.

My fan is still a blessing and I loathe and despise this Connecticut sultry heat. Please write soon and thanks a lot for all

15 The owner of the house at 28 West 10th Street.

your entertaining letters. I hope to see your story next week. Oliver of course would never get around to mailing it here. I don't see why you thought I had gone so far away. It certainly would have been simple enough to get my mail if I'd been in New Canaan. I just fed the little baby and by the way I saw about thirty Pekes in a kennel at Gloucester. I am happy that you are not disappointed in your trip. That would make me sadder than anything.

Much Love

Jane

P.S. Have you heard from Gordon — where on earth is he — and with whom? Will he join you again?

I hope Touche doesn't bamboozle us into getting into your place. It will be difficult if he's out on the street but maybe you'd want him there? Donald [Fuller] is not with him. Forwarding mail under separate cover. Some air mail.

21

Jane Bowles to Paul Bowles
[Treetops, Merriebrooke Lane]
[Stamford, Connecticut]
[Late September, 1947]

Dearest Bubble,

Your letters have been truly wonderful and so profuse. I wish that I could say the same of mine. I must hate the written word no matter how I use it, and you must enjoy writing, or I'm sure you wouldn't do it. I shall get the worst part of this letter over with. Since I went to see my mother on the ninth of August I have never really got back on my novel except for a week. It is terrible, but there it is. I might certainly just as well have gone to Africa — I know that now. When you wrote me on the twenty-sixth of August I had about ten more pages typed than you did at the time, and some more in a notebook (maybe fifteen but in bad condition) and I have not added a page since. It is terrible, but I think you must know it so that you don't keep writing me "Come in January if your

51

novel is finished." I did naturally no work during my two week trip with H. and then when I returned I set to work on a short story after a day or two or three of catching up on my correspondence with you and Mother and Saks Fifth Avenue, my tenants etc. I was going along with that as slowly as usual for a few days and then Ollie came down for the weekend. He stayed in my room with me so there was naturally no work done. We had a great deal to talk about since I have not seen him at all this summer. I started on a short story after my return from the Helvetia trip because I feel I should earn some money. I have a doctor's bill to pay and a Saks bill which would take just about all the money that I have in the bank, and with the fall coming on and the cleaner's bill (he has stored my fur coat, reconditioned it and done the same with my winter suits), I feel that I must make a little money. This is not an appeal for money but an explanation of why I would veer off my novel which I'm sure you don't approve of. I want to be able to take care of those little things myself, because it is a terrible feeling not to be able to earn enough to pay for even the details of one's life at the age of thirty. I am not frightened because it is not as though I were out on the street or could not ask for money. (Even my mother would give it to me but I would never ask her!) It is simply a question of *humiliation*. The Saks bill is something I ran up a year ago very gradually. It amounts to about fifty-nine dollars and was not an extravagance at the time, since I did need shoes etc. However I should have paid it then when I had enough money in the bank to cover it without getting down to my last dollar and I feel that because of this I have to get out of it myself. I have written them and asked them to give me until November for the payment and sent them fifteen dollars on account. I hope by then to have the money by selling (first writing!) a short story. There *is* a chance that George [Davis][16] or Mary Lou would buy it, after all. Libby says they can not attach *you* for the money unless we have a joint account, and she's right because I could do nothing about making Mr. Denny pay Mrs. Denny's telephone bill, morally or legally. I hope someday to get back to my novel. Naturally I know yours will be finished years ahead of mine and will be wonderful. Probably mine will never be done so you had better stop writing about it. Still I hope that the month of October however will be a good one and that I can make up some lost time. I work well in the fall. There were some terrible weeks here in

[16] Fiction editor of *Harper's Bazaar*.

August and during the first half of September. Muggy and breathless. The worst possible kind of weather for thinking or writing. In fact the weather man said that this was the worst summer we have had in twenty-five years. I must say that such weather, the really damp heavy kind, does have a particularly bad effect on one's energy and even after writing a letter I would be exhausted. I don't know whether all these things are excuses or whether I simply can't write. It is not, I am *certain*, for lack of trying. But I know you would rather have me blame it on the weather than on a complete lack of talent or imagination—imagination really because if I can imagine anything I can write it. So much for that. Perhaps I wrote all this to you in my last letter, probably did, but in my next I hope that maybe I'll be back on the novel or at least finished the story. After Oliver left I hung about for a day and drank brandy with Mrs. Swazie, the sixty-three year old deaf secretary who is leaving. It was her farewell night and I had to be with her. But that relationship is too long to tell about. I recovered the next day and just as I was getting down to work Libby appeared from New York, sky high and filled with excitement. Viola Rubber had just introduced her to Echols and Gould and given her the *Folle*[17] to read. She read it that night, part of it, and decided it was something I might have written myself. I don't know how in the world she reached such a conclusion because nothing could be farther from me as you will agree—except that there are some crazy old ladies in it, and *that* I suppose is what gave her the idea. Into town she went the next day and out again that night with the fantastic idea that I should do a new adaptation for it. She had finished it by then and seen Echols and Gould once more, who half promised her a part (one of the minor lunatics) in it, when and if they got it on. They are as you know still looking for the perfect adaptation.[18] She had the fantastic conviction that I could do it but not only was it an idea of hers, which would have been easy to waive, but unfortunately Echols and Gould also had me down on their list, although their first choice is S. N. Behrman whom they can't thus far get hold of. I tried to convince her that I never could do it and that they as well as herself were wrong but she finally put it to me as a particular favor to her and with such

[17] Giraudoux's *The Madwoman of Chaillot*.

[18] Paul had previously been commissioned by Echols and Gould to do a translation.

insistence that I could not or would not refuse to at least try my hand at a few pages. Oy! I don't know exactly why it would be such a favor to her but whatever it is I would do anything for her if only I could. Gould came out here and brought me the two translations, the potpourri that is a combination of yours and their own and one other by a New York lawyer who did it in four days. I told Libby there was naturally no point in trying unless there was some way of improving on either of those scripts without even going a step further than that, so I insisted on seeing them. I can recognize certain sentences in the potpourri one as being yours. The rest they've made a scramble of mostly. I asked them what they didn't like about your version and they seemed to think you hadn't gotten the Giraudoux spirit very well. I should think you would have hated the play in any case, the first act, particularly, the part before the "Folle" appears. Anyway there was nothing for me to do but to give up a few days and translate three or four speeches as a sample of what I could do—mainly the prospectors. It took me forever as you can imagine but I was very surprised to find that I did have some ideas about them. I showed what I did to Gould and he was very noncommittal about it. He said he thought I was on the right track but it was hard for him to say really, because he had thirteen other translations and adaptations whirling around in his head. I am sending in the final version of these speeches (they take up only three typewritten pages) with Libby today and she will meet the boys at her apartment this afternoon. I don't think for a minute they'll accept me because Gould was completely without enthusiasm but at least I know I will have done my best as far as Libby is concerned and that I have not in any way shirked my task. So now I am ready to return to my own writing (ossir). I must mail my play off to Gian-Carlo this afternoon and forward what little dreary mail you have. Before I finish writing about Echols and Gould, *I don't think they are ever going to get what they want*, because I feel they want it to be as elliptical and complicated as Giraudoux's style and yet to be written like a straight detective drama at the same time. If one *is* "fancy" in the adaptation they say it won't "play well" and yet they want to keep Giraudoux's quality. I am sure it won't play well anyway, and find much of it very tedious indeed. Mostly I can't bear it, but there *are* some charming moments and even moving ones. Well, enough of that. I think it's terribly funny that it should have turned up again, and I have a feeling it's going to be like one of those dreadful thick necked people who are seen first with you and then with Buzzy

[Aaron Copland] and finally with Touche or Charlie Ford. They are not dreadful people but unattractive. But then I shudder to think of your impression of my friend at the Inn; I would simply love to see your expression. In fact I cannot help laughing aloud when I think of it. Although I myself find her very attractive I can see the whole thing through your eyes.

About coming to Africa, I don't think there is a chance that she and her friend would, although I mentioned it to her. As for the novel influencing my decision, I shall surely not be finished. I can only hope that I shall get as much done during October, November and December as I didn't get done in August and September. If I really do, I should have a pretty strong grip on it and could decide in December whether or not to go. I told Oliver to get passages anyway and then we can always cancel them. You know how likely he is to change his mind the last minute and then too you may have to come home for something or other. With prices as they are I cannot honestly advise you to come here without the assurance of a job, but I can't say what I'll do either. I *won't* go on a small boat in winter and neither will Ollie, but the American Export lines are getting ready and I think if you could pay half my fare Oliver might pay the other and even I might be able to contribute. I would however not count on that and I should keep my money for clothes and the things that I have to get for myself through the years, if the money is very little, and so far of course it's exactly nothing. Helvetia and I will probably spend November and December together in the country if her furnace gets in. We could all then go up there in fact if you were in this country. She's having another bathroom put in and there are three more bedrooms than there used to be. I'm supposed to ask Oliver up there for Thanksgiving or anytime and you of course would be invited too. Naturally if you came back for a job it would be a nice place for you to go to for a month or two and work if you could stand the boredom, particularly if your apartment were occupied. Oliver says you can't wait to get me into the desert. Of course I'm sure that when I get there, if I do, all the part I would have liked will be over—like the wine and the nice hotels. I would like to stay in a hotel in Fez, I think rather than Tangier, and I still refuse to cross the Atlases in a bus. But if O. came maybe we'd take a cab. I wish to hell I could find some woman still so that I wouldn't always be alone at night. I'm sure Arab night life would interest me not in the slightest. As you know I don't consider those races voluptuous or exciting in any way, as I have said—being a part of

55

them almost. The architecture is another thing, and I think I would love the daytime there, and the very early morning, but I'm sure it is just the opposite with you and would be with Oliver. It is hard for me to think of going anywhere by myself of course, and I'm not even *going* to think about it yet. If my novel is not coming along at all by then it would be more painful than pleasant to go over there and see your manuscript almost done or even half done. I don't think I could bear the sense of failure made so palpable, but I couldn't bear it either to have you in such a terrible state about yours as I am about mine. I really am very glad you are coming along with it and I don't believe any of the things you say about the value of it, but aside from that I also think it is very important that you have this extra source of income if you can really develop it substantially, because it will permit you to do much more work out of the country than your music does which is after all what you want, and in a sense a good way to keep alive with prices here the way they are. None of this makes my life any simpler perhaps or maybe it will but that's beside the point. It will all work out, or it will never, I can't imagine. But certainly I don't like to see you miserable and bored, which you are in New York. I myself cannot get into New York at all. It is almost as difficult for me as getting on a boat to Africa. That is why I hate you to send things to Oliver. I did write you that even if I *weren't* here that I could not understand why you imagined they would not forward my mail to me; I wrote that in reference to the story which you sent Oliver because he had written you that I was in New Canaan (which is ten minutes from here, anyway). Now of course he's read the story, promised a hundred times to mail it and will lose it before I ever see it, probably. You must know that much about him. Also, I'm sure I'll never see the books. Half the packages he receives are lost because they're left in the hall forever. He completely mislaid the whole set of silver John something or other in the theatre (C. Wilson[19]) sent him and I am bitter about your having sent the books to him. I did write you too that I would only go in for a while to sublet the apartment if I had to. Even if he does receive the books they'll go into his library and be amalgamated. Don't you *believe* I'm at Libby's, or do you think it's in the mountains and on a mule trail? I wish that you would explain your logic. It is not that Oliver would purposely do these things but his apartment is like the dead letter office. Everything disappears. I do want the books so badly

[19] A Broadway producer.

and I've been waiting and looking forward to them so much. I think it was sweet of you to send them too. I am really frantic about the whole thing. When I saw Oliver he said that he thought he had rented your apartment definitely to Paul Godkin who would get out whenever you wanted him to. He was to let me know about it a week ago and hasn't. I wanted to be sure so that I could do something about it if it weren't rented. But then you know Oliver. He said also he was going to try and get you a job in Hollywood and that you shouldn't come rushing back yet because there was nothing in sight. He is supposed to take care of the boats and passages from New York so you might keep in touch with him about it, if he remains interested. I shall spend a week or so with him at some point. After *Bonanza Bound* opens end of November I shall suggest a rest to him in Vermont. Libby heard an audition of it and hated it but then she has very violent dislikes in the theatre and she seemed to hate this because the people in it were so greedy. Both Oliver and I think it would be nice, the next time there is any money around to get a house maybe in the town of Nyack, and give up New York entirely. The subletting business is a real headache and there is never any place to leave one's things. It is nice to have a place to come back to and I think a *house* in Africa or any other country is silly. I think hotels or temporary places are more fun. But we *should* all have a permanent one which could be closed up without being rented every time we moved. Particularly as we grow older and more feeble. I myself never go out of Libby's house very much and am still the same old home body. I asked Louisa Carpenter if she would like to go to North Africa but she said she wanted to go to South Africa and do some big game hunting. If Sister Bankhead goes down to Alabama, Louisa may fly me down to Maryland in her little Bonanza plane for a few days to catch the last of the fishing season (which of course I can't bear to miss). I would only go if I can be there with Louisa alone or with Libby along, but I can't face being there for three days just with Sister and Louisa for several reasons which wouldn't interest you and are not very important to either your life or mine. The little farm down there is charming and I would like to know Louisa better since she is a sportswoman and such a type has never entered my life. Later she will go duck shooting and I imagine she even goes after deer. And then think how jealous John Uihlein[20] would

[20] Jane and Paul had spent the summer of 1946 in Uihlein's house in Southampton.

be. (She's a DuPont as you know and you remember the fuss in
Southampton about that Ruth Ellen in the big beach house.) She
is really a very attractive plain woman and of course terribly broke
all the time. Touche is now after my apartment and I worry about
that. He was furious when I asked him if he could pay regularly
and I feel it would end up in a big fight. Do you think he would?
Maggie was cross with me because she said you wrote someone
that I had written you she was going to be married. I denied the
whole thing and I don't remember writing anything of the kind
nor in fact even hearing such a rumor. What could I have said?
And do be careful of what you write, although I don't see why the
hell Maggie should get so huffy about it; it's not an evil thing to
say about anyone. I might have said something jokingly to you,
what was it? I can't imagine. Anyway if there was something write
it to me but not to Maggie or anyone else and I'll explain what I
meant by the remark – if I ever made one. I miss you a great deal
and hope to see you here or there but it's hard to say just yet what
will happen for the various reasons I have mentioned. I hope Oliver
is doing something about boats in any case so that we do at least
have passages. And I hope to God I can get back to my novel and
that it will move along. If Oliver goes he will have to rest up first,
at Helvetia's perhaps, before taking those shots. But don't for
heaven's sake count on anything and do whatever you think wisest.
I am taken care of as far as my food and living quarters are
concerned so don't worry about me. I have not felt you were far
away thus far, in fact I feel it's much nearer than Mexico but I'm
sorry you're going into the desert. It will take longer to hear from
you now I'm sure, or it *will* when you get there if you are not there
yet.

The day is windy, at least, which I like more and more as I get
older. H. has been terribly sweet but she is very broke until March,
having had all those things added to her house and cannot take
any kind of trip before then. She will have to stay in Vermont most
of the winter to save up so I imagine by next spring she'll be ready
to go somewhere, after the asparagus is up. Of course the news
about the world is bad these days, and I must read all the papers
which I put into my closet week after week and never read. I intend
to study the Marshall Plan one of these days but I'm so far behind
now it's going to be difficult. Please write me *here* and you might
write O. that the books are a *special* present for me and that I want
the pleasure of opening them when they arrive so that they won't
be scattered to the four winds if he does ever get them out of the

front hall. I prefer not to think about it because I get too angry.

I saw Puppet; Helvetia spent the night here day before yesterday. Her sister lives not far from here and was giving a party on her birthday. Now that one can drive, Vermont is no longer so difficult to get to. No distinguished magazine has ever written me and complimented me on a story, or asked for a contribution, nor have I certainly ever won an O. Henry award. I seem to be completely ignored by the whole literary world just as much as by the commercial one. Nevertheless that would not stop me from writing. But I might have heard from someone all these years even though I have a publisher (ossir). I seriously doubt that Knopf will ever take anything of mine again.

Much Love — as ever —

Jane B.

P.S.   I sent all the music I had — but can't remember details. I'll call Helen Strauss. Maybe I'll have better news for you next time about my work.

O. says your story ["A Distant Episode"] wonderful — but I don't ever expect to see it: subject matter sounds fascinating but scarcely material for a magazine! You'll have to wait to bring it out in a book.

I remember there were some either black or green music sheets I sent you from the place in California, I believe.

22

Jane Bowles to Paul Bowles
[Treetops, Merriebrooke Lane]
[Stamford, Connecticut]
[October, 1947]

Dearest Bup,

I have been away for a week but shall forward your mail tomorrow. I usually wait until it accumulates somewhat. There is nothing of importance, you'll see. I have waited to write because I have been in such a boiling rage with you having spent most of this week

59

trying to make some order out of the havoc of your clothes and pure junk left around the apt. none of which I dare throw away. The number of filthy articles that were simply stuffed into the closets is unbelievable. It was like cleaning out an old Vermont farmhouse — the dirt left by two generations of maniacs. I am not even speaking of the laundry in the cardboard box which May is going to do gradually, since there are five hundred dirty things. If you did not have so many clothes such a laundry and such dirt could not accumulate. Naturally at this point it *would* cost a fortune to have everything cleaned. Paul Godkin and I packed away all the clean shirts and woolen stuff, clean and dirty, in grips with moth balls and then for the other things we used cartons. We had to have an extra maid in and even so it took three days and the place is still loaded. There is however room for Arthur [Gold] and Bobby[Robert Fizdale]'s things and for Paul's who is very kindly allowing five or six of your suits or coats, whatever they are, to hang in the closet. We emptied the bureau completely. However when May has finished with all your laundry there will be enough again to fill another bureau, so she had better keep it at her apartment until I get back eventually because there is no room really for anything more in the apartment not even a pill box and the boys are entitled to a little comfort since they are paying the rent. I thought that perhaps I could ship some cartons up to Vermont with Helvetia's permission. Every book was taken down and dusted and the floors scrubbed. Paul Godkin has sent everything (curtains etc.) to the cleaners and is really going to a good deal of expense. You are indeed fortunate, really born under a lucky star because had the apartment been sublet to a stranger I *don't* think with all the good will in the world I could have handled the job of making room. I would simply have given up in despair and wept, or disappeared for ever. Even without facing strangers, to have made ready for Bobby and Arthur alone would have been hopeless, because Arthur came down while we were in the midst of clearing space for their clothes and almost collapsed, so I don't think they would have helped me the way *Paul* did. Luckily he had this wonderful maid whom he summoned and she did most of the work with May but still it took supervising and organization. And then there were all these junky old dirty vests — costumes — hats — bathing suits — mats: They marvelled at my not throwing them away but of course I didn't dare unless there was something completely hopeless. It is all very well and your business to keep hoarding things and collecting more but then you should not expect to just go away and have it taken care of. You do not live in an apartment but in a *storeroom* with a little space in the middle! You need once and for all to go over your things, to throw out what you don't really want, and find a permanent place for the rest. If they are all packed away in really good strong boxes and nailed shut absolutely air tight we could store them somewhere, either at Helvetia's or somewhere in Vermont for practically nothing. I'm sure she could make room. I don't mean the books but all the junk—masks—extra serapes—papers that are merely keepsakes at this point—clothing you never wear—or half of what you *do* (you couldn't get around to them all in a year), old shoes etc. Then you could move in and out of your apartment more easily or at least it would be easier on everyone else. Until you had enough money to either keep a place on in New York—whether you were in it or not—or else own a house, you would live without this great burden of things. You need a real house with an attic where you could store things to your heart's content but that would of course involve a servant staying in it or some caretaker near by. If Oliver buys a house in New York you will be in luck because there would be a cellar with plenty of space, I suppose, and judging from the kind of lucky solutions you find to your problems—like Paul Godkin—Oliver probably *will* have a house and you can pile in more things. I know you think I am stewing but you wouldn't really, if *because* of your vast accumulation and the state of chaos you walked out on there had been *no* possibility of subletting. I had to get this off my chest obviously or I would not have ever written you—I mean I could not get on to anything else without writing you about this first. Paul Godkin is a wonderfully generous and helpful person and never complained once. He has fine energy and did a thousand little things while *I* sat on the bed in utter dejection and exhaustion. I think you might write him a letter. *Also* if there is one word of complaint about him when you come back—if you ever do—you had better not voice it when I am anywhere near or could possibly even hear a *report* of your remark. Everyone seems to know about your buying a house in Africa except myself—and why on earth you would suddenly have written about it to Bob Faulkner whom you don't ever see I can't understand. I just *happened* to be in town when Oliver got your wire and I of course advised him to send the $500. I knew you were getting a kick out of the house and I cannot help but want your pleasure. I was hurt though that you had written to Oliver and Bob Faulkner about it and yet no word to me. In your letter to Oliver you don't sound at all as though you expected us *both* to come over but only he. He refuses however to go without me and perhaps you didn't expect that he would. I know that you asked me over in a letter to me but that was before this house came on the scene, and possibly now you feel instinctively that it is all wrong for me. Of course you know how I feel about houses—and living in quarters where I might be conspicuous. I don't of course know about the Arab town of Tangier (I *refuse* to use that Arabic word). It may be filled with European and American eccentrics in any case. That is all I would mind, being conspicuous. As for worrying about comforts—as you know or should by now, that is not the kind of thing that concerns me. Have you forgotten Mrs. Copperfield? I would prefer also that there be no food worth eating for the tourist who has dollars or other money that the natives don't have. I have no interest at all in that and I would feel the proximity of starving France too keenly to really enjoy it. I should keep to a simple couscous and some cheap alcoholic beverage or a dope of some kind since it is impossible for me to live without such aids. I have lost interest in all foods, although I am more plump than ever. Recently I have been drinking quantities of buttermilk. Oliver I don't think will want to live in a house without a bathroom but I discouraged him from having one put in before he got there. I think he might better stay at a hotel and see how he likes it all, before making any more expenditures. This way it is still low enough in price to come under the heading of a "lark" because "lark" it is—which is all right—but surely it will end up costing more than not having a house. I don't care naturally how either one of you spend your money because I have no sensible suggestions actually or anything that *I* would like except perhaps a permanent house here with a servant or farmer in it where we could leave our things forever. Something in a small town. I don't see how an Arab house could be even a "headquarters" as you term it unless you keep a permanent servant in it because surely you would be robbed of all your things the moment you left for the desert or any of these "points" it's so convenient to, as you say in your letter. That is why I consider it a "lark" and not a practical arrangement. I will be only too glad to hear that I am mistaken however and that you *can* leave your things there or intend to have a faithful servant. I hope you will write me the details about just how frightening it's all going to be. I am *bitter* that I have missed the hotel part of your sojourn (all for nothing too) and that I shall arrive in time for the mess. I know now it was a mistake to stay here.

Sometimes I am in despair and sometimes very hilarious but I have a terrific urge now to go to Africa in spite of the house, although even the house I would like in the day time I imagine. The plans are to come in Feb. I hope maybe to have done enough writing by then so as not to be completely ashamed and jealous when confronted with your novel. At the moment I can't even think of it without feeling hot all over. And yet if you had *not* been able to do it I would have wrung my hands in grief—I say this sincerely. If by Feb. I *haven't* done enough maybe I shouldn't come because you'll view me with such disgust but *Oliver* keeps saying he won't go without me. Please keep plaguing him about securing boat *passages*. There have really been a series of plane accidents again. I had a letter from Gordon. Oliver seems to think he'll go to Italy and to Egypt. I would like to go to France as well—food or no food—eventually. Maggie Dunham seems to be interested in coming too. I am simply *dying* to be there now and perhaps I would come alone right away if it weren't too exhausting to think of doing the whole thing by myself—and also if it weren't for my work—but I may inquire and wire you.

However little I have done I am pleased with but shall probably throw it in the rubbish heap when I see yours. The story I am working on to get some money is nearly 60 pages long in my notebook already—and they are large pages—so I worked at a good rate but have not touched it in over a week. I flew down to Maryland for two days and when I returned I tended to your things at the studio for three or four days. I feel like getting back to it. It is utterly unsaleable but I like it thus far if I can only work it out! It's coming out much better than the novel did—and I know why: it's because I tried to put myself into the novel—in the guise of a boy—which somehow throws the whole thing off. I shall go back to it eventually but with grave misgivings. Possibly I am meant to write plays—or short stories. *Two Serious Ladies* was after all *not* a novel. I must also spend *some* time with H. who is flat broke because of all the work she had done on the house and therefore obliged to spend until March in Vermont. If I can spend part of Dec. and January with her it will at least pull her through half the winter. I imagine she'll go somewhere actually by February. She *can* borrow on her income after all. Oliver seems to have mislaid your story. He tried to find it for me when I was in New York. Don't scold him because he is so very helpful and caters to your slightest whim. He says he won't go to Hollywood unless you can go with him which I think is very sweet. He is really wonderful to you — and you are *not* wonderful to him. I am grieved however that he has mislaid your story. I want to read it. I am slowly disintegrating I suppose — but all the time marvelling more and more at American womanhood. It is nice to find as many miracles as I do but perhaps it is time I rested my overblown heart and looked at some Arab houses.

Heaven knows I shall be made nervous over there by the absence of any charming possibilities, whereas for you and Ollie it will be just the opposite — or is there a chance? Write me *everything* — including about the house.

My Love, as ever,
Devotedly

J.B.

P.S.   I am at R——— Inn for 2 days. I hope to have a letter when I get home. Don't mind my scolding — it is kind of a literary exercise in precision. Perhaps you don't want me to come? I shall naturally not mind the house when there's more than you and me in it. And it does sound beautiful because you can see the water — yes I think I would have worked much better over there. I have had too much the burden of my entire life here but in a sense I have learned far more by staying.

23

Jane Bowles to Paul Bowles
[East Montpelier, Vermont]
[December, 1947]

Dearest Bupple,

Your letter from Tangier — the one written on Thanksgiving day — has thrown me into a state. I think it is rather mean of you not to be more careful of what you say when you know how easily upset I am and how quickly guilty even when I know I'm not in the wrong. I don't know where on earth you got the idea that I would arrive suddenly in Tangier. Surely unless it is just wishful thinking — because you were bored and ready to have me arrive —

64

it must have been Oliver who confused you. I enclose a letter (an excerpt from a letter rather) written in September, late September to Helvetia. To come around January if you did not return had always been my plan—at least since I began to plan at all. Before that it was *"le néant"* because to begin with you were originally going to return. Not that I think you should have. It is only in the last six weeks or so that your letters have become so pressing and one in particular written during the period of the "Villa"[21] when you suddenly said that I should not come so late as Xmas because then the hotels would be full. That startled me greatly, because if I had been able to get there as early as Xmas, even if only because of passage difficulty, it would have been a miracle. After that there was a long blank period when you seemed to write Oliver and not me which I mentioned to you in another letter and which I decided was due to the fact that you didn't think I liked the house idea one bit and were temporarily avoiding me. Perhaps Oliver has been announcing all kinds of arrivals that I never even knew about? I told you too that I would spend a month or so with H. before leaving, otherwise that I would not be happy leaving. January always seemed the wisest to me from the time I thought concretely about the possibility of your not returning, and then Oliver put it off until February. I may have nebulously referred to a fall arrival much earlier in the summer but nothing definite I'm sure. Everything took much longer than I thought. Perhaps you have found it so too. But to finish with this so that it is clear in your mind that I don't feel I've kept you waiting for me in Tangier, I had planned to come possibly in January without Oliver *with your approval* naturally until this operation of Julian's [Julian Fuhs, Jane's stepfather] came up. Only because I always felt O. might not get off even in February. But then Julian knocked out the possibility of Jan. until mother suddenly decided it wasn't too serious about J. a few weeks ago—all of which I wrote you about in my last letter. I am again trying to get away in January but the Fern Line holds out no hope at all, they say however that I may as well be down on the list just because of the barest possibility. Now however since the letter about the Clairvoyant[22] I feel no matter what I do I will not go at the last minute and this worries me terribly because I

[21] Villa de France, hotel in Tangier.

[22] A letter from Paul had mentioned a warning, a prediction—of illness or death in connection with a journey—by a clairvoyant.

feel that it will concern Julian's illness if I should get a ticket on the Fern Line for January and then not go. I am fortunate in that Cory is now in New York and working on all this for me so that at least I can work. The work seems to be going well at last as though somehow all those little marks like flies' legs in my notebook were at last turning into sentences and paragraphs. That is also why I wish at this particular moment you hadn't worried me about keeping you sitting in Tangier. It is so extremely irritating and unfair and untrue—not untrue that you took it into your imagination but untrue that I said, "I am coming any minute." Naturally all during the summer there were moments when I thought of simply rushing off and other moments when my deep despond about my own work and your reports about the slow but steady progress in yours somehow combined to make me feel "que ce n'était pas le moment encore." Particularly as I knew you would be out all night all the time. In my present more optimistic mood I wouldn't mind a bit. I want to get there and feel I would if it weren't for the Fortune Teller. You should never have written me that of course. I can't imagine what will make me change after I've bought my ticket except the illness or death of someone very close so you see what a mood I'm in about the whole thing. Do you think he's infallible? I may of course not be able to get the money in January anyway because I don't know about Ollie and you'll be in the desert, maybe, but I'm pretty sure I could. However I can't make it before the middle of the month so I wouldn't get to Tangier till Feb. which would give you time to come out of the desert to meet me or soon thereafter. If I come in Jan. Cory will be with me, as I explained, so I could wait in Tangier. If I can't get away by the middle or end of Jan. it will then be the end of Feb. or March. (Have decided definitely against the Feb. 13th sailing which I mentioned in my last letter) I too might take a short trip, six or eight weeks, with Cory by motor. (Or if we could find a little boat that went to Haiti or Jamaica that might do but I expect we will just have to go somewhere around here.) Of course I feel very frustrated when I think of Mother alarming me so about Julian and then turning round and making me think it's silly to stay for that. (Not her fault really since the doctors seem to have made a mistake at first and I'm glad naturally), but I *could* have had my passage by now I think plus a travelling companion and gotten to see you and Africa all at once! It is infuriating. Also if I had only decided or you had been more urgent about my coming earlier in the summer I might have stepped up everything and got going sooner too. But then what is the use of writing all that. If by some miracle I do get off in January we will go straight to Tangier and you will get there when you can. I will wire you. By February you will have had time to see enough I imagine. I hope you understand that if I don't come by then I will skip February. It would mean everything to my new friend and after all only a month or so to us – which God knows seems like nothing at this point. Don't think either that it is because of her that I have been delayed. Au contraire. 1. I never expected until last month that she wouldn't be going to South America with her partner (they have travelled together for sixteen years). 2. She would have *preferred* most to leave on the first of December or as close to it as possible and asked me if I might not get ready by then but alas it was too late when she suggested this. I had not yet seen Helvetia and soon after that Mother's trouble came, so that even January I thought was out. Her partner has gone off to Honolulu in a semi-huff and it would be cruel of me to walk out on her in Feb. to get a month sooner to Tangier. About this I am morally certain. She could not leave in Feb. and be back by March. As for our getting to Tangier somehow in Jan.: I would naturally want you to be there when we arrived if you could but I don't want you to get hysterical if you are way off or if you get this letter (and) decide you can't go off because of my possible arrival, which I wouldn't put past you at this point. You might better just say, Jane will arrive in March (except that at the last minute she will give up her ticket so she won't! I am really furious that you wrote me such a thing.) Oliver has more or less decided on May for his trip unless he flies over quickly in February. He had the idea you should get all your primitive travelling done before we get there. As for Egypt, the *Vulcania* and the *Saturnia* go there so maybe it will have something to do with that, the Fortune Teller's prediction I mean. Oliver refuses to go on any freighter so he may want you to meet him there. I still can't believe that it takes as long to get from Naples to Tangier as it does from New York to Tangier. What are you thinking of? One has only to look at the map – particularly the big boats which call at Gibraltar. I think it would be fun to go that way. *I* can also wait until May and go with Oliver and Maggie *if* you think that's better but then I shall engage a passage for March in any case and we'll see what your mood is by then or mine, and what you're doing. I certainly *will* wait until May if you still want to be in the desert in March and are bored with the idea of coming out to meet me. If I go with Ollie all my expenses I think would be paid, in fact I know it, but he is undependable. I *am* sure however that he will do no more work for a while after this winter because he will certainly have knocked himself out by spring. He wants to do *Ondine* and my play next season and spend the summer around Africa and Italy if possible. I am working very hard this month typing my long story ["Camp Cataract"] and revising. I hope in January to work on selling it and perhaps getting an advance on some excerpts from my novel, but I must see Leo Lerman about it and also fix them up. He thinks I should switch to Viking. I really should finish all this work before leaving and if I could just sit here until the boat sailed I would, but leaving—even by January—always entails so much. En tout cas, we will see. Your book I have a feeling will be really wonderful. I should not actually worry about you too much. Are you not in the place you most love and writing about it, and do you not have a parrot? I am of course flattered that you want me there too with all those riches. So I will come in January or March but not in February. It is a short month anyway and I'm sure you see my point about that. (She would be in N.Y. because of me, instead of with her friend in Honolulu, so that for me to leave would be awful—and even Jan. is late for her to leave and get back by March—so Feb. is of course out. I have made no promises to her but I would not be cruel and I am fond of her.) I have as usual precipitated a holocaust and can't walk out just in that month. M. will be back in March when they return to the Inn towards the end of the month. Besides the idea of making this little trip amuses and enchants me though not nearly so much as it would to find a boat and get to Africa. She is getting a passport just in case we do. Do you think the Clairvoyant could have been wrong about my buying the ticket and then not going, and that it could have meant simply all this business about boats (I have the *Journal of Commerce* sent to me here in Vermont), all of which might have come out in his head as actually buying a ticket? I wonder. I shall never forgive him or you, really. I think I have said enough about this for one letter. If you, for some reason by the time you get this, think it advisable for me to wait and *not* leave in January even *if I can*, for God's sake cable in spite of cost. I don't know what reasons you'd have except that suddenly you might be coming back or be expecting to be gone until next June in the wilderness. I certainly hope not because as long as I hear from you I feel all right unless everything else is wrong which often happens but it's going to be awful from now on with you in the desert—and most likely months between letters. I shall never know what is happening or what to do if I should suddenly have to decide something.

I *loved* your story ["How Many Midnights"]. Everything that happened in it was perfect down to the man who was looking for Riley and her dismal return to her own apartment house (the janitor having to bring the elevator up from the basement!). You write wonderfully about this country I think, as well as you do about any other country. In fact I am convinced that you are a writer down to the marrow of your bone. Certainly I should never have expected this kind of story out of you. It is even more surprising than the one about Prue and the other two women ["The Echo"]. This is besides *sumamente* saleable I should say. The tension as usual is terrific. It seems like an innocent enough little story when it begins and the way in which you have shaded it so that it becomes steadily more somber, almost as imperceptibly to the reader as to the girl herself, is I should say masterful. I read it twice because I could not quite encompass it. The effect was so much as though it were almost that night itself and not just something written about a night that I had to reread it to see how on earth you did it, and if you really did. Of course I still don't see how, even now, except through the expert and naturally instinctive choice of the detail. The candles, the sound of the log breaking in two, the melting ice cubes, and some perfect word you use concerning her fingers in the ice bowl. I can't think of such a word *even* after reading it. It was simple enough but so accurate. The drawer and her running to the buzzer, and not pushing it, going back again to the drawer and then to the buzzer again and finally the man called "Riley," were so terrible and exciting somehow that I almost threw up. I think the artistry there was her not answering the buzzer the first time it rang, which started the suspense at just the right pitch. It is an exhausting story and the morning was really wonderful. It is even better reading the second time, too, because one notices little indications about the boy's character in the beginning which should actually be just as lightly drawn as they are or the suspense would be ruined and one would expect him not to return or at least expect some calamity. The whole thing is very wily and real short story writing, I should say. (We don't have to go in to your talent and originality because that has never been questioned.) Perhaps writing *will* be a means to nomadic life for you, but I hope you won't slowly stop writing music, altogether. I think you will do both. You have always wanted to go back to writing anyway and I remember your discussing it very solemnly once at the Chelsea. You were standing against a bureau. I am

69

furious of course about your other story but Oliver insists it isn't lost, just mislaid. Unfortunately he has to go down to the customs in person for the books as far as I know and I don't see him ever doing it. It is appalling but when I get down to New York I shall see what I can do. Meanwhile I shall instruct him not to lose the little slip from [?] in a letter that I shall write now.

Please be good and don't worry me about Africa. In other words don't be slipshod and get mixed up about what I tell you. Your letters can be very confusing too, but I do try to get the meaning out of them and not falsify. In the most recent one you don't mention your trip into the desert, only to Fez, and I understood from the other one you were starting out on a real Safari. I am so worried that I shan't hear from you for months. *Please* take care of yourself and don't for God's sake get sick down there. Also afraid I won't have any place to mail a carbon of my story when it's finished for a long while. Is there any mail delivery in the desert?

The dog is fine. I hope this reaches you. The neighbors (the bores up the road that have the little girls) came by two nights ago. I was a little tight so I insisted that I would love to go with them to a lecture on "Cooperatives in Vermont" or some such subject. Tonight is the night and I'm certainly horrified at having gotten myself into it. They will take me to the high school auditorium and bring me back with them and have a bit to eat here around ten o'clock. I have made noodle ring with beef stew in the middle. I cook little and mostly work and write letters. My energy comes from the fact that winter is here at last. I function badly in the hot muggy summer and this fall was warm all through September and during half of Oct. Libby also would like to go in May to Africa. I am of course torn between seeing you sooner and avoiding the trip alone, so will wait for your advice on that and meanwhile get on the Fern Line list for March as well as January. Helvetia wants to be on the list for July. I have more to write but I will some other time when I hear where you are. I shall forward mail to British Post Office, what little there is of interest.

Much much love, as ever

Teresa

P.S. I miss you very much indeed and want to see you naturally. If ever you are troubled or puzzled about my inertia just imagine everything you feel about "setting out" in reverse!! Of course I vacillate but I have come a long way nonetheless. I can now actually imagine the trip alone without exactly shuddering, whereas this summer I feared it even with you along. I should hate truthfully at this point not to get to Africa at all.

I am going to walk to town and mail this before I throw it away. I have as usual gotten too wound up about some remark which you have by now forgotten. I suppose it was your saying you were now at last "going to lead your own life"—as though you had been hanging about Libby's kitchen all summer. In the next breath you told me about the parrot's Thanksgiving dinner, so I know you realized that you were being unnecessarily petulant. I have noticed that whenever you are cross in a letter you atone for it quite automatically by describing some gesture of the parrot's. He sounds like another lunatic—thank God—how *will* you lug him all over Africa? Be sure to get a strong cage so that he doesn't stick his head and shoulders through the bars. Does he *say* anything? Is he pretty or just crazy? Your hotel sounded charming but whenever I get to Morocco I shall insist on Fez. You must let me know if you think the Fortune Teller infallible.

Love again,

J.

P.P.S. It is so beautiful here in Vt. You must come some winter. The furnace is being put in and as you know there are three rooms and two baths extra. H. is wonderful—no dramas—and she is eager to have you and Oliver here for long stretches of time. You will find it a most satisfactory place to spend a month in as far as work goes but undoubtedly you would be bored for longer periods. But it will be good for when you are obliged to be in this country between jobs etc. I do not accept *any* money from her—which has been an excellent idea. At the moment she's broke anyway because of her artesian well, new rooms etc. and could not even afford the Fern Line before July.

[*Enclosed, excerpt from pages 7 and 8 of a letter from Jane Bowles to Helvetia Perkins, with a handwritten note to Paul Bowles.*]

Dear Bupple, this letter was written to Perkins in the latter part of Sept. I'm sure I would have been writing you about the same sort of thing—so it must be Ollie who's done the confusing and naturally he has been instrumental in confusing me but I think it will all work out.

[To Perkins, underlining added for P.B.'s sake.]

Please forgive this letter if it is spotty and does not give you a clear picture of what I want to do. *All I know is that I may go to Africa in Jan.* and I may not *if I am working well, and Paul comes back.* Perhaps we will all be in the Chelsea again. I wouldn't be a bit surprised. Plus ça change — naturally I want to spend some months with you somewhere before leaving you unless you have changed your mind about coming along with me. You know how many hundreds of times we will all change *ours.* It might be a good idea to rent the apartment until January when I will know for sure except that I suppose that is just when you would *not* want to be in New York. Well it is too complicated to write about but you can bear all these things in mind . . . *Nothing being too imminent.*
[Letter torn here]

Paul's concert was cancelled because Arthur Gold had a gall bladder operation or attack, I'm not quite sure, but he's been ill. He's better however but they are postponing the whole concert because of lost weeks when they could not rehearse the programme. One more thing. We all think we would like a house perhaps in the town of Nyack on the Hudson from where we could commute and give up New York entirely — but this too has been going on indefinitely hasn't it? I would like that but only if it were big enough so that you could always have a room there which would be yours when you wanted it, which is of course not difficult outside of New York but so impossible in an apartment.

There are other little things to write about. As soon as I got over the hot muggy weather this cold spell put me right to sleep for the . . .
[Letter torn here]

From *Out in the World:*
(Emmy Moore's Story)

On certain days I forget why I'm here. Today once again I wrote my husband all my reasons for coming. He encouraged me to come each time I was in doubt. He said that the worst danger for me was a state of vagueness, so I wrote telling him why I had come to the Hotel Henry — my eighth letter on this subject — but with each new letter I strengthen my position. I am reproducing the letter here. Let there be no mistake. My journal is intended for publication. I want to publish for glory, but also in order to aid other women. This is the letter to my husband, Paul Moore, to whom I have been married sixteen years. (I am childless.) He is of North Irish descent, and a very serious lawyer. Also a solitary and lover of the country. He knows all mushrooms, bushes and trees, and he is interested in geology. But these interests do not exclude me. He is sympathetic towards me, and kindly. He wants very much for me to be happy, and worries because I am not. He knows everything about me, including how much I deplore being the feminine kind of woman that I am. In fact, I am unusually feminine for an American of Anglo stock. (Born in Boston.) I am almost a "Turkish" type. Not physically, at least not entirely, because though fat I have ruddy Scotch cheeks and my eyes are round and not slanted or almond-shaped. But sometimes I feel certain that I exude an atmosphere very similar to theirs (the Turkish women's) and then I despise myself. I find the women in my country so extraordinarily manly and independent, capable of leading regiments, or of fending for themselves on desert islands if necessary. (These are poor examples, but I am getting my point across.) For me it is an experience simply to have come here alone to the Hotel Henry and to eat my dinner and lunch by myself. If possible before I die, I should like to become a little more independent, and a little less Turkish than I am now. Before I go any further, I had better say immediately that I mean no offense to Turkish women. They are probably busy combating the very same Turkish quality in themselves that I am controlling in me. I understand, too (though this is irrelevant), that many Turkish women are beautiful, and I think that they have discarded their veils. Any other American woman would be sure of this. She would know one way or the other whether the veils had been discarded, whereas I am afraid to come out with a definite statement. I have a feeling that they really have got rid of their veils, but I won't swear to it. Also, if they have done so, I have no idea when they did. Was it many years ago or recently?

Here is my letter to Paul Moore, my husband . . . Since I am writing this journal with a view to publication, I do not want to ramble on as though I had all the space in the world. No publisher will attempt printing an enormous journal written by an unknown woman. It would be too much of a financial risk. Even I, with my ignorance of all matters pertaining to business, know this much. But they may print a small one . . . :

73

Dearest Paul:

I cannot simply live out my experiment here at the Hotel Henry without trying to justify or at least explain in letters my reasons for being here, and with fair regularity. You encouraged me to write whenever I felt I needed to clarify my thoughts. But you did tell me that I must not feel the need to justify my actions. However, I do feel the need to justify my actions, and I am certain that until the prayed-for metamorphosis has occurred I shall go on feeling just this need. Oh, how well I know that you would interrupt me at this point and warn me against expecting too much. So I shall say in lieu of metamorphosis, the prayed-for improvement. But until then I must justify myself everyday. Perhaps you will get a letter every day. On some days the need to write lodges itself in my throat like a cry that must be uttered . . .

I want you to know the whole truth about me. But don't imagine that I wouldn't be capable of concealing my ignorance from you if I wanted to. I am so wily and feminine that I could live by your side for a lifetime and deceive you afresh each day. But I will have no truck with feminine wiles. I know how they can absorb the hours of the day. Many women are delighted to sit around spinning their webs. It is an absorbing occupation, and the women feel they are getting somewhere. And so they are, but only for as long as the man is there to be deceived. And a wily woman alone is a pitiful sight to behold. Naturally.

I shall try to be honest with you so that I can live with you and yet won't be pitiful. Even if tossing my feminine tricks out the window means being left no better than an illiterate backwoodsman, or the bottom fish scraping along the ocean bed, I prefer to have it this way. Now I am too tired to write more. Though I don't feel that I have clarified enough or justified enough. . . .

My love,

Emmy

In January 1948 Jane Bowles arrived in Gibraltar with Cory and crossed over to Tangier by ferry. With Paul and Edwin Denby, Jane and Cory went first to Fez, then set out on their own tour of Morocco. In March Jane

74

*accompanied Cory to Spain, saw her off to the U.S., and
returned to Tangier, where she moved into the Farhar
Hotel. Paul joined her there and shortly received a wire
from Margo Jones, who was directing Tennessee
Williams'* Summer and Smoke, *asking him to return to
New York to do the music for the show.*

24

Jane Bowles to Libby Holman
[Tangier, Morocco]
[March 24, 1948]

Libby darling,

The dog[23] is wonderful. Very soft and made of wool inside and
out. The waiter thinks he's wicked, and a young Arab boy mistook
his pink ribbon for moustaches. Also he said the dog was a woman
because the front paws were breasts. He drew a picture of the dog
which I'll keep for you or send. I can't decide. I hope I didn't
discourage you with all the bus talk. You know how worked up
I get. I've worked myself out of any interest in what Paul or Topper
do as long as I don't have to be with them. Paul will make a wise
decision (ossir) I'm sure. Are you coming? I hope that you and I
can just be on a beach. Maybe that is not your intention. Now it
looks as though Paul and I would never go back to the States, but
there is time to discuss all this. No answer from Margo Jones so
far to Paul's last week's wire. I feel it has all gone up in smoke.
Perhaps you could find out what's happening through the agent
whose address he gave you. I have a dreary feeling that all kinds
of communications have been lost.

I hope I hear from you soon and that you are coming. This is
just a note partly about the dog. I imagine it *is* the way I look. Is
Louisa back—with or without that God Damned Milly? How is
everything and what's happened.

Much love,

The Dog

23 A present from Libby.

*In early May Jane and Paul went to Fez, where they
stayed at the Hotel Belvedere. While there Jane finished
her long short story, "Camp Cataract," and Paul finished
his novel* The Sheltering Sky.

25

Jane Bowles to Libby Holman
[Tangier, Morocco]
[May 10, 1948]

Dearest Libby,

I have been very excited ever since receiving your telegram. Also
if for some reason you don't come, after all, I will have had all the
pleasure of looking forward to it anyway. (I am not nearly so well
adjusted as I sound.) I think it good that Paul and I wrote contradic-
tory letters because now I feel that you know the worst and the
best and are deciding on your own hook. Actually I can't imagine
Topper not loving it, *even* if he saw only Fez and Tangier. Certainly
it will be worth more to him than staying at Treetops. I didn't mean
to make him sound like a mechanic to Paul, but I couldn't
guarantee any of his interests except the two Paul mentioned in
his letter (workshop and camping trips which you'd told me he
liked). I didn't know how interested he was in just travelling and
looking around. Lots of bright people haven't been, but have
preferred to stay in their own country. Marco Polo for instance.
Anyway you know what I mean. I am writing this for Topper's
benefit more than for yours because you understand, but he might
think I misrepresented him if you read him Paul's letter which I'm
sure you did. I think when he gets here Topper himself judging
from the heat on the coast can decide how much farther into it
he wants to go. We can discuss all that. Paul himself is against
taking native buses, since they are constantly tipping over and
going off cliffs. Since the war they are all broken down, and so few
remain that they load the sides and tops with people which is
naturally hazardous anyway. The tires are terrible and they are
built (the buses) high and narrow, so you can see how risky they
are on a curve. Half the time the brakes don't hold. Cars are very
cheap to hire, and it is in no way equivalent to hiring a car in the
States or Cuba. We could have lived on one hundred dollars a week

76

the two of us, including everything, *and* hired cars, if we'd wanted to spend more and thus stay a shorter time. I am writing this so that Topper will arrive with an open mind about everything, and not dead set on any way of doing things before he sees the country. I think he'll understand when he *does* see it (OY!). He needn't worry about luxury. Except in Tangier and a few beach towns, the good hotels aren't open. I told you that the best hotel in Tangier was about eight dollars a day or less for two people with meals included, and they are *not* like the Chez Roig[24] meals. Four head waiters and the hors d'oeuvres wagon is three stories high. This is to give you the scale. I am hoping that maybe Ollie will arrive and we can all take a trip together, in that way it will come to nothing. But whatever they decide to do will come to nothing anyway. I realize of course that you have to keep Treetops going whether you are there or not and I imagine that you want everything to be as cheap as possible. I think this must be the case because you were sort of worried when I left. I promise you that Africa will satisfy in this respect (a sentence I borrowed from Cory), but I don't want the men (boys?) to do anything really *dangerous*, whether I am along or not.

I finished my story and am typing it in one more than triplicate (quadruplicate?), so that I will have a copy here to show you. The other three go to my agent, Mrs. Aswell, and Helvetia. Paul has finished his novel as he wrote you, I imagine, and will turn out six stories tomorrow. Please telephone my little Cory before you come, if you do come. She always asks about you in her letters; the number is Lakeville 24. Tell her that you're coming here but don't forget to speak to Mary Anne too and make a fuss over her or there will be more strife. If you come will you be kind enough to bring me the two dresses I left in your apartment in New York, unless they make your luggage overweight. I wrote Scotty about them. The navy one with dots and the sheer black one with broken buttons down the front. At least bring "dotty" if you can't bring both. They should have been found in Ray's closet. I would also like a package of "Zip Epilator" just for fun. For God's sake if you should see Cory by accident in the middle of a field, don't show her ͟his letter. She might not like that sentence quoted. I hope your "Tzoris" (correct spelling?) is a little better and that you *do come*. Oliver wrote you had some success at your club. My love, Libby dear, as ever,

J.

[24] A restaurant in Varadero, Cuba.

At the end of May, Oliver Smith came to Morocco and joined Paul and Jane in Fez. Soon after he arrived he became ill and for some weeks lay in bed with a high fever. During this time Jane too became ill. She went to a local doctor, a Dr. Cheroux, who told her that there was "something organically wrong" with her heart, though her symptoms soon disappeared.

In June Jane and Paul and Oliver Smith returned to Tangier to meet Libby Holman, who had arrived from the U.S. with Topper. Jane stayed in Tangier while the others took a trip south through the desert and across the High Atlas mountains.

After the visitors left, Paul returned to Tangier, but on July 18 he was called to New York to work on Summer and Smoke. *Jane remained alone in Tangier at the Hotel Villa de France. Mornings she worked on her novel* Out In The World. *Much of the rest of the time she spent in pursuit of Cherifa, a young Arab peasant woman who sold grain in the market. It was Paul who had introduced Jane to Cherifa, shortly after her arrival in Tangier.*

26

Jane Bowles to Paul Bowles
[Hotel Villa de France]
[Tangier, Morocco]
[July, 1948]

Dearest Bup

It is stupid of me to take so long to get down to writing you. There seems too much really to write about—I mean Fez and money and Africa altogether and my failure to like in it what you do and to like what you do at all anywhere. I love Tangier—the market and the Arab language, the Casbah, etc. And I long to go now to Marrakech and Taroudant. It's a pity and since reading your novel I take it very much to heart. I hope you will not complain about me to Peggy Bate. I know you love to talk behind someone's back, just as I do, but oddly enough I don't get any pleasure complaining about you. On the contrary I am horrified and scared when people attack you because you are difficult to defend at times. Now that I've seen you waiting for O. to arrive and witnessed the subsequent disappointment I shudder to think of my own failure to react properly. I have reason to hope that you simply could not have been that excited about my coming or at least that your excitement was of a different nature. I can't believe that after ten years you would have secretly been expecting someone like yourself (or Edwin Denby) to arrive from Gibraltar. (I am sorry you had to stay there for three days). At the Farhar I was peculiarly disturbed by the fact that you lingered on in Fez with Edwin instead of rushing to the Farhar to see me. I felt very jealous and left out; I sensed that you were really better off with Edwin and that there would be an unfortunate comparison made at some future date. Alas! it came much sooner than I had expected it would and I have not ceased brooding about it yet; also I have never tried harder to be in your world — to see it the way you did which probably is why I was in such a foul temper the whole time. I wanted to be companionable and pleasant — a source of mild pleasure at meal times and otherwise calm and self-effacing. I am really and truly sorry that it turned out so differently. I don't quite know yet what happened but I do know I have never been so near to a crack-up before. It was not pleasant and I prefer not to think about it ever again. I daresay I won't want to be in Fez ever again, either, unless by next year I've forgotten it all. You are happier there without me anyway, but perhaps the Palais Jamai?[25] Also before I go on to new subjects, I hope that you did not really *think* I would "*pull* a heart attack" on the trip, as you said to Libby and Topper. It's the only thing you've ever said that I've minded, that and your Fez remark about visualizing me in a wheelchair or dead. I was so frightened by my heart anyway. I can find only two explanations for such statements — either you never believed for a minute there was anything wrong at all or else you were really worried and therefore mean. I am at my meanest when I feel the greatest tenderness. Seeing you dead in the novel brought out the spitfire in me at the Belvedere in Fez. Perhaps harpy would be a more suitable word. I was not exactly like Lupe Velez, after all, but more like my Aunt Birdie. Sometimes I find nice explanations like the above for your attitude and sometimes I feel that you saw the whole thing, I mean the state of my health, as nothing but a threat to your trip, which mattered to you more than anything. I wonder . . . It must be that

[25] A hotel in Fez.

you never believed there *was* anything wrong—but then you must have or you wouldn't have gotten so gloomy and had visions of me in a wheelchair. I thought I was *finished*, I assure you. It was different from thinking, "The war is coming so soon—" but I'm glad now that I did think I had so little time left to live. Cheroux should have never worded his diagnosis the way he did. I told him I was "pulling a heart attack," and he told me that on the contrary there was something organically wrong with my heart—that is why I was frightened. Much more frightened than I told you. I would so much rather have been the neurotic faker than someone really ill and I was still not sure whether I was really well when you mentioned my pulling an attack to Libby. Surely the English in this letter has gone to pieces long ago but I just can't worry about it. You can understand with a little effort what I've written.

I shouldn't mention all this perhaps but I can never write anything else if there is something that must come out and I'm sure you would not like to be without any letters from me at all. I hope that I'm a horror to even *think* of these remarks and that I should not invest them with too much importance but I cannot forget them, or some aspects of your behavior. I think a word from you would put my mind at rest on this subject. You have a way too of saying things easily so that it wouldn't take you much time. I am not attached to you simply because I'm married to you, as you certainly must know. If I were I could pass over these things conveniently. Oliver thinks that I'm "hanging on to you." I hope you don't think that or that it isn't the actual truth even without your thinking it. I shall approach the awful financial question some other time. Maybe not in a letter. I get upset because you say you have enough money for one but not for two etc. It's probably true, unless we live in a house—it's surely true when one is travelling. It is also true that I could have stayed behind in America indefinitely and have cost you nothing. But now that I am here I am damned if I'll ruin it by worrying about these things. I am extremely grateful to you for letting me stay and use the money. I don't believe I have it coming to me because I'm your wife. I just can't bear that idea and yet I'm not sure either that atavistically I don't probably consider myself—partly—entitled to this sojourn because I am your wife? In other words I feel both things at once. That you are completely free and someone who will help me when he can, out of affection, and yet also that you are a husband. I don't think about the husband part very much but I am trying to be *very* honest. I am not sure either that being confined a bit by the social structure is altogether bad for either one of us. We will see.

The view of the Arab town from my window is a source of endless pleasure to me. I cannot stop looking and it is perhaps the first time in my life that I have felt joyous as a result of a purely visual experience. The noise in the Villa is something I must fight constantly but I cannot leave the *lieu*. Certainly it's the only place in Tangier I want to be. If I left it I would go to the States I think. The [Old] Mountain, I know, would be bad in summer unless one found a tree to work under far away. I am just beginning to try to work now and the morning noises are very bad. It makes me frantic because I love it here, but I'm sure that I shall find some quiet spot or else reverse and work at night. Or say from five to nine A.M. I am going with Boussif today about the deed. Cherifa, I'm afraid, is never going to work out. I think she's very much in love with Boussif. She's in a rage because she expected that once his wife left he would marry her, and instead he's taken some woman to cook for him whom he also sleeps with. He brought her to the grain market and introduced her to Cherifa. They all sat in the hanootz according to [Jacques] Lantzmann (I was not there), and joked together. Boussif, however, said that his mistress told Cherifa that only *she*, Cherifa, could come to see Boussif while she lived there, because she was not afraid that Boussif would ever marry a woman who wore no veil and sold grain in the market. I asked Boussif if Cherifa were not insulted, and he said, "No, why?" They are definitely confusing people. I think Cherifa is afraid of me. I saw her sneak behind a stall yesterday when I appeared so that I wouldn't see her. Nonetheless I am determined now to learn Arabic. It is good exercise for the mind in any case and there are more chances that I will get pleasure out of it than not. Even if my evenings with Cherifa and Quinza [with whom Cherifa lived] turn out to be a pipe dream. I am so utterly dependent now on Boussif that it is foolish to even think about it. The pronunciation, Dean[26] says, is impossible to master—ever. One can just vaguely approach it enough to be understood because it takes years to develop certain throat muscles. I said my first words yesterday after Cherifa sneaked behind the stall and I suppose I said them in desperation. The older dyke was there, thank God (she comes to the market irregularly), so I walked over to her and somehow spoke. Just a few words actually, but immediately some old men gathered around me and everyone nodded happily. They said to

[26] Proprietor of Dean's bar, where the English of Tangier went.

each [other] that I spoke Arabic. I am slow and stupid but determined. I shall never of course be as clever as you are.

Customarily I will send your letters immediately upon receiving them from the British Post Office. If they are sent within twenty-four hours they are forwarded free. A few times I have not done this. Reasons: I didn't know it in the beginning, and then once or twice got there, couldn't remember address of Morris Agency, brought letters back here, didn't get them back on time. Have now committed address to memory so no mail will return with me to my room from now on. I must know about your contract. I hope and pray that it is all settled. Oy! I hate to think of it. Also keep me posted as to news about your novel. I shall let you know of any progress or total lack of it on my part (in writing) within a month. It is a little soon yet for me to know whether or not this was a wise decision. (Staying here—I mean.) Of course the less I worry about whether it was or not, the wiser it will have been—and I am more and more pleased that I've stayed so far. I am trying to get Helvetia to come over here, and still think she might be persuaded to come with you if you do come back. I am not very worried about all that, but very eager to see whether I can work or not seriously. If I can't I think I'd better just plain give up writing. Conditions here should be ideal. Except for the awful war cloud, I should say I was very very happy. Naturally, I am moody, but I'm savoring more separate minutes than I have in many years. I love this spot geographically and I'm always pleased to have lots of blue around me. Here there's the water and the sky and the mountains in the distance and all the blue in the Casbah; even in the white, there's lots of blue. The grain market is blue—blue and green. I have had a ladder built so that I could get up on our terrace—about seventy pesetas, and certainly worth it. It is the best view from the Casbah I've seen. The white dome cuts out all that Rif section, thank God, so a room there would be magnificent. I think it would always be small to live in for more than a few days except for one person but very useful as a garçonnière and very profitable to rent, if it were really done up properly. Plumbing etc. We should discuss it further when I've got the deed and when we see each other, here or there. There's no rush after all except that we must make sure the house is really ours. I am going there to cook lunch in a few minutes. Just a pot of ratatouille and some sausage—cheap and very nourishing. Quantities of tomatoes now, so that makes eating simple. It is unfortunate that a hole in the kitchen leads to the bathroom because of the smells. I think the whole bottom part would remain smelly but the room on top would be free of odors. In the bottom there should be a kitchen, closet, bath and room for a servant to sleep—caretaker—and on top the room to read, eat and entertain in—sleep in too, naturally, when one felt like it and there would be part of the terrace left as well. We will decide on all this later. I can't tell now really what I want. I might be fed up with Tangier in three months. But it might be a good investment to improve the house rather than to sell it even if we rented it to Arabs. I know we could rent it to Americans. They love to live in the Casbah and there are lots of bachelors wandering around. Also people like Jay [Haselwood], Bill Chase[27] and others. It's a sweet house and I am really beginning to understand now about your buying it very well. I enclose this check (Dutch royalties on *The Glass Menagerie*). The accompanying note was a mere business form. I have received no notice of your checks coming through but will in a few days go and ask about it. You had better write me the particulars in your next letter as I've forgotten the details. The amount etc. Why don't you call Pearl Kazin at the [*Harper's*] *Bazaar*? Maybe she could have a drink with you and you might find out whether she's optimistic about selling my story or not. Of course I don't even know whether or not she liked it. Thanks for library card, checkbook etc.

Please—Please write me

Much Love

J.

P.S.   Could you try to get Edwin's address for me? Please write my mother immediately. She will want to call you I'm sure so give her your number. Tell her you're coming back here and that I'm crazy about Tangier and therefore stayed behind.

Mother's address: c/o Mayor's

3rd and Main Sts.

Dayton

[27] Haselwood and Chase owned the Parade Bar in Tangier.

27

Jane Bowles to Paul Bowles
[Hotel Villa de France]
[Tangier, Morocco]
[July/August, 1948]

Dearest Bup,

This must be a short one. I owe letters to H., Libby and O., who wrote me a long Swiss one that was very sweet and interesting. "H" stands for Helvetia, whose letters have been getting better and better. I think if I just stay in Africa for a few more years everything will be fine. Even Mother seems to be calming down. This letter is to assure you that I do have everything you handed over to me in the long narrow envelope and that the receipt from the bank said two hundred and eighty dollars not three hundred and ninety seven or whatever the sum you quoted. I hadn't looked at it when I wrote you because I knew that unless I read the papers you left with me carefully—they're in Spanish—I'd get confused about which was the statement and which was the receipt for the checks. There were two things in the envelope besides the checkbook. I hate reading Spanish legal terminology; in fact everything Spanish gets on my nerves. I don't believe Spain would but you know how they are over here. Perhaps I couldn't stick them over there either—it would be depressing but wonderful to see, as you have assured me many times. The slip acknowledging that the checks had come through also said two hundred and eighty dollars so that *must* be it. I hope there isn't a different receipt. You did say something close to that sum before you left—I'm quite sure of it. In other words, both slips, the one you left inside of "long and narrow" as well as the slip that came through the mails last week, are marked two hundred and eighty bucks, so that must be right. No?

I don't know myself what I meant by aspects of your behavior. (?) I've forgotten. It is true that Oliver was a thousand times more solicitous than you which made me feel that you didn't give a fig, whether I collapsed in the street or not; you must remember that whether I brought it on myself or not, whatever it was, I did think I was going to die or have a heart attack and I was terrified, which I don't think you ever got through your head. I think I expected you to be more worried and concerned than you were, whether

I brought it on myself or not. I still don't quite know what the hell it was all about and I suppose the less said about it in letters the better. I am *not* brooding about it and take you at your word that there is no reason to. I don't want for there to be a reason to. I couldn't resist that sentence, because it is just the kind of thing I am longing to write all the time. I am glad that Mary Lou's letter pleased you. [*inserted*: P.S. Naturally I'm glad I reworked it— without your advice it wouldn't *exist* (Camp Cataract).] Not that you must expect a sale. There are many old women and old men at the *Bazaar* who must be convinced that it is the proper material for their magazine; even if Frances McFadden did accept it they could still refuse to have it published. Perhaps Pearl can give you an idea of what to expect. I continue loving Tangier— maybe because I have the feeling of being on the edge of something that I will some day enter. This I don't think I could feel if I didn't know Cherifa and the "Mountain Dyke" that yellow ugly one (!?). It is hard for me to separate the place from the romantic possibilities that I have found in it. I cannot separate the two for the first time in my life. Perhaps I shall be perpetually on the edge of this civilization of theirs. When I am in Cherifa's house I am still on the edge of it, and when I come out I can't believe I was really in it—seeing her afterwards, neither more nor less friendly, like those tunes that go on and on or seem to, is enough to make me convinced that I was never there. My professor has disappeared but I daresay he'll be back. Now that I've mastered a few words it's become an ordeal for me to go into the market. I am frightfully shy and embarrassed by the whole thing—my pronunciation, my inability to understand them most of the time. They each speak differently. All that is a terrible strain and I must steel myself before I plunge into it. I do not underestimate the importance of knowing Jay—who is really sweet to me—because I would not be able to just struggle with Arabic all the time. Also there are days when they disappear entirely and it is nice to know someone here. I am terribly happy because the Mountain Dyke asked me to go for a walk with her either on the mountain or by the sea. I was amazed because I had just about given up getting anywhere with any Arab women ever. I was in a terrible state of despond too because Cherifa had just rushed past me leading a mule to the country. She wore a pink embroidered vest and a new red and white striped blanket. She was on her way to visit her family in the country (three feet out of Tangier). She was supposed to leave three or four days ago and be back yesterday which is precisely why I

85

was hanging around there and instead she was just leaving. I wonder too if I would bother with all this if you didn't exist. I don't know. Surely I would not have begun it — got the idea without you, I mean. It is the way I feel about my writing too. Would I bother if you didn't exist? It is awful not to know what one would do if one were utterly alone in the world. You would do just what you've always done and so would Helvetia but I don't exist independently. I am *doubly* delighted with anything that delights me here because I feel that you are able to participate in my pleasure more than in any pleasure I might have in being with Margaret McKean,[28] or Spivy or simply wandering about New York (which I don't like now, but used to). You know too that I am no hypocrite and would not *pretend* to be pleased — in the first place I couldn't. I know you don't like Tangier much so perhaps it's silly for me to think you can be pleased with my taking any pleasure in it. Perhaps you are not at all pleased. But I think you do approve of my having some Arab women friends and you do see how boring it can be otherwise. I loved Fez as long as we were both working but somehow the whole thing went to pieces after that, as you know. If I ever go back there, I think I'd stay at the Jamai. When you complain about New York, for God's sake don't bring up the radios. Nothing could be worse than the radios here and in Fez. For the rest I agree. If you had any sense you would buy yourself some Birdseye corn or asparagus, some hamburger, canned soups etc. and fix yourself food in the house. Frozen strawberries you love and there are other cheaper fruits available. None of that would be any more difficult than making Klim, tea, "chocolate milk mixed with coffee," and handling the endless paraphernalia one travels with in Africa. Instead of complaining like a maniac why don't you try to solve some way of eating so that you will be stronger when you get to the next place you go? Even if it costs you a little more than the Automat, and it needn't, you would be better nourished. Libby says that Willy May would cook lunch for you and she also said you should call up Scotty[29] at any time and go out there to Treetops. You have no right in the world to complain so much when you've been away an entire year, and it's only the fact that you can be there and earn some money that will permit you to live over here. I don't mean this time but any time. You sound more

---

[28] A former lover.

[29] Housekeeper at Treetops.

spoiled than ever, ranting against civilization and the Americans and their noise (after having lived among the Spanish—MY GOD!) and in spite of the fact that I see exactly what you mean and that New York must *really* look hideous after this part of the world, it frightens me to think that you have no part of yourself you can retire into, though that is what you advised *me* to do when the noise and confusion got me down in Fez (on our way to lunch in the carriage). I don't like to see you so helpless and so unable to take one minute of something you don't like gracefully. Please do something about Treetops or your food. You can perfectly well and you will be stronger in the next primitive place you visit. If you think of it that way and not simply as spending money or any effort in New York, you might be able to do it. What do you mean by Peggy's ambivalence—about me? or you? I don't understand. Is she really worried about me? Does she think my coming back would keep you there longer? What's it all about? I have no plans. Do you think you'll come back here or do you prefer to go somewhere else. For God's sake go where *you* want to go and don't dare come to NORTH AFRICA just because of me if you'd rather go to West Africa. How can I say yet what I'll do? I refuse to. I am very happy— with moments of depression because I always have them, but very few. I am delighted I stayed. Tangier is wonderful in summer. I have certain ideas but it is all too premature to start trying to work any of them out. I am typing the little story for George and will send it on in a few days. Be good and please get yourself some decent food. All you do with Birdseye food is to plop it in boiling water. One box of corn or peas is enough for two meals and delicious. Then there are the package soups and hamburger you can make. I think too, that you should go out to Treetops. Helvetia is waiting for a letter from me before she writes you. She would like very much to have you out there if and when you can go. I shall write her immediately—and for God's sake get there and eat before you come back here or anywhere else—or don't you want to? At least get to Libby's.

Much Love

J.

P.S.   This was to be a short one.

If hamburger is too expensive why not tell Willy May to put a stew on for you in the morning when she comes—beef—carrots—

onions—vegetables are cheap in summer—celery—corn etc. She could easily do it every day, alternating beef and lamb. Débrouilles toi—enfin!

I don't remember about your coat—ask Scotty if by any chance it's out there—as for the cigarette cases—God knows.

I take for granted that you don't mind my being over here—will come home if money matters make it advisable for me to live at H's or Libby's.

28

Jane Bowles to Paul Bowles
[Hotel Villa de France]
[Tangier, Morocco]
[July/August, 1948]

Dearest Buppie—

I am off to Cherifa's hanootz. Our relationship is completely static: just as I think that at least it is going backwards (on the days when she sneaks behind a stall) I find that it is right back where it was the next day. Nothing seems to move. I have finally, by wasting hours and hours just hanging about mentioning the Aid Es Seghir[30] about every five seconds, managed to get myself invited for tonight. So I shall go soon to the grain market from where we will leave for M'sallah together. I don't know whether I shall walk behind her or in front of her or parallel to her on the other side of the street. I made my invitation secure by suggesting a chicken. I made wings of my arms and flapped them—"djdédda"—your phonetic spelling and mine are different so don't correct the above in your mind.

Later: It would take far too many pages to explain how the Aid Es Seghir came a day sooner than moon experts expected that it would, and how I therefore went to Cherifa's the very night after the carousing was over. Because in a normally arranged world the whole appointment would have evaporated. On the feast day they don't come to the market at all, and on that day we had fixed our rendezvous there which was in everyone's opinion the day *before*

[30] A Moroccan feast day.

the feast. I was to give her the chicken then so that it could be plucked and put with the olives for the following day. It is all so ridiculous—because others said it wouldn't come for five days. Then I worried about the chicken rotting—well how can I ever explain this? But somehow in this peculiar world where nothing is arranged there is a sudden miraculous junctioning, a moment of unraveling when terribly complicated plans—at least what would be a complicated plan anywhere else—work out somehow as if in a dream, where one has only to think of something for it actually to appear (your novel). It would take years to believe in this, and not to see it merely as an amusing mirage—I mean to believe that such things *do* work out for the Arabs *when* they do, not because there is a law of chance but because such a lack of concentration on even the immediate future would allow all sorts of mysterious rhythms to flower, which we are no longer in possession of. I wonder. The Herrera soup coming down through the streets from all the far sections of Tangier to the Arabs who remained in the Socco after dark—always on time, always warm, and always sufficient to serve the number of people gathered— just like Cherifa's tiny blue tea pot with its endless supply of tea.

Well, in any case I wandered down there at 7:30 A.M. just thinking, Well, maybe she has thought of our appointment and come to wait for me at some point. She wasn't there but the old yellow-faced mountain dyke was, and alas I had to eat quantities of perfectly terrible tortilla-like bread soaked in rancid oil, flies and honey!! Then I followed a parade thinking, "Well it's such a funny country, maybe I'll meet her this way." The policeman said the parade was going to M'sallah but of course it stopped a little above the Villa de France, and the next policeman—also an Arab— said they were *not* going to M'sallah but turning 'round and going back down to the Mendoubia. By then I'd already waited around for it an hour, while it just remained in the square behind the Villa. I was planning to follow it to M'sallah. It was thus far the hottest day in the year and the Tangier flies in August are terrific. Funnily enough I don't mind very much because I am having fun. The men in the parade, some of those wonderful old men, were really beautiful in pink chiffon over white, some in pointed red fez[zes] and others in the usual square (?) ones. The horses were wildly spirited even in the heat, and there were hundreds of women gathered all on one side of the road in beautiful djellabas. I went back to the market feeling that there was no chance of meeting her, but somehow I went anyway. She *was* there—no glimmer of surprise or pleasure in her eye when she saw me, in spite of the arrangements having been completely bitched up because of the Aid Es Seghir coming a day sooner. Probably because she'd forgotten there were any arrangements. I had to go through the whole thing again about the chicken "dar dialek gadi nimshi maak" etc. and she said I should meet her at 7:00 P.M. there in the grain market. At 10:30 we started for M'sallah with her cousin Mohammed (who is a good musulman), as our escort. He always steps in when she is on the outs with Boussif—which is now the case. I shall tell you the rest of the story some other time. I miss you and I wish that we could once be together some place where we could both be having such foolish days and yet days that are so full of magic too. It would be fun to come back and talk about them. I can see that I would *hate* to have some one waiting here at the hotel for me, with an eye on the watch and feeling very sad. How eleven women wandered in and out of Cherifa's house and all had tea out of the tiny pot in the morning is something I so wish I could make you see in *color*. But I'm afraid I never can.

I was delighted to hear from my mother that you called her up and that you *are* doing the show. I would have felt so terribly responsible if you weren't because I half pushed you into it. I appreciate your calling her tremendously. I imagine you'd be bored to tears staying with her in Dayton—she mentioned a possibility. You needn't put yourself through *that*. If you see her for God's sake don't mention *anything* about my being nervous or thinking my heart was bad—*nothing* remotely connected with that or she'll be right over here. Of course you wouldn't. Perhaps I *am* the "Dorothy Dix" of Tangier. But for the Arabs, the world's biggest "sucker"—I don't know. But I don't mean any "double entendre." I just realized with horror the pun. I have *no* occasion to make one. I am being extremely economical so don't worry about that. I would always be completely scrupulous about your money because you earn it. I continue pleased that I've stayed on but I'm in despair about Arabic. I can speak a little but understanding them when they speak to each other is another cup of *tea*.

Much love

Teresa

P.S.   Your checks came through so be at peace about that.

90

29

Jane Bowles to Natasha von Hoershelman
[Hotel Villa de France]
[Tangier, Morocco]
[August, 1948]

Natasha dear,

Thank you for the postal card from Fire Island which has practically
ruined my life over here in Africa, now that I've decided to stay
awhile. There are many reasons why I've stayed but since actually
I don't make decisions ever, I am somehow here because I didn't
leave. Paul's gone back to do music for the new Tennessee Williams
show. He'll return to Africa probably but that won't influence me.
My only reason for returning now, as I've said before, or haven't
I ever said it, is you and Katharine [Hamill] and as I'm off liquor
for a while I don't think it would be wise to rush home to see you
yet. I feel that H. can get here, I mean Helvetia. I am learning Arabic
although one can't really learn it at all—you could because you're
Russian. Still I can say a little. There's a harem I'm trying to get
into, after all our joking about that. There really and truly is. Two
veiled pitch black women (I've seen one of them only) and a yellow
faced savage down from the mountains who is their husband, I
think. It is hard not knowing the language to be sure—yet. I am
at a great disadvantage being a *Christian* (OY!) also a woman and
any of the market women are ashamed to be seen with me in the
streets. Actually I know only two of them. The yellow one and
my little Cherifa who is about twelve years younger than myself.
No one is fond of me at all, but I like to look at them and listen
to what they say, even though I don't understand. I see the Arabs
in the market mostly. It is right under my window, almost, so I
can run out and look at someone whenever I please. I expect maybe
to go to the house belonging to the wild yellow one's family for
a feast on Saturday that ends Ramadan (the month of fasting)—
God knows how I'll get back. It's way off in the poorest Arab section
and I shall never find my way home. They will probably just turn
me loose at four in the morning after eleven hours of tea and say
goodnight. No one I'm sure will accompany me since they seem
to wander all over alone. But then it is all right for them and tradi-
tional to do so (but not on the beach or in the country—just in
the towns). I don't know the yellow one at all but because she's

seen me in Cherifa's stall a lot she decided to ask me. The worst of it is I'm so mixed up by the Arabic pronouns and verbs that I don't actually know whether I asked myself to her family's house or whether she asked me. Surely I asked myself because they don't invite one. Not these market ones. She came over to the stall and somehow in my lousy Arabic I must have got myself into the feast without meaning to. It isn't sure that I'll actually go either—they will probably never mention it again.

Will you please send the enclosed letter off to Sylvia [Marlowe] immediately. If I were sure Katharine were not suddenly in Vt. I would ask her to do it. You can perfectly well take it to the office and stick a stamp on it. In fact I have decided to send this to the office where you must have all the necessary equipment. I meant to write you days ago about Mary Lou and now if you don't send the letter off it will be too late. Read it and you'll see why I'm sending it. Kiss Katharine for me. I miss you terribly. For God's sake don't send any more cards from Fire Island—

Much Much Love

Jane

Kiss Lola [Natasha's sister]—this is for her to read as well. How is she? It is very important that the letter go off to S. immediately.

30

Jane Bowles to Paul Bowles
[Hotel Villa de France]
[Tangier, Morocco]
[August, 1948]

Dearest Bup—

I started a long letter to you the other day, telling you all about my terrible afternoon with "Tetum" (the Mountain Dyke). We never did go to the mountain—in fact she never had any intention of going there. We went to a dry triangular square, right in Tangier, surrounded by modern villas and near a bus stop. It was too long and sad and funny and involved to write about, so I gave up. All

I can say is that I have never been so frustrated by anyone in my life as I am being right now—except by Iris Barry, and that lasted eleven years—so God knows I'll probably stick around here forever, just for an occasional smile from Tetum or Cherifa. I wrote you how exciting it was to feel on the edge of something. Well, it's beginning to make me very nervous. I don't see any way of getting any further into it, since what I want is so particular (as usual); and as for forgetting them altogether, it's too late. For me Africa right now is the grain market and being an obsessive maybe nothing will change that. I am still learning Arabic and I still love Tangier but I cannot tell how long it will take me to admit that I'm beaten. It is not any personal taste that I'm obliged to fight but a whole social structure, so different from the one you know—for certainly there are two distinct worlds here (the men's world and the women's), as you've often said yourself. As for Cherifa, I'm utterly dependent on Boussif as far as seeing her goes, and he's not around much lately.

I still have a dim hope that if I learned to speak Arabic she would be friendly *maybe* and I could sit in the hanootz with her when I chose to. She never asks me in unless Boussif is there and then he does the asking. Either she is ashamed to be seen with me alone or, quite sensibly, doesn't see the point because I cannot really speak to her. I don't know. I am merely trying to know her better socially (having given up hope as far as anything else is concerned). I can't bear to be continually hurled *out* of the Arab world. The rest of Tangier really doesn't interest me *enough*, though I am very grateful to have Jay here and Bill, but most particularly Jay. I would be lonesome otherwise, though I wouldn't be if they would let me sit with them in the market when I wanted to. Perhaps you have never been in this inferior position vis-à-vis the Arabs. I can understand how if one could get all one wanted here and were admired, courted, and feted, that one would *never never* leave. Even so, without all that—and you've had it—I have never felt so strongly about a place in my life, and it is just maddening not to be able to get *more* of it. How I would love to have walked on the mountain with Tetum (I realize it's a ridiculous name). Naturally she couldn't and never will, and I was a fool to believe her. She's a big liar, and each day she says just the *opposite* of what she said the day before. Do any of the men do that? I mean really the *exact* opposite. Whenever I suggest *anything* to her at all—even a glass of tea— she cuts her throat with an imaginary knife and says something about her family—at least she uses the imaginary knife one day, and on the next is prepared to do anything (verbally only). I am puzzled, vexed, and fascinated, but deep inside I have an awful feeling I shall never never find out any more than I know now. Still, it is only August. We'll see—but I haven't much hope. I wept for two hours after my walk with Tetum. So you see I am very different about these things than you are. I didn't realize how much I had hoped for and how vividly I had pictured the walk on the mountain until I started to cry. After I had cried awhile, I began to laugh. And if *only* you had been here it wouldn't have mattered, because frustrating as it all was it was certainly *ridiculous*, and you would have loved hearing about it. I wish to hell I could have the same sort of adventures in Fez or that you liked Tangier. I cannot imagine a better time really than being in a place we both liked and each of us being free and having adventures, even if mine were frustrating—they would be more amusing naturally if you were here. I wonder how I shall ever be able to leave the view of the Casbah. It means so much to me. Enfin—I do not have to leave yet.

I was delighted about H.B. [*Harper's Bazaar*] taking my story. Please speak to Pearl about it. She writes that when Mary Lou gets back she will talk price with the top ladies, and that in any case I shall get at *least* $350—and they hope more. I *certainly* think I should get more, don't you? I can do nothing from here. But talk to M.L. when she gets back. Under separate cover I am sending Ivan Von Auw a copy of my story. I want him to show it to Knopf too. Tell him it's going to be published and that I want an advance on a novel. If that fails, I want Ivan to approach another publisher. One of them is already interested (I forget which) and if he can't get me something then I want another agent. It's all too ridiculous—but I feel the time to strike is now. I have written the story for George Davis and am typing it. I don't work nearly enough—as usual—and keep hoping that the next day I will change my habits completely.

Please do get in touch with Ivan (under Harold Ober in the book). Just call Ober and ask for Ivan. Do you hate to do this? After helping me so much with the story, surely you won't mind this final effort. Knopf might be interested in seeing it—though probably not. I think I should get another publisher. Maybe you will have time to do nothing. I shall also write Ivan all this but I would feel better if I knew *you* were looking after my interests there too—that is, if you would speak to both him and Mary Lou. I have often suggested to Ivan that he speak to Carl Van V. [Vechten] about myself and Knopf. Carl's a great friend of Alfred's and an admirer of mine as well. I think the *Bazaar* can certainly afford more than $350. Don't you? But I don't want to make things too difficult for Mary Lou. I hope you'll be there long enough to see her before going on the road. If not, speak to Pearl. I'd rather sell it for 350 however than *not* sell it at all, naturally, so be careful. I suppose there isn't much you can do really. But at least speak to them all, *particularly* Ivan. You must write me about your own novel. I hope you are on the track of a publisher.

Pearl and Mary Lou both have written me wonderful letters about "Camp Cataract." I'm so happy about all that. Now that it has been fixed up, I *know* that it's the best thing I've ever done — and always was latently. But I don't think it would ever have been if you hadn't helped. I wish though that you had liked it more. I would try Knopf for the novel if I were you. He loves composers and that might help him to advertise a bit, though I know you don't want them to plug that. There should be a letter from you soon. *Are* you coming back? It would be so wonderful here with a car. Tangier weather is *perfect* in summer. I would like to buy some little mattresses for the house soon, and then when you come back we will discuss seriously whether or not to build onto it — that is, if you *do* come back. Or have you decided to go to Dakar? If you think the war's coming any minute, let me know. I daresay in that case I should hurry out of here. Try and bring H. back with you — if you are coming. I'm sure if you wrote her to come with you and chose a decent boat, she would come, particularly if you did all the arranging. I hope you have found some friends in New York since you last wrote me.

Much Love —

J.

P.S. Dearest Bup —

Just received your letter and was delighted to have it though furious at your agent for being an idiot. I think you should pick your own publishing houses. She must be mad. How lucky Carson [McCullers] is to have someone in love with her. I feel that no one will ever be in love with me again.

If and when I leave Africa never to return it will be because I saw exactly what I have always wanted and couldn't have it. The house is fine. I now have the name of the owner and have gone twice to the Mendoubia. But the right people weren't there.

Much Love,

J.

P.P.S. Don't see Mary Lou Aswell unless you want to about my story and don't mention the sum she quoted to me originally. She'll do all she can I know. However you can certainly say that you *personally* think I should get a better price than that.

Pearl wrote at *least* $350—which makes me feel they'll pay $400. I don't know. Mary Lou is always on the writer's side so perhaps there is no point in seeing her except for fun—and I would like you to. She's an angel and I miss her very much..

Do what you like. But definitely see Ivan.

31

Jane Bowles to Katharine Hamill and
Natasha von Hoershelman
[Hotel Villa de France]
[Tangier, Morocco]
[August, 1948]

Katharine dear and Natasha,

Will you get this to my agent—immediately? I have lost his address. Naturally you can keep it for one *night* if you want to read it *OR* if you get it before a weekend he will probably be out of town. I am sending it to *Fortune* [where Katharine and Natasha worked] in case you, K, are in Vermont.

It is important for me to get it to him quickly because I want Paul to speak to him and Paul *may* be *leaving*. The story has been accepted by the *Bazaar* but I'm trying to get more money for it. I want Ivan (the agent) to get the MS to Knopf—who will read it— and if he likes it I want Ivan to try for an advance on a novel. If he can't get it from Knopf I may try to change publishers. In any case Paul knows all this and will discuss it with him—the reason for the haste. *However* call Ivan up and ask him how quickly he can get around to reading it, and if there's a delay it might as well

96

stay with you for a day or two. Naturally I'd like all of you to see it (most of all *Kay* Guinness, the critic). But I daresay if both of you get through it, I will be lucky. If it does arrive on a weekend *OR* if he says to keep it two days, whoever sees it—Lola or Rosalind might want to or Angelica (she's gone?)—please make read it chez toi. (That means in *your* house—*fedar dialek* in Arabic—an impossible language for me to learn. You can see how unlike anything it is.) The agent is named Ivan Von Auw, c/o Harold Ober in the book—in other words not listed under his own name. Call him. I suggest handing him the script—perhaps on the street to avoid elevators.[31] The Ober office is near you.

Love,

J.

P.S. Thank you for letter. Will have Bubble telephone you. Let me know if MS reaches you—the minute it does. I will write more fully soon. Mr. Von Auw is pronounced Mr. Von Ow!

32

**Jane Bowles to Paul Bowles and
  Oliver Smith**
[Hotel Villa de France]
[Tangier, Morocco]
[September, 1948]

Dear Paul and Oliver,

This is a business letter that I am sending both of you in case it does not reach one of you.

One letter is going to Paul in N.Y., the other I shall send to my mother in Dayton, since she may be able to get it to him on the road. She wrote that they might see each other in Cleveland. I believe this matter regards Paul more than you, Oliver, because as I said you will probably never come here again. Still the house *is* half yours and you did say you were interested so I don't consider

---

31 Jane was terrified of elevators.

you out of it either, unless you want to be, in which case you are.

In any case, as it is, it is neither livable nor rentable even to an Arab, nor could I even invite Cherifa or Tetum there, it is so poor compared to their houses. I had a man come and see it, an Arab, very reliable, I *think*—at least the friend who introduced me I *know* is reliable, and he said that they had robbed Paul prettily on the house. He has lots of property here himself and estimated that you could sell it for twenty-five thousand pesetas, at the most. I know you bought it in francs but I didn't go into that. If you fixed it up you could sell it for that price plus what it cost you to fix it up. In other words you would always have the original three hundred dollar loss, no matter how many rooms you added on. However you could make up the three hundred dollar loss (say that it is *roughly* that) by living in it or renting it. I have a feeling too that it would be far easier to sell once it can accommodate a family. They all demand two rooms because of the segregation business, which means that now it is uninhabitable except by a bachelor. Perhaps I am mad to think of selling it to an Arab, but I know that lots of them buy property and then rent it and sell the key over and over again to other Arabs, which is a good way to live. The man I spoke to seems to know his business perfectly and gave me an estimate of five hundred and seventy dollars with a leeway of two thousand pesetas, including the fireplace. He could not discuss the water since I wasn't able to tell him exactly how far the pipe would have to be laid. Actually the water is the least of anyone's worries because all summer there isn't much anyway. Little boys come to the door all the time and one can keep great cisterns of it in the kitchen just as the Arabs do. This price would not include changing the rooms all around, as Oliver suggested. It would simply be the cheapest easiest way of adding on. I think eventually the present kitchen could be made into a bathroom and the bathroom into a kitchen—they don't really use kitchens anyway—but that could come later and could be done without changing all the plumbing around—or no plumbing—but there is some sort of pipe in the bathroom and kitchen even now. This same man is looking for a house for me to rent in M'sallah. (1000 pesetas a month is about as cheap as they come there or anywhere.) I thought I might try one out. Even if I loved the one in M'sallah I think that our property should be improved. No other place will ever have a view like that and I know that it can be terribly attractive. Once fixed I'm sure we can (if we want to) sell the key for three hundred dollars and rent it for five hundred pesetas a month or sell it. Also if any of us are flat broke it is a place to be. I'm thinking more of Paul or me now—during lean months when we wouldn't want to be paying any rent. I doubt very much that I can find anything in M'sallah but if I do I shall buy some mattresses that can be transferred to the other house *if* it gets fixed up.

I want an answer on whether you and O. or you or O. want to do this or not. I think you should consider it more from a practical point of view than in terms of my plans. To have everything depend on me would frighten me right out of Tangier. I would promise to stay and see it built and even place a reliable servant in it, if you want me to—if I were leaving and you were not coming. Naturally in case of war I don't know what I'd do. If I did find something I preferred in M'sallah I might rent ours once it were fixed up or leave it empty if one of you were returning. Two houses would be ideal of course for many reasons. I doubt that I [will] find anything in M'sallah, but if I did I would have a much easier time getting into a life with my one or two Arab friends because inviting them to the Medina is like inviting them to New York. I think if they grew to know me and trust me better eventually I could invite them to the Medina but I know that a séjour in M'sallah first would be indicated. If it turned out to be wonderful there it wouldn't interfere with our having fixed our house. After all that does belong to us or rather you and O. and nothing else will ever have that view. I repeat it will not only rent well, once arranged, but be a thousand times more saleable. Still I feel that watching the boats from the top room at night (the lights in the harbor) may be so enchanting that none [of] us would ever want to give it up— whether, when here, we live in various combinations, hotels and other houses as well, keeping ours for a garçonnière, or when broke if one or two or all of us squeeze in there which would be possible once the room was added. Certainly for short periods it will be perfectly livable à deux ou à trois. I would love to know your opinions on this matter. If you are both interested the investment would come to about three hundred dollars each. Tangier, by the way, is perfect in summer, not a cloud in the sky ever and mostly cool. If the work is to be done it should be done before rains come. I enclose the plans as he suggests them. They are inaccurate but give you an idea of what it will be like.

If he builds a room big enough to cover the whole roof (he says it *could* take the weight), the downstairs will have no light whatsoever, except from the only window, which would never reach the patio. The plan at present is to have a small room on the top floor (but considerably larger than the one downstairs) with the open terrace in front, as you and Oliver decided before leaving. The new room would cover the patio kitchen and bathroom leaving just a slice of the patio (dark checked space in both diagrams) for heavy glass, the kind you walk on. It will be the only way of lighting the patio once the skylight is destroyed to make the flooring for the new room. Otherwise there would be literally no éclairage at all, except in the front room. Even though he doesn't seem to agree about the front half not supporting the weight, I personally think it better not to render the bottom part of the house almost useless, and I think too that a terrace in front of the room would be very nice. The stairs would lead out of the dark windowless room one door going into the terrace (arrows) and the other into the new room. (I mean "opening into.") I prefer reaching the terrace from the stairs and not through the room. It will be prettier to have three little windows across the room's front than a window on either side of a door. The stairs would be in a turning double flight with space under them for shelves and storage. I think too that storage space could be built into either end of the terrace for practically no money at all. Or a little kitchen or bathroom — but all that could come later. The house would be unbearably messy — small rooms always are — and all Arab houses derive part of their charm from the impeccable order that reigns within them. Naturally if Paul chooses to live in it with everything spread out, it is his privilege. I would not care to be in it under such circumstances, and he *himself* would I hope prefer it neat. There is a radio that plays Egyptian music constantly until about ten thirty at night but it is not very bothersome from the top floor. Please let me know if you want this done. I know that whatever else I find — although it may please me because of size and the fact that I don't want to live alone but eventually with one or two Arab women as well as you and O. — the view from the house we have will never be duplicated. Certainly not in M'sallah and I know how much that means to both of you and myself too. If you think I should sell the house let me know too or if you think I should go ahead on the building I will then use my own judgment about waiting or going ahead. Naturally if I saw something else that seemed perfect it would be silly to go through the bother of building on ours, though the money I'm sure we could get back. The cost in material is low at the moment — the only reason for deciding shortly. If you are definitely sure you want the room built, one or both of you, I will do it even if I decide against it — but I should at least know

100

whether you want me to go ahead should I decide to. I am furious with Paul because he hasn't written to say he was glad my story was accepted. Please write both of you.

Personally, fixed up I know the house would be charming though small. Perfect for love affairs, little parties and to paint or write in. If Paul is returning he should try to get passage back on American Export to Casa. It's only two hundred bucks. I hope you don't take forever to answer this letter. If I could sell another story and get an advance on my book I too would divide the expenses of the new room, which would make it ridiculous to even consider not building because even now by using it for half a year or less we would get our money's worth out of it, if we then sold it, in spite of the loss. You must write soon.

Much much love,

J.

Paul: Just received your letter. Your novel is *not* a bad novel— don't be ridiculous. I will write you further on that. The deed is virtually ours—remains only the signature of the grand Vizir of the Mosquée—he's been ill—purely a matter of form. The deed will tell whether we can build directly on our neighbor's walls or *not*. If not, the cost will be a little higher. I *should* have the deed within a week they say: *Also* if you want me to go ahead before you come back and if for some reason I can't stick Tangier any longer (frustration) I shall go back and leave the work to you. *But* if I start it I will see it through. I will know a great deal more in a few weeks. I can't go into it now. Much Love J.

33

Jane Bowles to Paul Bowles
[Hotel Villa de France]
[Tangier, Morocco]
[October 1, 1948]

Dear Bup—

I was naturally very upset when a check I'd made out to the Villa de France bounced back (1000 pesetas). I called the bank up and

101

raised hell and then when I went down there I found out they were right. I spent one hour poring over the accounts and verifying with my own eyes the checks you drew *after* the statement made out on the 30th of June (the only one in my possession and which you left with me in the long envelope, thank heavens—although I know the bank is honest). In any case your balance then was $497.90 and with the additional $280.24 that arrived afterwards, the total added up to $778.14. Your own checks however, cashed after June 30th, added up to $524.00. (I enclose the little slips with the checks jotted down—and I did insist on seeing them though they wouldn't *give* me the cancelled checks.) You probably don't remember now what they were for, but I know two of them were for me (the ten and the fifty). Anyway that left me with exactly $254.14. I'd understood there was much more or I would have known I was soon coming to the end of the supply. I naturally have all the slips that I get each time I draw money but they never send out statements telling you how much your *balance* is. Since I have all my slips in order, I thought eventually I'd ask for a statement and add them up to see if they tallied. When you left you said that you hoped there would be some money left when you came back. I don't understand—you said I should budget myself at 100 pesetas a day. I checked in here on the 18th of July (my hotel bill started then), roughly 11 weeks (75 days), and according to the money allowed me I should have spent in that period of time (counting the peseta at 30) roughly $223.00. (Figure it out yourself if you like—say eleven weeks at 700 pesetas a week—or ten weeks—it's pretty close anyway.) Counting the money ($25) I have left, I find I have now spent 234 dollars of the $254.00 you left for me. In other words I'm about ten, eleven, or twelve dollars over my budget. I bought a skirt for nine, so actually I think I have done very well. When you went away, I thought 100 pesetas a day was an enormous amount but that was during Ramadan when I ate bread and soup every night in Cherifa's stall. (I had done that while you were on the trip.) But then to eat bread in one's room alone every night is quite a different matter. I eat at *least* once a day in my room, and *usually* twice. Anyway whatever extra money I *had* went to Jacques and I have all his pictures in return. I couldn't let him starve—after all—and it was nice having him in the house. I bought him paints three times. Whatever extra money I ever will have, I shall spend, from now on, on presents—maybe. I doubt that I ever [will] have any extra though. My room with service and breakfast comes to 55 pesetas a day, which leaves me 45 pesetas to live on.

102

When you figure in tips, laundry, drugs, stamps—you can see very well that I can't be throwing money around. A decent meal costs 30 pesetas, as you know, minimum. Still one can get an indecent one for 12, 22, or 18 pesetas, and I have eaten at the Parade *free* and a lot at a special rate. I am not complaining but saying that 100 pesetas (unless one is in a house) is less than I *thought* it was. There are days when I spend only 10 of my 45 pesetas. But then suddenly the next day I spend sixty for one reason or another— laundry or the maid is due for a tip or drugs—or plain boredom with eating junk in my room, and I go out and have a decent meal. I think the Farhar would amount to the same money or more but I'd get fed. However I would prefer eating the way I do to spending every cent on their awful cooking. With the ten percent service there I'd have about seven pesetas leftover a day to spend (within the budget), and the truck down to town costs five. Still I may go there, though I would gain nothing financially. I cannot decide whether to come back or stay on here. Naturally I can live at Libby's in the States and I would not be such a drag on you.

Still I am not sure you wouldn't prefer me to wait if you are coming. I have done no work lately because I am in a very poor frame of mind, suffering from what you suffer from in New York— except that it does not seem to interfere with *your* work. I find I can think of nothing else and yet I cannot *bring* myself to leave. I refuse to face the fact that there is no hope for me other than a *slightly* increasing social life with Tetum and Cherifa. By offering a present at the right moment, I manage to keep my oar in. Perhaps if I were here long enough and I really learned the language thoroughly (I now speak I suppose about the way you did—or less—which is hardly conversation), I suppose I might get further, though I doubt it. Tetum has her friend Zodelia, and Cherifa is mad about Boussif. That no longer bothers me since I am crazy mad about Tetum—a hopeless hopeless situation. I feel a kind of fever and I even wonder if she hasn't given me a gri-gri to eat—a gri-gri made for Europeans and which prompts them to give away everything they own. Fortunately I restrain myself. But it's the war situation that has been driving me frantic, mainly because I think at every second that I should go home before it's too late, if it isn't too late already. I shall write you again about all that but please, if you are in New York, go down to the bank (address enclosed) immediately and deposit at least $100 to your Hassan account. Then tell them to wire Hassan (deferred) that the money has been deposited. Until then I shall be eating not very well because I don't want to borrow, and my hotel bill will be coming up soon—still they will carry me. But it's awful being here with only twenty-five dollars. So don't delay. Enclosed are the dates when Hassan will be closed, so you can judge whether an air mail letter won't be just as expedient as a wire. In case you can reach Tangier just before a holiday (several are coming up), I would appreciate a wire. The cheapest rate won't be so expensive. I am writing Scotty to do this for me, if she finds out you're not in town, which she can find out easily enough by ringing you. I feel better about the war today, but I've had a very bad unsettling week. You must write what *you* think. Oliver seems willing to go into building on to the house. Get together with him about it. He seems to be doing it to please me but how do I *know* how pleased I'd be? I think it should be on an investment basis. I'll try to find the old man at the Embassy when I've got the deed or maybe before. Are you sure the radio won't drive you crazy? There is one quite near. I know exactly how I'd like to fix the little room downstairs. I may wire you—suddenly—but God knows where you are. I don't see *how* you could have made such a miscalculation on the money really or why you didn't think to warn me but then you thought your checks amounted to much more than they did too—the ones on the New York bank. I feel very deserted and unadvised somehow. Have you seen Ivan? I wish you would help me on a talk with Knopf or *get* me another agent if you think Ivan hopeless. I can't bring myself to send the story to George. I suppose if I were dead sure I could never have Tetum I'd leave but it is the nature of Cupid not to allow those who are stricken to see the truth, so that I do see and I refuse to all at once. Still socially I am making some headway, particularly in a new role that started last week—that is of a procurer for Cherifa. I procure Boussif for her when he disappears, which he does for days at a time. Tetum doesn't touch liquor by the way. If she did it would have made things easier. Still my being European makes everything almost impossible. Are you coming here or not? I know you'll go on to French Morocco and I might go along for a while anyway, depending on where you were headed. It is all too mixed up for words. Naturally if I started building the room, I *would* stay until it was finished—no matter how unhappy I was. Then if everything was awful, you could decide whether you wanted to keep it or not. There's an Arab who wants to buy it now—Mohammed Ouezzani told me—but he looked very doubtful when I told him how tiny it was at present. What about this Mohammed Ouezzani—is he honest? Jay swears by him. He did his contracting for him. I think that I shall spend the two feast days (the Ayd El Kebir) at Cherifa's house—except that it's going to mean buying a sheep. She's trying to get one out of me already. She makes a horn out of her hand and says "Baaa" and then "Thank you." I shall certainly try to avoid buying a whole sheep, even if I have some money from Mary Lou by then, though I expect to have to invest a little money in the Arab part of my life—the *only* reason for being here, at least the most important one—though the view of the Casbah and being able to see the ocean remain very important to me. And somehow I do *love* Tangier. I might be just horrified to wake up and find myself not in Africa. It is all very odd. I shall write again.

Love,

Jane

P.S. Please, please attend to the money—I don't want to be embarrassed at the hotel.

I've started on my novel and as usual getting back into it is hell! The new war crisis doesn't help either. In two weeks or three I should feel more definite about things (ossir).

There is a Jewish holiday a week from Wednesday. I *really* would love it if you had the bank wire Hassan, as I'll be getting jittery if I have to wait very long and the hotel may raise hell. Letters can take nine days!

34

Jane Bowles to Libby Holman and Scotty
[Tangier, Morocco]
[October, 1948]

Dearest Scotty and Libby or one of you or nobody,

Through some awful miscalculation on the checks he cashed, Paul left me with the impression that I had twice as much money here as I actually do. I think he forgot that he'd drawn out about five hundred dollars of the seven hundred he left. Anyway I'm overdrawn and sitting in Africa without cent one. I've written Paul about it naturally and expect to have the money soon, but in case

105

he's on the road would one of you send me some immediately? He may be in Vermont too. He'll pay you the minute he sees you (ossir). I could try Oliver on this too but you know what reaching him is like and Paul said something about *his* going on the road.

If Libby is away, Scotty, call her and get the O.K. on it or if you can't get hold of her would you advance me the money yourself. I assure you you'll really get it right back from Paul. Libby said I could do this if I got stuck and couldn't reach anyone. In fact she told me to write Polly [Bennet Polikoff, Libby's lawyer], but I think this is better and more intimate. The only trouble is that the banks are closed *here* today and tomorrow. Stupidly enough I lost the address they gave me of their corresponding bank in New York; I didn't lose it but sent it off in my letter to Paul and now have to wait until Wednesday before I can find out what it is. The point is this: by depositing the money there you can have them wire the bank here that the money has been deposited to Paul's account and then I can draw it out here. Otherwise the money has to be wired which costs a fortune. This way you can just have them send a deferred cable (cheaper rate that way) saying the money has been deposited, but the *actual money* doesn't have to be wired.

I'm almost certain their bank in New York is the Irving Trust Co., Number something Wall Street (number one I *think*). Please call them and ask them if they are the ones who handle the accounts for Salvador Hassan and Sons, Tangier, Morocco. If they say yes, please have someone deposit one hundred dollars to the account of Paul Bowles, Salvador Hassan and Sons, Tangier, Morocco and ask them to wire Salvador Hassan and Sons, Tangier, that the money has been deposited. As soon as the Hassan bank here gets the wire I can draw on it. The Irving Trust Company sends the wire of course and pays for it out of the money deposited. The only other thing to do is to wire the money straight off. If the Irving Trust Co. has never heard of Salvador Hassan, then I'm really stuck. In that case take out of the hundred whatever it costs to wire the money. (Twelve or thirteen dollars I *think*, which is why I want to avoid it.) If I'm wrong on that it would be simpler to wire the money straight off—I mean if the sum isn't that important. I don't know who could go to the Irving Trust Co. for me, unless Polly has runners in his office. I don't understand much about those things or what a runner would wear if he did go down to the Irving Trust Co. Be sure and tell the runner to tell the Irving Trust Co. to wire that the money has been deposited. They must not write a letter and then toss it out to sea in a bottle. I should be uneasy

if they did that. Naturally try and call Paul first (at Libby's[32])
because he has probably done it all already. If he *hasn't,* although
you do reach him and he is in New York, give him hell and tell
him to please hurry. I need the money in time for the feast of the
lamb which is twelve days from today (or eleven if the moon shows
early). You can also try to reach Oliver who will pay you back if
Paul's away but it might be easier to come over here with the
money and we can spend it together. I am terrible sorry to bother
whomever I am bothering and frightfully annoyed at this whole
thing. I have no idea what to do, whether to come home or stay
here and I am not in a very good humor. I would like Libby's
itinerary which I have lost. Are you—is she on tour now or not?
I miss everybody. When I do return I don't think I'll leave again.

Much love,

Jane

P.S. Please reread this carefully and call in an expert if you don't
understand and do hurry if you can. I really have no money.

I hope it's clear that if you do this and the Irving Trust Co. *is*
the right bank that *they* must wire El Banco Salvador Hassan and
not *me.* Nor must you wire me or Hassan. *They must wire Hassan*
that the money has been deposited.

I will explain to Libby why I haven't written. I've been in a kind
of funk though different from the one she saw me in before and
incapable of doing *anything.*

35

Jane Bowles to Paul Bowles
[Tangier, Morocco]
[October, 1948]

Dearest Bup,

Just an extra letter because the other was written in haste and
agitation. I am still very agitated and wondering if you or Libby
will get some money here to me by the Ayd el Kebir. These feasts

---

[32] At Libby's New York townhouse.

are so important since the social lives of the Arab women are otherwise reduced to the family and immediate neighbors. One is so rarely invited to their houses and it is certainly necessary for me to make some little gift. I am also worried that you are going to write either a scolding letter or a "I couldn't have cashed that many checks, the bank is wrong" letter. Knowing you and your inaccuracy I was therefore careful and made sure to see the checks as I wrote you, so don't write me anything like that. If you now feel that one hundred pesetas a day is too high as a *budget* please say so. Perhaps when you stated such a sum you had imagined that it was less in dollars than it actually is. Recently the exchange has been at thirty-three—this week I mean. Also don't imagine that I've been *trying* to spend that just because you allowed it to me. I assure you by balancing two lean days against one extravagant one I just about manage. I *could* manage on less at a different hotel (*not* the Farhar) naturally, but I would only do that if I were *dying* to stay in Tangier. As for that, I can say merely that I am playing possum still—and the less I say about it the better. I will soon have the use of Jay's upstairs room and I will try and see if Cherifa and Tetum will come to tea. I don't think Cherifa will come with Tetum but then perhaps Tetum will come with her own friend Zodelia (another blackie, much *darker* than Quinza). I would lose face inviting anyone to our house in its present condition. I find myself in a constant state of inferiority vis-à-vis these women. Of course they live in wonderful long high rooms (the kind I used to hate and now love). Their beds are massive and covered with printed spreads (very Matisse) and white couches line the blue walls. They have hundreds of white frilly cushions too and they put very beautiful seashells into the water pitchers. The room we sit in when I visit Tetum is always the color of early evening because of the blue walls. I know only that room actually but I imagine it rightly as many rooms—there must be hundreds like it. It must be like Ahmed[Yacoubi]'s house, so much more beautiful that the Ktiris'. I know I have written all about this before. Never mind. It is a result of the repetitive note in the Arab life here. In any case even if she does come to tea several times, I have little hope that she will ever come to tea *alone*, and if she did—even so . . . The average American woman would be revolted I suppose by a Negro man, and I think I suffer from the disadvantage of being "different"—all of which made your success years ago. Naturally I admire the women for being this way, so much more dignified than the men, or are they just more conventional? I don't know. I suppose I could banish all hope from my heart and get it over with but I hate to and I never regret being with them. I can't quite explain to you or anyone what it is like to be in one of those rooms—I mean how I feel about it. I suspected I would in the beginning at the wedding, and I loved Cherifa's little house. Mr. Ktiri's on the other hand never had any magic for me really. Perhaps he was too rich, and all those men. The women look wonderful in their homes. I had not intended writing this sort of letter at all. But briefly:

(1) *Please* get in touch with Mary Lou. I am so frightened now that she won't publish the story at all. I have heard nothing from Ivan. Have you helped me on that? If not I think you're mean. He should try to get me an advance from Knopf or a different publisher. If you haven't done anything about all this then who will? I should have a different agent if Ivan won't help me. But please, speak to Mary Lou anyway. I am awfully worried really. Also the Berlin crisis drove me out of my wits last week. What do you think of the war at this point?

(2) I can't reach the carpenter for the Embassy, he is apparently loaded with work for the moment. Perhaps it is best to wait. I don't know.

(3) Are you coming here or going elsewhere, or don't you know?

(4) I have a way for us to live in Spain for as long as one year on a cultural passport twenty-five pesetas a day minimum *au lieu de cent* and all the pesetas we want sent us from Tangier. I met some Spanish "Intellectuals" who live in Madrid and are dying to meet you. They expect us to come this fall or winter and I think it might be fun. They will help us. (Very good families— Franquistos, I suppose—at least they have to pretend they are, I never asked them.) They are only twenty-three or four. I gave Jacques a few hundred pesetas, the only way he had of leaving Tangier. As I said whatever extra money I had left over from Libby and Oliver's donations and whatever I saved skimping went to him. *Perhaps* you feel I had no right to do this. Personally I have no regrets. It would have gone on something else. I don't think I'd want to stay here and never have any extra money at all. I mean I think it would get very dreary. I have very cheap big lunches now. The Parade is closed to the public at noon but several of us have got together and by chipping in I can eat there for what it would cost if I had a home. I live entirely on starch and vegetables and fish. I have forgotten what meat tastes like and I don't care, except that right now I don't have supper. I don't need it really but it makes an awfully *long* day. About 6:30 or 7:00 they leave the market, so

I can either go to the Parade or home to bed. At the Parade I have a special price when I do drink, so don't worry about that. I am always so terribly gloomy when Tetum ties up the grain sacks and says goodbye. Often she and Cherifa leave the market together and we part in front of the hotel. I watch them disappearing up the road in the beautiful soft night and I just can't *yet* go to my room. The Parade is a warm spot to go to thank God, otherwise I would be too lonely I think—I *know*. My breakfast comes in at six and as usual any work that isn't done by twelve isn't done at all. I rarely get tight, in fact I can't digest much liquor in Tangier. I am buckling down on the work but I daresay something will upset it. I wish you'd write.

Much love,

Jane

P.S. By all means try to get your book away from Doubleday-Doran.

36

Jane Bowles to Paul Bowles
Tangier [Morocco]
[October, 1948]

Dearest Paul,

Thank you very much for the money which arrived so very quickly, I was amazed. I still had money in my purse and needn't have worried at all. I hope that you have found the accounts I sent you satisfactory and that you were not too disagreeably surprised at my needing more money. I am waiting to hear what *you* would prefer me to do. There isn't any use in my going into the reasons I would have for staying here or returning to New York (at least for the winter). There are too many pros and cons and all of it would bore you. If I spend the winter with Cory and she *is* willing to be with me, I should like best in one way to be where I had friends: Paris or New York. I think the idea of being with her in Marrakech or the desert is a little frightening and I don't think Tangier's winter weather would please her. Still, I might decide to do that. I don't want to be with Cory in Africa really unless you are coming back

110

here and it is convenient for me because of that. I mean perhaps we could discuss the house and do something about it in the spring. I shall never stray very far from Tangier, my idea being neither to travel a great deal nor to live in Fez or Marrakech. I think we should decide one way or another about the house. Mohammed Ouezzani has a buyer for it, supposedly, and I have been advised by my dearest friend here, Kouche Saïd, to sell whenever I had a chance because you were really rooked, *unless* you want it for your own pleasure. Well I guess we know by now that it was not a good investment, but still if we ever get any fun out of it I think it will have been worth the expense. I personally would prefer a house in M'sallah eventually but then my reasons are all mixed up with people as usual, as I've written you, but I do like M'sallah very much besides and the kind of house one gets there. I heard of one for fifteen hundred dollars with Arab bath, patio and I think little garden (two stories); so you see considering that property in M'sallah is far more expensive than in the Casbah, it must be a bargain. I think however it will be sold long before this reaches you. Houses there are impossible to get and the rents run very high. I cannot get hold of your old man. He is busy working on a palace somewhere. By the time I reach him I suppose the rains will have started and it will be too late to do anything. Perhaps his estimate was lower because he was going to use poor material. The man who estimated it for me was going to make no profit whatsoever. He suggested that I buy my own material and only gave me the estimate as a friend. He has a great deal of property and actually advised me not to build but to sell. Kouche Saïd introduced me to him. Kouche I love and trust as I would any of my really close friends. One cannot compare him to Boussif or to anyone else here in fact. I would put every cent I had into his hands gladly. I know your concert is being given on the fourteenth of November. I don't know whether I could get back on time for that or not. I would appreciate it very much if you would let me know how you feel about it. If you would prefer me to hang on here until you return, I will probably do it, or if you prefer me to return and go to Libby's or somewhere where the financial burden will be reduced to a minimum, then I will start thinking about that. If I should decide I want to stay anyway for a little longer I could use my own money. I mean that I should know at what point I would be staying here against your will or at least contrary to a preference you might have. Perhaps you are never coming near here again. That would naturally influence me immensely. Or perhaps since you will

111

always be in Fez you'd prefer me back in the States. I don't know. All this needn't be decided by mail. We can talk about it if you come here but I should know now at least whether you are coming or not and whether you'd prefer me to be still in Tangier or if you are utterly indifferent one way or another. If the house were livable I could be in it and would be right now. Meanwhile I may move to Jay's in November *if* I don't return which will make things cheaper. I would soon know if I could *ever* hope to have any visits from Tetum. Once I am more certain of that I shall be very decisive, one way or another. Well you will probably be writing me soon. I would have felt better if I'd heard from you.

It is difficult being so very much in the dark—financially too. If I can't depend for *anything* on you here in Tangier next winter, or shall we say Africa, I might feel better and less embarrassed in New York. Unless of course I had a house here to live in. I am thinking again of Cory because I should write her what I can afford. Libby told me earlier I could stay in her apartment in New York with Cory. In that case I know Cory would foot the other bills. But I don't want to get her all the way over here, find out that sentimentally it doesn't work very well, and be financially dependent on her besides for everything. Thank heavens I have some money but if I have to spend it *all* on being in a hotel with Cory I'm not sure I wouldn't prefer returning to the U.S.A. and then coming here again, perhaps in the spring. I don't know what in the devil to do really, and the more I think about it the more complicated the whole mess gets. I *will* stay here to supervise the house *en tout cas* if you *want* it built now, and they say there is still time. I doubt seriously however that the old man, in any case, will be available before spring, and probably the whole thing will be delayed. Please answer me soon. Throw some light on the house, what you expect of me financially if I remain here, if you'd prefer me to remain here, or if you think I should leave forever or leave and return here in the spring. Maybe financially, with the passage, *ça reviendrai au même*. I have four hundred dollars, roughly, and I would like to keep some out for clothes. You can understand that—for a few little follies. I hope that you are well and that your book is with New Directions. Believe it or not I am working. I get up at seven or eight and work between nine and twelve, which is all I can manage a day. But it is best doing it this way. I am still amused by Tetum and Cherifa, also in love.

Jane

112

P.S. I am going to Cherifa's house for the night and Tetum's house tomorrow. The mutton festival is in full swing. I am simply terrified of the food I'll have to eat. Will write all about it. Tell Oliver and Helvetia, can't write everyone the same thing.

37

Jane Bowles to Paul Bowles and Oliver Smith
[Tangier, Morocco]
[October, 1948]

Dearest Paul and Oliver,

Today I saw the house I would like. I daresay you will be not interested, but I think it is a real bargain. In francs it comes to a little under two thousand dollars, the lawyer's fee included (the 5 percent that the city takes out for transference of ownership). It has two floors, each with large patio (about four times the size of the one in our house) and each with two rooms, one smaller and one larger giving on to a closed patio. There is a generously sized room on the ground floor which is now a "Moorish" bathroom, in other words the floor is constructed to permit steam baths—a private Turkish bath, I gather. The room was warm when I went into it, so someone must have been in there just before we arrived. I would much prefer that to having a lot of plumbing that doesn't work. The slaves bring in buckets of hot water and the whole room heats up. It could be converted into a bathroom with modern tub, but I think it is foolishness. The Arabs are extremely clean without all that nonsense. The best feature of all is a little garden space off the ground floor. It has a grape arbor and with a few hundred pesetas one could have wonderful flowers growing in it, and it would be charming to eat out there. There are excellent stairs already going up to the terrace which is about three times the size of our present one, and a room could be built there eventually very cheaply since actually the stairs are nearly half the cost, for some reason, of the entire thing. It is a real honest to God house that we could all live in very happily right now.

The disadvantages: The view is not as spectacular as the one from the present house (one can see an apartment house), though one does see the "Charf," which I think is pretty, and a lot of surrounding Moorish houses. The color of the Arab quarter, which is what I care about, is all around one. The Charf is a kind of hilly section in the distance. I love the house and the garden is so very unusual and to me such a great luxury. It is also very important to own actual ground. We don't, you know, in our present house since it is over someone else's, so if in the future it were torn down to be replaced by a *modern* building we wouldn't get any money because we don't own the actual ground. Our house, now, begins in the *air*. I would love to have this house and would certainly live in it often with Moors while you were all on your various trips. Jay says it's the cheapest buy he's ever heard of, but I would certainly make sure there was no hitch in it. The tiles on the stairs are not pretty as are the ones in our present house. The patios however are just plain black and white tiles. It is in excellent condition and the stairway tiles could eventually be changed. Though it is on the edge of M'sallah and therefore valuable as property because right near the European sections of town, one has to go down some narrow winding streets to reach it, and so it is, thank heavens, not accessible by car. It is at a dead end and would therefore be quiet. With an extra room or even two on the terrace it would be large enough for four of us and servants. It could be a place to live for some months out of the year, whereas our present house could never be that. Still it is naturally more of an investment than adding a room on to ours, but that will *never* be big enough for you, Oliver and myself, let alone Helvetia at one time. I know she too will be sold on spending some time in this part of the world once she gets over here. If she cared to join us in the investment it would come to about six hundred to six hundred and fifty dollars apiece for all three of you, and whereas I think that to buy jointly is usually a poor idea, in a place like this it is an excellent one since we would probably not all be in it together very often, hélas.

Any *hole* in M'sallah rents for about eight hundred to one thousand pesetas a month. God knows even at that rate there *is* nothing. The market is being moved down there by the way, and I fear that in ten or fifteen years, or twenty, they will be widening all the streets and tearing the properties down. I am going to see the plans for M'sallah if you are interested. Some of the streets are already being widened, but this one won't be for a long while. By then we will have got our money's worth a hundred times and can sell at a huge profit because we own quite a large plot, including the garden. Perhaps Libby might be interested if Helvetia isn't, although I doubt it. She already has two places anyway and she is not alone like Helvetia. I *really* think that if the three of you got together then whatever happened wouldn't be so very tragic. As we couldn't move in for three months *anyway*, I would only need to make a down payment now to hold it. He has had one offer of 750,000 francs but is holding out for 800,000 (about). I fear that this letter will reach you too late, but if you are at all interested you should wire me and I will get a lawyer at the Embassy to look into it *thoroughly*. Helvetia, if she is *not* in Vermont, is at the San Jacinto Hotel (East 60th). But most likely she has got in touch with you. Perhaps she would hate living Arab style for a few months out of the year but it would [be] a marvelous contrast to Vermont. I would eventually find the right servant or servants to leave in it when none of us were here. Anyway I have written you about it, so do what you can, but if you are at all interested do it immediately and wire me. I hesitated one day on renting a horrid black cellar-like place in M'sallah (with a horrid toilet one had to *crawl* into), and it was rented for double the amount right from under my nose. I have no doubt that some other house might turn up eventually but probably twenty times as expensive. There's someone trying to buy our little one now who hasn't seen it yet, but we can discuss that later.

Much love,

Jane

P.S.   You can get this letter to H. if you think it's simpler than explaining.

Will send my story to George. If I could sell that I would actually have earned enough to buy a third of the house, and I would prefer that really. Then H. could simply be there when she wanted to be. If she liked it she could help towards a room on the third floor. Naturally if you are through with Morocco and moving on to West Africa, there would be no point, as I think of it as a focal point for you and one which would be possible for me, much more than the desert, for some of the year anyway and for the others as well.

Write me Villa de France, Tangier.

Love again,

J.

115

38

Jane Bowles to Paul Bowles
[Tangier, Morocco]
[November, 1948]

Dearest Paul,

I had certainly hoped for a letter from you before this, but either you or the British post office is impossible. I have some ideas again for my novel which stopped dead after the Aid, and the wedding that I missed, because I was so bitter and because I'd reached an impasse anyway. Now I feel like working again. It will always be this way I imagine, so I must take advantage of these brief oases. Helvetia's letter upset me very much and so did and (still does) the fact of missing your concert. It began to obsess me, but I didn't dare leave until I heard from you and besides I felt the least I could do was to clear up the house matter. I thought you would be furious if I came home without the deed or at least the assurance that it was waiting for you, because I am not sure they will let me sign it. That finally decided me and of course the fact that there was nothing left on the *Saturnia* by the time I inquired, still hoping I might get a wire from you or a letter from you in answer to mine, but of course you have all disappeared again. To finish with the house: after weeks of going to the Mendoubia they told me I was to go to the qadi where everything would be ready, then started a real Kafka in fancy dress that went on for several days. I wandered between the adoul [notaries], the qadi and Mr. Lairini's store from which he had suddenly vanished. I can't go into it, but the whole thing seemed to be moving backward instead of forward as in *Through the Looking Glass*. The adoul kept asking where the Rue Maimouni *was* with a kind of dreamy interest, as though the deed were tucked under the cobbles there. It was all ridiculous and Boussif was divorcing in the next booth. It made me love Tangier. Fortunately a very nice gentleman, an Arab belonging to one of the richest and best families here, took the matter into his own hands and started running about for me the other day. He was worried that something *louche* was going on because he did not think very highly of Mr. Lairini. He doubted however that he would dare do anything really dishonest to an American beyond charging twice too much for the house; *enfin*, his brother being the Nadir of the Mosques himself, he jumped right into the very thick of it.

It seems that the Mendoubia lost the Nadir's letter and therefore the number to the house (210) but now it's all beginning again. They are writing everybody and soon I should be ready to go down to the qadi and the adoul. I hope they don't ask where the Rue Maimouni is. No one ever seems to have heard of it and yet it is an endless and important street. The important thing is that my friend has seen Mr. Lairini and he says that happily there is nothing *louche* going on and that the deed should soon be ours. He has been perfectly charming and accurate in all his appointments. He wants nothing, being very rich himself and not interested in women. I know that I am not explaining it very well but then I have never understood any of it. I think it is important to get the thing over with and registered and I'm sure you will be pleased that I have stayed to attend to it. Meanwhile I have calmed down and am again in good spirits. There was a terrible time there however when I could perhaps have got the boat and tried to guess which you'd prefer me to do when I almost went mad. I am looking forward to your next letter but for God's sake don't just say "do what you like." Cory writes that she will be coming over here the earlier part of December (unless of course I go back). I will put whatever money I've earned toward being here or my passage back and just forget about ever getting any clothes. I don't feel I deserve them anyway, for various reasons. I am deeply disgusted with myself. I don't know what will occur financially with Cory here actually, perhaps the same thing as last year, but I do think I should have some base to live on and therefore perhaps it might be better in New York because there I wouldn't need to fall on your hands at all. I know you hate to figure out anything in advance which is maddening, of course, because there are certain things that must be. If I only got a word from you I would fix up the house even as is (without another room) and move in. Naturally Mr. Bucurri has upset my plans of doing anything since he is *introuvable*. If we had a place to live Cory could join me in it, and then if she insisted on travelling or living in hotels she could pay for it. I know she probably plans to pay for anything we do anyway but then maybe I might better be somewhere else. I shall write and ask her what she prefers. I suppose instead of going into all these complications I might just say that there is a boat leaving on the twenty-first and one on the third of December. If you have any opinions about it you had better write me immediately as there are already no cabins available on the one sailing on the twenty-first. One has to know the captain by the way as far as the American Export ships are concerned, but Miss Fried is inquiring about it for me. I'm almost sure they won't take a woman. Otherwise all ships are about three hundred dollars minimum. I hate in one way the idea of returning. If you were interested in really establishing a headquarters here in Tangier I would be delighted to fix it up, either this house or buy another one and live in it part of the time. If however you are merely dashing through Morocco and starting off on one of your trips around the world, never to return here, then what is the use? Perhaps now is a good time for me to return, as I should otherwise go in the spring (Mother is getting terribly lonely), but I can't bear the idea of leaving Morocco unless I *can* return. I can't explain it at all. I met a man yesterday who has lived in Egypt for years and knows the Near East very well. He was delighted with Tangier and said it was so very much more Oriental than anything around there. Strange. I too feel it very strongly here, though you don't find it exotic at all. I prefer M'sallah to the Casbah. Many things may have happened too, and you yourself may not be returning yet. If however I am to take the boat on the twenty-first there may not be any cabin class left and the one on December third is either first class or third; I shall probably need another hundred dollars to get myself out of here with a margin, or maybe more. I haven't figured it out. Perhaps I should just not think of going any way but second class. I shall try to work now, whichever I do, but my success will depend on knowing whether or not I am staying or leaving very shortly and how much money you think I should allow myself for passage. I am sorry to involve you at all, but as you say yourself one is somehow not alone in the world and if it weren't for you I would never have come to Tangier. I do not regret it and hope when my heart is healed to resume my Arabic lessons if I stay, or when I come back. I did not go near the market for a week, then the other day I went and spoke to Tetum for a while. She is so very beautiful to me. I don't care how crafty or mean she is. I am happy just to look at her. I know you think she is a hiddy. If we go to Fez later I am going to take Cherifa and her sister along for a few days. She would naturally not come alone. Her sister has elephantiasis and wants to go to Moulay Yacoub. I am considerably cheered by the fact that Truman was reelected which I think is better than Dewey, don't you? Mary Oliver is supposedly arriving here today. Mr. McMicking reported this to me. He came through on his way to Fez from Gib, having spent all summer in England. I have developed a great feeling for him and I believe he likes me too. It is *pénible* to be with him of course because of his affliction.

Please write me here at the Villa de France, Tangier and immediately. The suspense of not knowing whether you care or not what I do or have any opinion on the subject at all that might help is too much. If I came back would you wait and go up with me to Helvetia's for a fortnight before being on your way? I would cook wonderful things for you and then you could leave and I'd join Cory. I shall see presently whether she has any preference about where to be. If in America we would, I think, go for a month or so down to New Mexico. If you were here I'd come back in March or April and perhaps build onto the house then.

Much love,

Jane

P.S.   Oliver's money order has not arrived: I still have some hope because they told me that it took twenty-five or thirty days to get through London. Please thank O. and explain I've been waiting to write him when it arrived to thank him. When did he send it? Is it over a month now? If so we must take steps.

39

Jane Bowles to Paul Bowles
[Tangier, Morocco]
[November, 1948]

Dear Paul,

Since I wrote you a twenty page letter last night which of course I shan't send, I feel better, and more important still I think this one can be brief and to the point. I must ask you to please keep it for answering purposes because everything I write you seems to go down the drain and I do take pains to keep you au courant and make it easier for you to answer me. Since the end of October I have been waiting in vain for a letter, some indication of what you wanted to do and what you hoped I would do. You say casually that you have neglected your correspondence because of your work but surely you could have found time to scribble a line. I hate to think anyway that I am part of that correspondence of yours and that you only write me when you pull out the list. I am being nasty because I have suffered intolerably for four weeks — anyway, ever since I might have taken the November fifth boat. I received your wire which I appreciated very much. It said letter following and of course that took another ten days. "Will you wait Tangier?" I interpreted in a million different ways. If it had only said *hope* you'll wait Tangier, or *please* wait Tangier, but I suppose you worded it that way purposely. Also I didn't know whether you meant wait and then leave after we've seen each other or what. I didn't worry much because I thought the letter would come in a few days since you announced it and I would know more precisely what you meant. That last bit of waiting finished me off I guess and when Mary came and there was this sudden opportunity to leave I suddenly thought well, why not? It was a good excuse anyway to wire and I suppose I hoped you'd answer that you weren't impartial or that you were because "leaving for Timbuktu upon arrival," but mainly I hoped you weren't impartial. Still, *that* is not your fault and I don't expect you to have guessed that. You may very well not want to be with me this winter because of Cory and would *prefer* me to come back in the spring. I had hoped you would express yourself on that in a letter but you didn't. I asked you about it before. Because you mention really nothing about all this I have a feeling that you have something up your sleeve and are therefore just not saying anything. I know you want to go to Timbuktu but I don't know *when* or if you are planning to go with Gore [Vidal] and Tennessee or what. Between Spain, Marrakech, Fez, the desert, etc., I think we could have a wonderful time either three of us or five of us. (I have no idea about Tennessee's plans of course.) But you don't even mention this possibility in your letter and probably for good reason. If you are going off alone with Gore and Tennessee for the winter, then I must decide whether I would rather be here with Cory or in New York. She has a car there after all. Maybe Tennessee won't be staying long. You have either mentioned him in your wire to indicate that you had a travelling companion and were more or less making your plans with him and would not be lonely, or else you were mentioning it as a temptation. I can't imagine why you would have stuck him into your wire otherwise. I'm inclined to think you were showing me that I needn't be involved in your arrival at all. I don't know. A car is always a temptation to me as you know. You mention it in your letter but you don't say whether either of us or three of us would ever have a

120

chance to get into it. Perhaps it would be too small for five people and that would leave me out because of Cory. Of course Cory is the whole complication in this. If you think the three of us or five of us or twenty of us (Gordon is in Tunis) can have some fun together for part of Cory's stay here anyway, I shall remain, but if I shan't be seeing you much then I think Cory should decide what she would prefer doing. I personally think it would then be better for me to take the bull by the horns and leave, but maybe she doesn't have the car in the States this winter and maybe she would hate to change her plans. If I don't go back on February third, I mean December third, I shall return in March and try to get over again with Helvetia in summer. Otherwise I shall return here with Libby and Helvetia in the spring. Do you think it's silly that I should have spent all this time here and not see you, which will happen if I leave on the *Saturnia*, December the third? I have missed my chance to return with Mary and in any case she may not be returning. I will know today whether she is nor not. As by now I have pains in my head from this problem and I am in a pathological state I may try at the last minute to do something anyway. I keep interpreting your telegrams differently. All at once I think you are trying to influence me to come home and then again I think well no, he is trying to make me feel I *can* return if I like without guilt. I think this time I feel more guilty about staying than I would about returning. Why? Whatever it is it's terribly neurotic but once the cycle starts there is no stopping it—only the departure of the boat—and then I have a few days rest until the next one comes along. I wish I knew what I could do to help myself but when I reason myself out of it for awhile and enjoy a few hours of false peace I am even more tormented afterwards for having forgotten my pain. If you read this carefully you will certainly be able to advise me. Did you understand when I wired I was "miserable" that it was because you seemed to *want* me to come back which confused me? I don't understand also your last telegram. I asked you to wire me if you were *pleased* that I was remaining but you wired in answer: WAS MERELY CLARIFYING SITUATION IF MISERABLE BY ALL MEANS COME IMMEDIATELY. Well, I can't come immediately now but you know this time how I feel and if you think because of Cory and your own plans I'd be better off home right now then wire so in answer to this but first call Cory and give her a chance to say what she'd like. She may *hate* at this point not to leave. Once she gets started on one track she usually can't conceive of a volte-face. As for her boring Tennessee if he's around (or Vidal) she could never bore anyone. She is a character and has fine sentiments. The trouble is I don't know how it will work between Cory and me. I have promised to take Cherifa and Quinza to Fez. I have to buy Cherifa a djellaba and shoes eventually. Also I am taking her to the doctor's right now which is ruining me. She has a skin disease from grain. I have to spend money on something that's "fun!" It's all too ridiculous. I don't know about fixing up the peseta thing from here with you in Gibraltar. The Madrileños will be in Tangier for Christmas and actually suggested February for our meeting in Spain as a good time. That would be perfect if Libby would come then. Couldn't you suggest to Tennessee that he come here first or is he going to drive to Tunis and then go to Italy? I suppose so. I'm sure they could fix the peseta thing for Tennessee too if he was interested. In any case they want records of yours so that they can play them on some radio program. Also they can arrange to give you a concert, they think, so bring sheet music. I imagine I mean scores! A visiting celebrity always has many privileges so I think you should take advantage of their interest in you. They are mad about Tennessee too. Naturally you can do this whether I am here or not. Poor Cory, I suppose, will have to pay the full rate but maybe we could manage something. But if she must I don't expect her to pay for *all* my expenses in Spain. Whatever money I have left will naturally go into the pot, whatever pot I'm in next winter. My tapeworm was yards long but we are not sure of whether I've got rid of the head or not. It didn't come out with the rest but it may have got lost. Since I'm gaining weight I daresay I have got rid of it. *On verra, il n'y a qu'à recommencer autrement.* It's a revolting thing. I feel like a total failure and will try to work for the last time right now, and according to you letter, I will either sail or not on the *Saturnia*. Naturally you don't know exactly what will happen, one never does, but you have a little better idea than I do at this point. Will there be any chance of staying somewhere and working for a month? Jacqueline Cramer, by the way, is taking the Ede house or rather an old man is, and she is going there with her daughter to keep him company and run the house. She is throwing in a lot of beds and some of us or all of us could stay there. Three or four of us anyway I think. She has a little car and would like to drive down to Marrakech in January, or somewhere. Personally I'd like to drive to Colomb-Bechar and into the desert a little way. If Mary Oliver isn't leaving she's going to take a house in Marrakech. She's a holy mess. What about the house in M'sallah? I wrote you about

122

that but now I suppose I won't hear because of all those wires. I wouldn't visit Carson now because I can't write. I'm sorry she's ill and why does she send me her love? She doesn't know me. I suppose it doesn't really matter what I do. For God's sake write or wire soon, and consult Cory. Oliver's money never came. He must do something about it. For heaven's sake reach him and thank him for me. I miss him but I am too upset to write just now. With George gone there is no point in sending my story. I enclose an errand Mr. Ede wants you to do. I hope you will, they have a wonderful new house and may invite us to stay eventually, if you're nice. Mrs. Ede adores you. They think I'm a yenta but I don't think it matters. It will mean everything to me, to my peace of mind and my chances of working, if I hear from you immediately. If you think it is worth the money you can send me a deferred wire, unless you feel that what you have to say cannot be formulated in a wire. Because of the God damned Gibraltar problem, I should start leaving a week ahead, which does not leave so much time after all. I won't be annoyed if you think Cory and I are better off not here this winter. The whole clue is in your wire—whether you mentioned Tennessee to warn me off or to entice me and whether you are going off to Timbuktu now. God knows. Surely you could not have stuck an extra word in for no reason at all, or did you mean that because of him you couldn't change your passage? In your letter you said you were sharing a cabin with Gore? Perhaps you thought I wouldn't know who Gore was (I know only too well) and would therefore understand better if you mentioned Tennessee. *Kif-kif.*[33] In other words, you might have been trying to show that you were involved with someone in a cabin and could therefore not wait over in New York. That would explain your mentioning Tennessee. In other words, neither as an enticement nor as a hint that you were off with a group of men and that I should make my own separate plans with Cory. Perfectly understandable if you are by the way, it is just that I would prefer knowing so, if it *is* so and I am not going to be seeing much of you. That is the marrow of this letter. Please answer quickly as I said. The horror of it is that if I do come back it will have been wildly ridiculous to have missed your concert. Give my love to Libby, Oliver and Helvetia. Tell Helvetia she must come here later with her car. Perhaps the whole thing will pan out better if I go back in December, but after you've read this carefully you can surely

[33] Kif-kif—Moghrebi for six of one and a half-dozen of the other.

write or wire me something helpful. I shall stop now before I get into an agonizer. How was the concert?

Much love,

Jane

P.S. It is too bad you didn't get back sooner. I guess suddenly I just got lonely and now everything has gone to pieces. I won't mind whatever you decide and please if you want to have this winter free for a land trip that *can't* include Cory and me, then say so and I'll return in spring. I just feel in my bones that Tennessee has a small car! If you can go anywhere with them you *must*, but let me know in time! A letter won't reach me in time unless you write it very quickly! Don't forget, if there is a possibility of a trip by car, other than over that road to Marrakech, we'd like that, but you would have mentioned it if there were.

If I have left anything out, for God's sake try to imagine what I'd like to know yourself.

40

Jane Bowles to Paul Bowles
[Tangier, Morocco]
[December, 1948]

Dearest Paul,

I feel so happy and relaxed now that I feel I am staying. Perhaps you have written me not to because you don't think you'll see me for more than a week or two? I seriously doubt that, though it may be so and I hope you will be truthful if it is. It is not your fault after all that Cory is coming. Perhaps she will prefer being here in any case, so I might not be leaving whether you are with me or not. I would take a train to Marrakech or the desert, but I don't like the "idea" of train travel in Spain—it will doubtless go through many tunnels—still I can *force* myself on one. The Sicres, by the way, are driving to Madrid in time for Christmas. You mentioned Tennessee and Gore driving through Spain before coming here. Did you want to go with them? Or did you want us both to (or isn't there room for two)? Perhaps you and I being in Spain had nothing to do with them, in that case come here first. If you have a chance to go alone with them for heaven's sake do. I don't want to spoil *that* possibility. Cory gets here ten days after you or eleven so I'd have to be in Gibraltar at that point anyway. I shall find out if there's any possibility of fixing the pesetas *here,* without you. You would want the rate for yourself as well wouldn't you, or are you willing to spend one hundred a day at their official rate—whatever it is? I shall find out what I can do. I hope to God I hear from you soon this time. As I said in my other letter I shan't feel really at peace until I do.

I am so worried that you will think I want to come *home* because of that wire, but it was just a result of being fed up with not hearing a word from you and not knowing what on earth your intentions were. Actually it was meant to get some reassurance from you, but of course you did just the opposite. Well, I'll see what you have to say in your letter. I would like very much to have the house in M'sallah. Have you talked to Oliver about it, or Helvetia? I just don't expect her to be interested, but it's a good investment. Quinza and Cherifa will live with me, I know, but probably Quinza will refuse to climb up into the Casbah. It is quite a pull. If I live in a house here I *insist* on a harem. there is no other way of doing it. They cope with all the details and keep one company (I am quite happy with them without any kind of romance). We can discuss all that when we see one another, but I wish some one of you would be interested in the house. I suppose you think I have quite lost my mind. I missed living in a kind of basement right next to Cherifa's house by hesitating. It was during the days when I was so wretched at having missed the *wedding* in the country with Tetum. I didn't care about anything I was so miserable so someone else took it while I sulked in my room. I am afraid every move I make is wrong, at least recently I have been running in bad luck. I hope it won't continue. Had I moved into that house I would have had quite a nice life, eating every night with Cherifa and Quinza. I am slowly becoming part of their household, but I *must* study my Arabic again. It has gone all to pieces these past weeks.

Living here I have to walk back around eleven at night, or sleep there, which I must say is not amusing after a while. The hip I sleep on is always black and blue in the morning, my couch is so hard. I seem to be the only European woman walking out of there at that hour of the night, and often I carry back my empty briefcase (I take them one bottle of wine in that). I don't know what the Arabs think, and it is very unlike me to be doing something like this.

Naturally some call out to me, but I am not too upset by it. Still I would prefer living in the quarter. I am terribly upset about Oliver's money not arriving. I am afraid I've gone way over my budget what with doctor's bills and food being more of an item now that it's cold, and then when I got very depressed I bought some things, and I have also contributed money to the sheep, as you know. It will come out of my own money, but then I suppose that is just the same as if it came out of yours. I don't know. However, I think now and then when I make some I should get some fun out of it. It just can't support me anyway. I wish you would bring me two large size cakes of *Zip*—wax hair remover (not the tubes)—the one that advertises "It's off because it's out!" It's called Zip "Epilator" and a bottle of "Adalin" (Bayers). It's very expensive but unlike aspirin it does not affect the heart nor is it habit forming. It is a "calmant," quiets the awful turmoil in the solar plexus created by panic, and will be excellent for trips. One does not need a prescription for it so you can see that it's not dangerous. I think it would be a good thing for me to have around.

Don't let Mother load you up with a lot of things. There's nothing else you can bring me really. If I need things for winter I can pick them up here.

If you have advised me to return I shall regret terribly missing your concert. It will seem too utterly ridiculous for words and I shall probably brood for years because it was just the time here when everything was going so *wrong* that if it hadn't been for a feeling I had that you would like to find me here I would have fled. Of course now with Tennessee coming everything is changed for you, though *my pleasure* in seeing *you* will be very great. I shall write Libby and Helvetia, and you keep Oliver informed about everything. I have avoided all the bars where I might run into Mary for the last two days, although she invites me to meals. I felt terribly like some real food for a few days but I never enjoyed a bite of it, and part of my hysteria was due to being around her at all. Any drinks I had with her just made me frightfully ill. Don't forget, if possible bring whatever records you have.

Love,

Jane

P.S. Have just wired Cory. Her letter received this morning made me feel you'd be glad to see me here. It clarified your wires so I shall just take a chance and stay even if I do see you for only a little while. I'm wiring her because I'm afraid she may be upset. Thank God for Cory!

You may think I'm crazy, but I was terribly hurt and just more and more and more depressed at not hearing from you, and your first wire which was clear to me in the beginning wasn't after a while, and the promised letter took forever arriving.

I really don't understand about the pesetas. You had better wire me if and what you want me to do about them. For me? For you? For both of us? It is quite a different question if we don't start off from Tangier together. You must forgive my wires and when I see you I can explain more about it. This morning I walked through M'sallah. I am longing to walk through it with you. Maybe you'll understand why I want some day to live there. I can't imagine ever being away from Morocco very long and I know now that in my heart I have *never* wanted to leave. Otherwise I wouldn't feel so happy. I hope to God you haven't sent for me.

Love again,

Jane

41

Jane Bowles to Libby Holman
[Tangier, Morocco]
[December, 1948]

Dearest Libby,

Your letter was one of the sweetest and most inclusive I have ever received, in great contrast to Paul who must have entered the secret service he's been so mute about everything. You must have heard all about our wild cables back and forth. Your suggestion that I decide everything on my own hook without him was a good one, but you did say that I should wait over here and see him first (at least you suggested it), and alas I had to decide to either be here or there before seeing him or else come home before he left because of Cory's plans. I could not keep her waiting on a perpetual hook. Well why go into it? I had an opportunity to come home with Mary Oliver

(I thought), and John Willis—you know how I loathe travelling alone—and it would have helped a bit financially, at least I could have sat in their suite all the way back and just taken any old bunk myself. (She wanted me to come in the suite with them in fact, *if they got one*, since she said the difference in my ticket and the extra amount she would have had to pay to keep me in there would have amounted to a night's drinks, so I might even have done that.) Actually she gave a five hundred dollar tip to a taxi driver just before coming here (100 pounds) so I had no scruples about it. She's quite insane and ordered up fifty sandwiches for the two of us the minute I saw her. That impressed me most. Touche can tell you about her, except that she's such a mess that I thank my stars not to be on the boat with her. Aside from that she finally the other day decided not to leave, after all, so it is a wonderful thing that I did not decide to take advantage of the opportunity presented me. I have not been able to decide from Paul's cables yet whether or not he liked the idea that I was staying but wasn't saying so because he had gathered that I really *wanted* to come home. I got awfully tired of not hearing from him and then when your letter came I thought it *might* be better to come back. It was a terrible strain and just last week I thought maybe this time I really was going to crack, but I made a very big effort and I'm working again. That's all I can do to save my brain. It just gets going around in too many circles. Maybe I shouldn't be staying but it seems to me it's too late now. My only hope is that you will come to Spain in February. I will certainly join you there. Cory is meeting Mary Anne on the Riviera, so she writes, after her stay with me, and then the two of them are going on up to Paris and then on to the boat bound for New York. It's too exhausting. By then I suppose I'll be just stuck in the middle of Spain or back in Tangier again. Paul will be off to Timbuktu, if he isn't on his way there now. Had I known all this shit about Mary Anne I would have come home now and alone. I would have it behind me instead of hanging over me. I was so pleased to have my own private travelling companion (Cory) to return with. I have written her asking her to ask Mary Anne if she would mind terribly, in case that I was alone by then, if we all met on the Riviera or in Paris and I returned with them. It is a very undignified thing to do, but I think it wouldn't hurt Mary Anne to spend a little time with me just to see how it works out. If I'm to be with Cory every year for the rest of her life, I think it would be more convenient for all of us if M.A. took a more friendly attitude, don't you? But she won't; please, please try to come. I may even just plain fly back with *you* as I daresay that's the way you'll do it. Oh! My God! An entirely new *tsuris* has come up! I see seven possibilities. Please call Cory and ask her to reach you in New York. She leaves the Inn on the eighth or ninth of December and writes that she can't give me her New York address. (She leaves New York the 13th of December by the way.) That means of course that she's with her brother. I feel that it would be better to have some way of contacting her. Would you ask Scotty to call Canal 6-8050 and ask for the doctor there? She'll get him eventually (I forget his name, it's a Jewish one and very common) and when she does would she ask for Mrs. Bowles's eyeglass prescription, and have her inquire if it's all right to make a lens and have it poked into the frame over here: I need my *right* lens. If he says you can't do that then I'll just have to go on the prescription (I don't know how good the glasses are here but I can try). If he says it's better to have the whole thing made then I suppose I'd better do that, but I doubt that he knows my size of frame and naturally the other way would be less expensive. I do have two mediocre frames over here which will last out the winter and anyway he might get the wrong size and just *say* it's better that way to make more money. Be very *careful* of him. The address is 191 Canal Street. It has a very sort of Left sounding name, the store, like the People's Eyeglass Store or something like that but I'm not sure that this isn't entirely in my imagination.

I can get chicken heads and giblets for a penny a pile but have no eating companion so what's the use? I'm God-damned sick of having no one to eat with except on odd nights, and no reason to eat at one time more than at another. I don't see how Helvetia makes out on her farm. I have hit the bottom here but that's as it should be. I shall really have a fit if you don't come over because part of my decision to stay was based on the knowledge that God willing I would see you either way. I realize too, Darling, that many things might prevent you from coming so don't *worry* about it. I just hope I will see you, that's all, and I know how you long to spend a little time with Cory. If you can get the lens to her in New York, which would mean communicating with her right now at R——— Inn before she leaves, it would be a great help. Also if you could see her and make lots of charm to her it would help our being in Madrid when you are—*if* you are to be there. You can also tell her about when it will be so she can warn Mary Anne about meeting her in Paris rather than on the Riviera if the time of your stay there works out that way. Madrid is nearer Paris than the Riviera as you probably don't know—mapless. Or isn't it? Oy! She will suggest reaching you probably because of her brother, though don't let on that you realize that because she's very embarrassed about it. Just say "How will we reach each other?" in a very offhand natural voice. I think it would be a very *clever* move to ask *both* of them up for a drink. You can give Mary Anne an Alexander. I want you to start thinking about this and preparing for it. You might bring Claudia and Johnny in for the occasion. Try to find out the dates of Cory's departure so that if I can't go back with her I can go back with you maybe, or at least be left with you, that is if you plan to spend only a certain number of weeks in Europe and it doesn't matter you might as well arrange it so that you don't go back *before* Cory. I don't know of course when your tour begins and what other reasons would prevent you from arranging things that way, but just in case when you see her or talk to her you can get the details. The last time she left me alone here I was truly desperate and the mere thought of it is ruining whatever pleasure I have in her coming. I do find that I am very eager to see her and excited. If only I don't have that awful departure on my head—at least I hope it can be arranged differently this time. Paul hasn't written me yet and I'm just plain puzzled.

Now that I've got all the complications over with I must tell you how happy I am about your tour. Paul told me too about the raves you got. I'm terribly excited about it and I know you are happy. I don't like what you wrote about "that certain party" being highly psychopathic. Were you exaggerating a little—I hope. I am worried now and hope you can give me some reassurance. Also did you really mean that your ulcer is back? You must write me about that at once. Paul of course will tell me what the Lorca plans are (if he recognizes me or has time to call at the hotel). I am glad that you have respect for him and that you like him. I love him very much though I could smack him at the moment. I probably confused the poor thing with my wires but I do wish I had known long ago how I felt. Do you like Tennessee? I like the sound of your beau and am glad he continues to make you happy. You wrote in a previous letter that Helvetia didn't like him? Did she tell you so? She said she saw you at Oliver's party and touched your cold dress. Who is this Wanda? Did you meet her? Was H. drunk as a hoot owl? I am ill about missing Paul's concert and think he should have somehow—*if* he doesn't care about whether I'm here or not—said something so that I could have arranged to come back for it. Helvetia writes that it was wonderful. I don't think being anywhere near Louisa with Cory around would have been exactly fair to Cory. I might have just become obsessed by Louisa which would have spoiled everything. Won't she keep? Anyway I think it is very dangerous for me to make any plans with *her* in mind. I feel that she is just as hopeless and unattainable as Tetum whom I have finally given up. I could not keep up a friendship with both Tetum and Cherifa. Cherifa just made it impossible. I go to Cherifa's house three times a week with food and wine. She is my sister. Between her and Tetum they have all my scarves, most of my money, my watch, and I am now taking Cherifa to the doctor's twice a week. I shall have to stop however unless he is willing to make me a price. I think he will. I have promised her a cloak (djellaba) for the Mouloud and shoes. I don't mind being liked for my money one bit. Being the richest woman in the world has certain disadvantages but I accept them. I feel that I have done everything, absolutely everything wrong, but perhaps something nice will happen anyway. I *would* like to have some fun again some day.

There is a very nice man in Madrid who knows all of Lorca in Spanish. He is the head of the Trans-World Airlines there, has an apartment and can show us everything we need to see. I think you will like him. He has a fireplace and serves cocktails. I think it would be lots of fun. We can fix up the money thing, tell Cory, so that she needn't spend more than six dollars a day for living. The "Parade" is booming with business but Jay only gets two hundred pesetas a week out of it and his food. Bill keeps the accounts and Jay's too lazy to ask for more money, he says he doesn't care. (That's about seven bucks!) He's quite wonderful really but I shall put the bite on him because he owes me five hundred pesetas (four), and I refuse to have Bill keep it if they've got the money in the box there — it will buy Cherifa's cloak. Ira Bellin got thousands and thousands of pesetas out of Mary Oliver, enough to send for her Russian family. She sold her jackets and pictures. Mary fell in love with her and has gone to buy a house in Marrakech. Cherifa wants me to buy her a taxi, after the djellaba. However I do save a penny a week on eggs. She gets them for me a little less and also knows how to look into them to see whether or not they are rotten. She is getting quite plump because of my affluence and every now and then instead of looking like a boy she looks like a complete Oriental woman. The minute Tetum saw that I was taking Cherifa to the doctor's she wanted to go too. I asked her what was wrong, and as far as I could gather she merely wanted a *thorough checkup*. Last month they were burning

131

crocodile dung and pig's bristles and now they all want x-rays. Cherifa was wild and said I couldn't take Tetum to the doctor because it would be a disgrace and that the doctor would be horrified if I came with a *second* Moorish woman. I have never understood why, but I am terrified of going against her orders and have therefore made an enemy of Tetum. I have more fun at Cherifa's house (the food is divine, ossir), so I thought I'd better give up Tetum. She is more of a conniver and mean all the way through. Besides that, she's too damned conventional and penny-pinching. She brings her own coal to the market and other equipment for making tea. Cherifa is much more grand and orders hers from the tea house, though she has actually less money, I believe. I am working because there is no sense in my brooding about whether I have done right or wrong in staying here. I, too, am *only* happy when I work and of course now that Paul's arriving I feel like it. Perhaps Helvetia and I can accompany you on your spring tour. Write me soon.

Much much love,

Jane

P.S. If the doctor isn't there at the "People's Eyeglass Store?" surely they have my name on their files. I want my prescription whether they can get me the lens on time for you or not. Cory might go and pick it up there. But mail prescription in any case!

42

**Jane Bowles to Katharine Hamill and
    Natasha von Hoershelman**
[Taghit, Algeria]
[March, 1949]

Dearest Katharine and Natasha,

I can't tell you everything that's happened because if I tried to I wouldn't write at all. I have tried to before and simply stopped writing because it was too exhausting. No one could have been happier than I was to receive your Xmas wire. It was wonderful to know you thought of me. (I sound like a real cripple or "Public Charge.") Certainly you were the only ones who did. Then I started many grateful letters and Cory was with me and—it was all very complicated. Now I am in the Sahara desert. I got to Marseille in February, stayed four days and came back to Africa, scared to go to Paris because there is a very long tunnel outside of Marseille. Lola can appreciate this. Of course I'm not neurotic any more, which is a good thing, but I do find it very hard to go *North*. This place we're in is an oasis—a very small one. We had to walk to it from a bus, with donkey carriers for our luggage. It is not a bus but a very interesting and solidly built *truck* that goes to Timbuktu. The dunes are extremely high, and I shall not attempt to climb them again—well maybe I will—because it is so beautiful up there. Nothing but mountains and valleys of sand as far as the eye can see. And to know it stretches for literally hundreds of miles is a very strange feeling. The sand here is a wonderful beige color. It turns bright pink in the evening light. I am impressed. It is not like anything else anywhere in the world (and I do remember New Mexico), not the sand—or the oasis. Anyway the rest is all rocks and rather terrifying. We saw a mirage called "Lake Michigan and the New Causeway" on the way here. I suppose there are mirages in New Mexico but I can't remember. We are going on to Beni Abbes (Paul and I) next Friday. The hotel here is kept up for the army since no tourists ever come but occasionally army people stop by for lunch. There are just Paul and me, the Arab who runs the hotel, and the three soldiers in the fort, and the natives—but *they* are just a little too native—and frightfully underfed. It is very very quiet, no electricity, no cars. Just *Paul* and *me*. And many empty rooms. The great sand desert begins just outside my window. I might almost stroke the first dune with my hand. Friday we are going further "in." (Oy!) But I am looking forward to the next place, though I doubt that it will be as beautiful as this oasis— nothing could be. The little inn there is run by a woman, a *Mademoiselle* Jury. Paul says she's a yenti old maid. Hoorah! I think there are eight or nine "whites" there—a real mob. Paul thinks there will be too much traffic because the truck goes through twice a week. There is no road leading *here* at all, so he's gotten used to it. We plan to be in the desert about a month and then back to Fez. Then to Tangier, where I can resume my "silly" life with the grain market group: Tetum, Zodelia, Cherifa and Quinza. You remember them. I have gotten nowhere—but Cherifa calls me her "sister" and I eat with them several times a week. I bring the food and the two heavy quarts of thick sweet wine. I had Tetum x-rayed. She was determined to go to the doctor's because I'd taken Cherifa ten times about her foot. I spent all morning in the doctor's waiting room among women wrapped in sheets. But I love to be with her — anywhere. She was happy because she had caught up with Cherifa. She felt the x-ray equalled the foot treatments Cherifa got out of me. It is all really about prestige — their life I mean — but I cannot tell them even that I know they are making an ass of me. I am always scared that they might find out I know. I'll tell you about it when I see you. Forgive this disjointed letter, please, I have had a fly after me and then in the middle of it the Arab who runs the hotel asked me to write a letter for him (naturally he can't write) to a man living in a place called "Oil Pump Number Five." It's a famous hell hole south of here. I hope we don't go there to live.

I spent five or six weeks with Cory. I shall always be very devoted to her. The business partner is quite a problem but I shan't have to face it until I get back — if then. I don't know where I live at this point. If I ever have any money I shall buy a place near the one in Delaware. How far is it from New York? Can Natasha and you *really* get out there for weekends? Can we go to Fire Island just once? But only if Kay Guinness is there. I am determined to be famous because of her and Janet Flanner, and I am simply sitting here in Africa biding my time.

I am actually full of plots and plans and have forgotten none of my enemies in the United States. I shall not be here forever. I refuse to spend fewer than three days with you both at a time. I am sure that I am now *utterly* incapable of getting around New York. I have written some, recently, and hope to see "Camp Cataract" appear in summer. How much land is there in Delaware? I am interested and surprised by this purchase of yours. Oliver wants to build a house with the next money he gets, and he is more likely to have some than I am. It would be nice to be settled near you — or would you hate it? I want to know where Dione is and Miss McBride. Please Katharine call up the *main* Y.W.C.A. headquarters and ask if Miss McBride is there. Tell her Jane Bowles was trying to locate her in order to write her a postal card. If you get her, *or* if they say she's out, at least I'll know she still works there (50 something street East, I believe), and you can write me her address. I keep thinking about her. Give my love to Lola and to my dear Florence, whom I should have written. I wrote Lola once — she never answered. Tell Florence I am going to be in Paris by the 24th of June to hear a piece of Paul's. I expect to come back home (?) next summer—middle or end—it will depend. Miss McBride used to be my teacher when I was fourteen. I've seen her a few times since. I miss you still—if anything, more than ever—and am getting rather eager to return for some nice evenings. (Three nights in a row at least—*please*.) Write me British Post Office, Tangier. If I'm still here they'll forward the mail. But I think it will take quite a while to reach you. I don't know. But much love—as ever—

Jane

P.S. Tennessee Williams got me a thousand dollars from the "Author's League"—$100 a month for ten months. He liked my play. I love him. Send me Rosalind's address if possible. Will write Tennessee to give her a message via Natalia, whom he's naturally met. Oh! my God—it suddenly occurred to me Janet Flanner is over on this side of the water and *not* in the States at all. I *know* I shall run into her. I'm sure she'll ask about the Arab nationalists and what their attitude was about Palestine. I shall certainly go into a dead faint right over again. I suppose Rosy will be back before I can reach her. And why get excited because she's in Italy when I'm four days away from Tangier—nearer ten days actually because the train to Colomb-Bechar only runs three times a week and trucks once or twice? Oh well. Give her my love in New York. Ask her for Esther's program. I should so much like to be somewhere when she was. Is Sybil with her? Please write about land or a house near yours. Maybe you could sell a couple of acres or do you want every *inch* of it? I'm furious already because I feel you're going to be difficult. Will mail this from Beni Abbes (six hours from here) when we get there, and you can judge by the postmark whether you're to answer me there or in Tangier. I daresay Tangier is best. We won't be down here more than a month, and we will have spent about twenty days of it by the time this goes, so unless it reaches you fast, write me British Post Office, Tangier. I love you for writing me and I love you anyway. The picture of Natasha is a dream. I have it with me. Please write again. Miss McBride might also be in the book under her name, Mary Frances, but try the Y. first. Kiss Betty and Lola and Florence— haven't Betty's exact address.

Much love again,

J.

43

Jane Bowles to Katharine Hamill
[Farhar Hotel]
[Tangier, Morocco]
[Late Spring, 1949]

Dearest Katharine,

I was very surprised and distressed to hear about your operation but happy you are getting along so well. Has it affected your drinking or eating? Since writing you I have come out of the desert and am back in Tangier—or have I written you *twice*? Now I'm confused so you see it is better really if I don't write at all—then there can be no mix-ups. *Who* is sending me the cards about Palestine? Is it Billie Abelle or all of you? Please let me know at once. If you don't know about them, take Billie aside and ask her if she has sent me two postal cards asking me what I intend to do about Palestine. I smell Janet Flanner of course but does Billie know about that? If not, you must have been up there or told her about it. I think of Billie very often but hesitate to write her because I can't remember whether I'm supposed to or not—because of Virginia. Does Virginia care? I don't know any more. But give her—Billie—my love when you see her, and I will send them both an official postal card.

Katharine dear, I am still sitting here in Africa and have given up the idea of going to Paris—too expensive—too complicated—and I want to work for a few months at a stretch now before returning, which I daresay will be in the fall. You will be without Natasha in August but I daresay you have sewed yourself up with your sister and several others for that month by now but if not why don't you call Helvetia? She'll be on her farm if she doesn't come here (and I doubt that she will) and you can certainly visit her or perhaps she'd visit you. I would like to think of her with you but I'm sure you will have other plans. Why doesn't Natasha retire too when you do? We are having some little rooms built on our roof so that we could all live in my little house in Tangier. (The taxes are $1.20 a year.) It costs nothing for the food, and liquor slightly less than in the States. Wine of course—nothing. We could be here for part of a year or one year and in the States the next. I think you *must* come to Africa sooner or later. There is a Russian woman here with her father and brother (all of them over 8 feet) and her four dogs (each dog bigger than two Arab houses put together), and she wishes she could make 1500 pesetas ($43) a month, which is what she needs to live on for all of them. Seven hundred a month rent and 800 for food—that's 21 dollars monthly for food; rent of course is non-existent in my house.

This "estimate" does not include meat or "Mrs. Crocker's Vegetable-Noodle Soup." But it does include fish, vegetable oil, and stones. Also please continue hunting around for Oliver's Pennsylvania country seat. What is all this about gardening? You are going to be gardening all the time. Helvetia's getting her garden in now and I'm furious. She goes right on with her life and here I am year after year in Africa.

When the rooms are built I shall have Cherifa and Quinza over to sleep. Tetum won't come I'm sure but this time when the rooms are ready I shall offer her a present if she lives with me for a day, two days or a week or more. One month—she gets a whole sheep. One night is going to be a toothbrush or a key ring. Two nights— socks, one week—pyjamas. The addition to the house (it is unlivable now) will cost 350 dollars roughly and we will have one more decent room and two more little rooms large enough for beds. There is one decent room downstairs—well not very decent—but long enough to contain Oliver, and another tiny room large enough for a bed. The bed however would fit only a Latin man or most women but no cowboys can get in there. I had planned to come back sooner thinking that I would go to Paris and then on to New York but it hasn't worked out that way, particularly since we're adding on to the house. I would like that done before I leave and then I will know it's there. I expect I'll come back here in summer very often. In any case it is not a great investment! And it can be sold at any time so I do not feel tied to it either. I am trying to get on with my novel and if it isn't reasonably far advanced by fall I shall chuck writing forever—but I am working now and did in the desert but then I stopped again for three weeks in Fez and one week here, so I've decided no moving about for the moment. The trip back was awful! You must be very exci.ed about your house. I am not neurotic except about hooking the bathroom door (we have hooks and slide-bolts in most W.C.s here) but otherwise O.K.

A boy called Themistocles Hoetis has come here to join us. He hated France, particularly Paris. He is twenty-three and was shot down in a plane during the war. He edits a magazine called *Zero* and had corresponded with Paul though he'd never met him. Well—here he is, and he can get out of his body whenever he wants

137

to and turn around and look at it. His name is *really* Themistocles. I am toying with the idea of having diphtheria shots. We are in a hotel up on the "[Old] Mountain" (an elevated part of Tangier). The straits are below us and across the way Spain. It is unbelievably beautiful here. How is Lola? Are you continuing to get stronger? Will you kiss my darling Natasha and yourself. I have no one to sleep with as usual.

Much love and *write* me —

Jane

44

Jane Bowles to Libby Holman
[Tangier, Morocco]
[August 29, 1949]

Dear Libby,

My letter and Paul's should arrive at the same time. If I don't get an answer *too* this trip I shall kill myself. "Cold actress thwarts comic writer." Tell *Ollie* to recall all pink and blue scripts of my play, am writing a new third act, cutting out that "treatise" at the end which stinks and has been holding us all up for two years. Cecil Beaton thinks I look like Gloria Swanson. I told you I got old out here. *Please*, darling, will you do me a great favor? Cut out "Camp Cataract" *if* it's in this issue and send it to me airmail. I don't know how much it will cost, but it won't be exorbitant like sending the whole magazine, which they will undoubtedly send me, but by boat and it won't get here for two months. That's O.K. if only you will airmail me the story. Scotty can cut it out. Give her my love. Naturally we are waiting to hear *what* you are going to do about Spain. If you do come over call Helvetia up and her Pekingese and ask her if she wants to come along. *Do* run in and see Cory, and fuss over Mary Anne if you are up that way. Kiss Touchie and Ollie. Delighted about T's play.

Love as ever,

J.

138

45

Jane Bowles to Katharine Hamill
[Farhar Hotel]
[Tangier, Morocco]
[Late Summer, 1949]

Katharine dear (and N. *if* she's there — but I doubt it):

What a *Beast* I am not writing. I've become very British, by the way, these last weeks. Our English summer crowd is here (2 people), one of them Cecil Beaton, and the locals are all going to a masquerade very soon given by C. dressed as *events*. Isn't it awful? For me, I mean, because as usual I don't remember what's happened. We have a fifty year range. I can think only of Lindbergh's return but need New York City for my costume. I wrote Oliver an alarming letter about the house next to yours and I've not heard a word since. I have no plans — more mixed up than ever, writing off and on — mostly off — when it's hot. Also have my drinking stomach back — God knows why — probably because I stayed off it for so long. Everything has changed since Truman Capote arrived. I wrote you about his staying here. Then all we needed was "Cecil" on the opposite hill for Africa to pick up its skirts and run. So I feel that though I have not gone to Paris it has come here, which is perhaps a good thing. Happy to find myself as uncomfortable, shy and insecure as ever — I mean it almost makes me feel young again to know that I must still have 4 drinks to feel at ease. I am as indestructible as an armored truck, in that sense, and it is a kind of relief to know that it will never change. Cecil Beaton is shy too, tell Natasha. I had a letter from Helvetia which worried me badly. It did not sound to me as if she were very well. I have no idea *exactly* when I will come home — March the latest — but most *likely* in the fall. I am afraid to see Helvetia and also don't know how on earth I shall get from one place to another in New York. Will you *please* write me whether or not I can *always* stay with you or N. or both for 3 days whenever I visit? I've asked you this in every letter. I just simply won't start that shunting back and forth anymore. Anyway where on earth am I going to be? Oy! I wish you would make a casual visit to R——— Inn. There's Cory too, in the middle of winter. I wish we could have a little apartment together just for a couple of months. My love Katharine darling and to Natasha when she returns.

J

P.S. I had a letter from Iris Barry, the first in the twelve years of my *courtship*. A friendly note. Do write any news you hear of Margaret and of yourselves of course. Do you play cards? Paul bought a mah jongg set. Can't you both get sabbaticals? Give my love to Billie Abelle always—she is a wonderful girl—and Rosie and Betty and Frances.

46

Jane Bowles to Libby Holman
[North Wales]
[November, 1949]

Dearest Libby,

I was horrified to read in your letter to Paul that you had not heard from me. I've written *twice* now without answers from you and have been waiting and waiting for a reply. My last letter gave you an address for Paris *and* London, as I was not sure you would reach me in Tangier. I shall repeat that I am spending the winter in Paris, which is now arranged with Cory, who has probably called you up about my coat by now. Paul (I wrote you this too) is hell bent on going to Ceylon. I think it would be fatal if he hung around until February—for Spain. It is the wrong season there, and he doesn't have any place he wants to be in winter except the Sahara where there really is no piano. He can surely find one in Ceylon. He wants to meet you in spring, either in the U.S. if you can't leave there or Spain and Tangier. Surely unless you have a tour you can forfeit the Connecticut spring—just once. I am speaking entirely against myself, as actually I shall probably return in the early spring (late March) and then come back to the old world just as fast as I can get out of the new one—late spring. It would be ideal of course—May and June in Spain—for you and Paul, and we could come back together but wouldn't that be too late for you? I mean wouldn't April suit you better though it wouldn't *me*? Of course I don't know what mid-April plans you have in the new world, but if it's the tulips or Easter I shall be furious. If you do come over— early spring—please let me know. I shall then probably wait for you. I am terribly confused now as to where I live, Libby, it scares me just a little to think of it, so I don't think of it. If you would only move the entire *shebang* to Tangier I'd be happy. Paris was beautiful and depressing, and despite a really wonderful reception in England and here in North Wales I am eager to get back to the "soupe hôtel"[34] in Paris. I stayed there a few days on my way here and am returning on November the 28th to Paris with David Herbert and Michael Duff. I think you know David — at least he's met you — but it was many years ago. You probably know Michael too. Oliver would love this house [the Duff family estate]. It is still run on a pre-war scale. I mean the "staff" are all here, but I feel that tomorrow they may vanish. I shall tell Oliver about it, the luxury of it will make him furious, and he will never dare to mention those bells at Jack Wilson's house again and those two wretched servants of his. As for myself I am almost dead from having my little scarf pressed which is all I brought for three days. It's the little pink one you gave me. I don't know what "Nanny" thought when she unpacked me and found Olive Oil — Popeye's girl friend — in my suitcase, but she laid her out diagonally on the dressing table. Olive Oil is made of wood. If I can judge by the few British I have met — who have been either of the aristocracy or the theater or of the "servant class" — I am all out for them. Paul is a *great* success here. He said that naturally his trip to England and the preparations for it slowed down his progress on *Yerma*[35] and he is sorry about that but after all one only writes a first novel once and I don't think he's ever had such a success before in his life and so I am happy he came here and I'm sure you will be too. Parties were given for him every second in London,[36] and though he was very tired after a week of it I know it has done him an enormous amount of good. I think when he gets down to work again it will go very quickly. Please write me. I wish to hell you could come to Paris but I guess you wouldn't.

Much love, Libby darling,

Jane

---

[34] The Hôtel de l'Université, where Jane could cook.

[35] Paul was writing an opera based on García Lorca's *Yerma*, in which Libby would star.

[36] Paul's *The Sheltering Sky* had just been published.

P.S.   Forgot to write you that Paul is all for my allowing Audrey Wood to represent me on *Summer House*. He thinks it will help both me and Oliver and that I'd be a fool not to. Oliver wired me that he thought the new third act wonderful and that he had definite plans for the play, but Paul thinks he is more than likely just keeping up my morale. Audrey Wood wrote me last week (probably prompted by Tenn). Love to Touchie.

47

Jane Bowles to Libby Holman
[Paris]
[January 11, 1950]

Dearest Libby,

At last! I won't go on about how puzzled I've been by your silence — and worried. My reason for not thanking you immediately for the clothes (which did arrive) — there was still no letter from you, only a more than confusing message from Cory, namely that you had not heard from *me*. All right that's over and I shall write without going backwards which is always a bore. I did write a long one from England and so did Paul explaining about Ceylon, and there was a lot in it about the Lorca opera too. He did lose some time on it in London but he will catch up now on the boat and I know it did him a great moral good to be at last a *lion* which he has deserved for many years and had somehow never gotten in music. He is now a famous literary figure in England (well-known anyway) and probably will soon be in New York if he isn't already. He took the translation with him on the boat to finish and expects to find a piano in Ceylon so that enough songs are written by spring for you to work on. He would like you to join him in Spain then. He is returning to Tangier around March, approximately. All this was written to you in a long long letter that I saw and which was sent from England (Wilton-Salisbury). From the sound of *your* letter I would judge that you never received it. If this is the case, I *can* write almost everything he said to you in detail since we discussed whether or not it was fair or right of him to go to Ceylon for hours on end, and he was against waiting around until February for several reasons. Please let me know Libby whether or not you received this letter. It's the one in which he even suggests your joining him in Ceylon (!) but is most in favor of meeting you in Spain this spring. In my letter I scolded you and said for once you could miss part of April at Treetops. It's a far better month for Spain and Paul will have enough music done by then to make it worth your while and his too. Now I've gone and repeated all this but I do have a feeling you've received no letters or only half of them. *NO*, Paul did not leave from Tangier, he left from Antwerp, and if Gore goes to Tangier he will not see him there. What *are* all these hog-wild rumors anyway? According to Audrey Wood, Ollie was going to take out an option on my play again beginning January 1st but now there is no *word*. I have overspent myself a little too, thinking the money was coming, so I hope it will. I think it will but if you see Ollie please ask him whether it is coming or not so that at least I know if it is coming. There are a few little things I'd like to buy and also my spring plans depend a little on that and also on whether you want to visit Paul in spring or not. He's already bought his passage back for March. I thought you might come over a little earlier, pick me up in Paris and then we could all go down to Tangier, or you could go from here direct to Spain. Anyway something could be worked out. I wrote Oliver that I was sad to hear you felt you couldn't take a "pleasure" trip, but I think that's one of your big troubles—that everything has to be connected and too complicated to unravel—it may even be necessary for you. I may share this trouble though it expresses itself differently. I forget how!

My plan is either to return to America in early spring, late spring or summer, for a while anyway. This depends on my work, money, you and my play. If Oliver did manage to get a fall production going then I might, if I can, just stay on in Paris or even go down to Tangier before returning to New York and being stuck there for a long period of time—maybe ten years?

As for my life I don't know where I live and I am sorry in a way that you *do*. I am having a very quiet time naturally with Cory here. I saw quickly enough that lots of parties would be out even if I *did* want them and even if I were invited. I know I could get about through Peggy Reille, but I can't put Cory through such evenings and perhaps even not myself. I work and I walk a little and I see a few friends who live nearby. (About 850 of them.) Paris is very beautiful and the only city I think to live in. Except to see you, I have no desire to return to the States ever. Not that I *love* it here, I just hate it there. I love Morocco best I guess. I don't know

143

what will happen to me—not really. *Please, please* write—if only a card. How I wish you could come over, perhaps in February or March. After all, perhaps I could count as "business" and it could be on your way to meeting Paul. Force Ollie to give you a third act, or else ask Audrey Wood to lend you her copy. I had one letter from you which I got (about three weeks after it was written) at American Express disapproving of her, but by then I was pretty well up to my neck. Don't worry about it. Much much love Libby darling and please let us keep in close touch. You *must* come in February.

J.

P.S. Will certainly buy Van Gogh if you want me to.

I don't go to nightclubs since Cory came so I haven't seen G. [George] Lloyd except once when I first got here and was taken to the Boeuf.[37]

Expect to have Paul's address any minute, soon as he reaches Ceylon. I'll forward any letter, just send it c/o Mrs. Jane Bowles here.

48[38]

Jane Bowles to Paul Bowles
[Paris]
[January 17, 1950]

Dearest Bupple,

I suppose I should single-space this, though I hate to. There is no room for corrections. I shall get all the disagreeable things off my mind first. My work went well last week. I had got into a routine, but this week it's all shot to hell again . . . not because of my life really, but because I have come to the male character again. I must change all that I wrote about him in Tangier. Not

[37] Le Boeuf sur le Toit, a Paris nightclub.

[38] This letter transcribed not from the original, but from previously published material.

all, but it must become real to me, otherwise I can't write it. I have decided not to become hysterical, however. If I cannot write my book, then I shall give up writing, that's all. Then either suicide or another life. It is rather frightening to think of. I don't believe I would commit suicide, though intellectually it seems the only way out. I would never be brave enough, and it would upset everybody. But where would I go? I daresay the most courageous thing to do would be nothing. I mean, to continue as I am, but not as a writer. As the wife of a writer? I don't think you'd like that, and could I do it well? I think I'd nag and be mean, and then I would be ashamed. Oh, what a black future it could be! That is why I have to use some control, otherwise I get in a panic. I am trying to write. Cory's being here is a hindrance and a help. A help because she gives a center to my day, and a hindrance because if I read, and wrote the letters I should write, and simply wandered around chewing my cud as one does when one's writing, I would have very little time left for her. We have been seeing too many people . . . not many different ones, but the same few over and over again. There have been very few dinners alone, and it has taken me some weeks to realize that Cory just doesn't want to have anyone much around. Though if they must be around, she prefers them to be men. Gordon she likes, and Frank Price. I have miraculously avoided a real bust-up drama, and have kept the most severe check on myself. I think now that things are well adjusted, and I am clear in my mind about how to conduct the rest of the winter until she leaves: in solitary confinement as much as possible. Strange that when she first arrived I thought we had a whole lifetime together; I guess that threw me into a panic. And now I feel I've done it all wrong. It would have been pleasanter and better for my work seeing no one else (the strain of wondering whether she was enjoying an evening or not gave me a headache), and instead getting into the habit of eating dinner in silence (unless I talk) which is, after all, not so bad. I don't know what I was afraid of. Despair, I guess, as usual. Now there seems to be not enough time left. I have grown used to her again, and fond of her, and we have moved into Frank Price's flat, which will be much better. I had taken my own room on the other floor because our room was not suitable for working; and because of a scene she made about my "walking out" on her, I felt guilty every time I was in my room and was not strictly working. She later explained how she felt, and tried to reassure me that she no longer felt that way about it, yet I could never be in my own room with any serenity. The fairies on the other side of the wall drove me crazy anyway, and turned out to be almost as bad as the children in the courtyard who had made work impossible for me in the room we had shared together (the same arrangement you and I had). It wasn't big enough anyway for actual living, though it was fine just for a week.

I want desperately to get another "clump" of work done in the next four or five weeks. There is simply no time for anything, ever. I know that I shall be terribly upset when she leaves. There will be a week of agony, I suppose. Changing from this charming flat into a cheap room, financial insecurity which I don't have now, and so on. I am sending you O.'s letter so that you know what's going on. If this option does get to me, instead of tearing up roots again, I may spend part of the spring in Paris . . . how long I don't know. I may also go to Tangier, depending on whether you're there or not and a few other unpredictables. If however the play does go into rehearsal this summer, I *would* prefer, as Oliver suggests, to go back in July rather than in the spring. It would be better sailing, would give me longer to work on Yenti, if I'm still working by then, and I'd see you sooner, as I'd most likely get down to Africa eventually.

I see Alice Toklas now and then, but I'm afraid that each time I do I am stiffer and more afraid. She is charming, and will probably see me less and less as a result of my inability to converse. This is not a result of my shyness alone, but of a definite absence of intellect, or should I say of ideas that can be expressed, ideas that I am in any way certain about. I have no opinions really. This is not just neurotic. It is very true. And Alice Toklas gives one plenty of opportunity to express an idea or an opinion. She is sitting there waiting to hear one. She admires your book tremendously. In fact, she talked of little else the last time I saw her. She won't serve me those little bread sandwiches in different colors any more because she says I like them more than the cake, and so eat them instead of the cake. I do like them better. And now I must go there and eat only sweets, which makes me even more nervous. Maybe she'll never speak to me again. Eudora Welty came over to dinner with Mary Lou Aswell and told me she was a great admirer of yours. She asked for *Camp Cataract* and took it home with her. After nearly a month she returned it with a note explaining that she failed on it, but would like to try something else of mine some day. I had met her on the street in the middle of the month, and she said then that she was having trouble with it, and so she never did finish it. I was disturbed by that as I have, since seeing you last, turned into an admirer of hers, and it would be nice for me to be admired by an established and talented American writer, instead of by my friends and no one else. That was upsetting, and also the fact that a friend in the hotel didn't like it really. (A very brilliant and charming girl called Nora,[39] who is now in Paris but whom I met long ago in New York.) This evening Sonia Sekula is giving a small party in her room. Mary Reynolds will come, and Lionel Abel and Pegeen. (Pegeen has two babies, apparently by her husband Hélion.) Cory will attend, perhaps, but I can't, because I am dining with, of all people, Sidéry, who was very excited when he heard I was your wife. I met him at one of the few cocktails I've been to, at Peggy's. He is quite charming, I think. I wrote you about Manchester, but you must simply have forgotten. I gave him to Truman, not because T. wanted him (though if he did it was for my sake, not his) but because I didn't like his face or his nature when I returned. Though Donald was never a real Peke, he was cute from the very first minute, and this one was cute only because he was a little fluffy ball. His muzzle had gotten much whiter, and his face definitely more pointed, and his eyes closer together. I thought I had better give him away while I disliked his looks, as I'm sure he would have been a nuisance. I have a few clippings which I'll enclose, though I'm sure you have them already. The book, though second from the bottom, made the best-seller list, which I think is wonderful. Your literary success is a fact now, and it is not only distinguished but widespread. I think to have [Cyril] Connolly and Toklas and a host of other literary people, plus a public, is really remarkable and wonderful. You should soon write another book. I hope that you are pleased at last, and not simply because it is a way to make some money. You do deserve a success of this kind, and I think you are at the right age for it. I can get no news out of anyone in Tangier. Have written Ira and Jacqueline and the fact that I hear from no one confirms me in my belief that Esterhazy[40] has gone. It is rather horrid not knowing what is going on. I am glad I have a little money down there because if anyone ever writes me I should like to send checks for Fathma. I have just about nothing left here, and I know this will horrify you, but it just happened, and without my going to nightclubs either. I am waiting from day to day for the option money to arrive

[39] Pseudonym.

[40] A Hungarian nobleman in Tangier as a refugee; he was to oversee work on the Bowles's house.

from Audrey Wood via Oliver, rather than send for more from Tangier. Naturally I would have been more careful if I hadn't had a letter from Wood that sounded pretty definite about the option. *Blondes* is not only a hit but a smash hit. Laurence Olivier's head reader saw my play and wrote that it was morbid and depressing, and though not something to be dismissed, certainly nothing they could think of doing. Truman hates New York, and wrote: "Honey, even if your play is done I hope you won't have to come back for it." Alice T. was delighted that you didn't really care for him very much. (I told her.) She said it was the one thing that really worried her. She could not understand how an intelligent person like you etc. She doesn't seem to worry in the least, however, about my liking him. So I'm insulted . . . again.

Paris is so very beautiful, particularly in this dark winter light. I'm surprised you don't love it more. I still love Africa best I guess, but there one must shut one's eyes against a great many things too. Here there is the Right Bank, and there the Villes Nouvelles, the buses, and the European shoes. You know what I mean. To cross the river never ceases to excite me. I went to see *Phèdre* at the Comédie Française with Nora. I am wildly excited about it. The only thing I have enjoyed thoroughly in years. I have never heard French *grand théâtre* before. I don't know how good the players were, but one must be good to do Racine at all. I shall go there now as often as possible.

I have gotten rounder in the face from the nourishing food. I'm upset about it, but perhaps it is becoming. Poor Michael Duff's son was born dead. I don't hear from them. Just a funny postcard now and then. I am terribly sorry that I can't give you more information about your book. Certainly friends in New York can do better. I might as well be in Ceylon with you. I love the descriptions of it, by the way, though at the moment I feel no need of adding any country to my list. I am puzzled enough with the Seine River and the Grand Socco. Oddly enough I still love Morocco best, though I do not admire it more. I think and think about what it means to me, and as usual have come to no conclusion. I dream about it too, in color, all the time.

Much much love, Bupple dear. I miss you very much. Write me your plans and don't stay away forever. I hope you'll return sometime this spring. Will you?

P.S. I had my tooth fixed. The dentist hurt like hell. Is Gore really joining you?

49

Jane Bowles to Paul Bowles
[Paris]
[Late January, 1950]

Dear Bup:

I don't know who else is sending you the enclosed, most likely everybody, but rather than take a chance on your missing out on it (or them), I shall send them along. I'm deeply sorry that I have not been nearer to the source of your criticisms, publicity etc. I should certainly have seen to it, that you received them immediately. I enclose Oliver's letter so that you keep up with the plans which as you see are in the air, but not very worrying. I have a feeling that Libby will be coming to Spain in spring. We should have a charming reunion in Morocco, all of us, if it ever works out. Of course nothing will be charming if I can't get my novel written. Yesterday the whole thing dried up on me again and I had the terrible pain in my head that I get—not a pain exactly but a feeling of tightness in my scalp, as if it were drawn tight over an empty drum. (My head is the drum.) It happens too often really and I'm afraid that it is the physical expression of sterility. I go on trying though it is a terrible fight. I had suggested this suite to Oliver (Frank's rooms) for himself though he seems to have misunderstood me. Because of my work, I don't think I could be even in a suite with anyone. I am sorry that he is not coming in early March, particularly for such gloomy reasons. If however he were delayed by something pleasant I should in one sense be glad. I think it will be good to have a few weeks completely to myself. I do feel very strongly that I should I give up writing if I can't get further into it than I have. I cannot keep losing it the way I do, much longer. This is hard to explain to you who work so differently. I may really have said all I have to say. Last night I felt so bad about it, I drank almost an entire bottle of gin. I had gone back to my desk after the most terrible *crise* of despair and forced myself to work after I had very nearly thrown everything in the fire (mentally). It was an effort and after that I just started drinking. I felt better as a result and by eleven o'clock I was very cheery indeed. Nora, who lives in the hotel, came by, and we all three of us went out to the Monocle. It has gone down terribly and the tough proprietress I was so crazy about whose name was Bobby and because of whom I hung around Paris for weeks (you remember) after you had left for the South [In 1938, on their honeymoon trip], has gone. "Elle n'est plus dans le métier," the bartender told me; he had known her too. "Elle s'est mariée et elle est propriétaire de deux énormes châteaux." Why would she have *two* castles? She was the most masculine woman I had ever seen. I would have been depressed if I hadn't been drunk. Ironically enough I had not been there twenty minutes when "La Zöora" appeared on the little dance floor doing an Algerian belly dance. I was wildly excited and spent the rest of the evening talking Arabic with her though God knows how, because there is practically nothing left of mine. She said *Gol* by the way instead of using the correct *Tangier k*. I wanted so badly to rush somewhere and tell you about it. It was certainly not what I had expected of the Monocle. And to think twelve years ago I sat in that place night after night drunk as a lord and partly because I didn't want to go to Africa—in the beginning entirely for that reason—until I met Bobby "aux deux châteaux." Last night I was more excited finding the Algérienne than I was by anything else. We talked about Colomb-Bechar and the Aid el Kebir. She said she couldn't live in Algiers because her family wouldn't allow her to dance. I can just see them. We are going out to eat cous-cous together one of these days. I have her address. She was the only entraineuse who did not ask for a tip—and I danced with her more than with any of the others—and she warned me against a restaurant that one of them was taking us to after the place closed. She said in Arabic, to me "matimshishi temma—Fluz besef—hamsa miat francs."[41] And so I warned Nora and Cory and we went home instead. She seemed so delighted with me. We were two yenti Algerians meeting in Paris, and helping each other out. Of course she would be called Zöora. I think she might be able to give me the real low down on Arab women and their habits though Algerians may be very different, but surely they have almost everything in common with Moroccans. Alas she is neither a Cherifa nor a Tetum, she's the other type, but terribly nice. Cory ended up the evening dancing with an entraineuse from Martinique, quite fat and dark. Isn't it all ridiculous? The evening cost roughly about ten thousand francs though it needn't have, but we were suckers. It wasn't my money so don't get excited.

Ira has told Tommy Esterhazy to fetch your package. He *is* in the house. Both Jay and Ira have written saying everything is fine

[41] "Don't go there. It's very expensive. 500 francs."

150

though I can't understand why Esterhazy doessn't pull himself together and write. It seems to me that (unless he has written you) it is a piece of uncommon rudeness. I don't understand. Two heartbreaking news items. One: they have sold the space between the Place de France and the B.P.O. and an enormous apartment building is going up. It will be the end of my enjoyment on that end of town. I loved that view so terribly—the rugs on the wall, the Algeciras boat coming in; the whole thing is too damn upsetting. I shall never go to the British Post Office again. The second item is even more horrible. Cherifa, Jay writes, is planning to move to the *new* market. So that will be the real end of everything. I just can't bear to think of her empty stall. Do you think he could be teasing? I am awfully upset and am writing Kouche Saïd about it. I shall enclose a letter to her which I'll ask him to translate, saying that I dreamed a terrible misfortune would befall her should she change her stall. Do you think it would be a sin to try and play the Deus Ex Machina in this? You think I am joking probably, but I am not. I am terribly upset. If one by one all the things I loved about Tangier disappear even in a few months, how can I even look forward to going back ever? The terrible thing is that I love it still just as I did when I left. I am no less hysterical. What is it do you suppose? The fact that I do not rush back at once is no indication of how I feel. It is in my heart and we do own the house. As I wrote you, now that I'm here there are things I must benefit by and that I hope to enjoy—always of course if I'm working well.

I hope you get a good boat, Bupple, otherwise I shall worry. Write me please.

Much love, as ever

Jane

P.S. Terribly worrying about O's mother. What on earth will happen to Ivan [Bernkoff—Oliver Smith's stepfather] if something does happen to her. I hope NOT. And what about Oliver? Will he take it terribly hard if something does? All the more reason for him to come over.

I really can't get *over* the French cats and that is why I keep writing you and O. about them. Do you like them? Toklas has given me up. A blow I scarcely need at the moment. I hate the writing paper you used last. Think of the money I spend happily on overweight for you and then *you* save a few—pence, I suppose— by using those HORRORS—you know I *hate* them.

151

50

Jane Bowles to Paul Bowles
[Paris]
[February 13, 1950]

Dearest Buppie,

I am happy to have news of you again, though I'm sorry you feel a bit lonesome. There is nothing I would like more than to be alone at the moment (or with you) but then when it happens (my separation from Cory) I probably shall miss her. It is going to be ghastly this time since she knows by now that everything is all washed up. I have never been through anything quite like this winter. How I ever got myself into it, I don't know. But by the time I reached England it seemed too late to wire her and too cruel. I was not *sure* either how really over it was. Perhaps even recently I thought something might be saved. I see no one now but Cory; this I wrote you was my plan, but I had counted somehow on routine and solitude hiding the absence of love or even inviting it again. I was quite wrong, but at least I think Cory can stand it better this way and there is less drinking. My close friends know the reasons for my seclusion and others think I've become a hermit, I imagine. Peggy Guggenheim has called me several times since my one lunch with her but I have more or less told her to try me in March! I could not be more isolated in Beni-Abbes, in fact Bidon 5 is probably a better parallel. Today I had lunch with Sybille Bedford because Cory went to see her friend at the other end of Paris, the only one, a WAC with a new born baby. It was wonderful to have someone to talk to. Sybille, though you hate her, is one of the better minds, I think, and very entertaining. She is rosy cheeked and gay too. God, I just can't take many more gloompots. I am not complaining really about my life, at the moment. I would not mind anything if only Cory did not look so sad. I am doing everything I can, but nothing will make up for the one terrible lack. She is often pleasant but most of the time gloomy and if even slightly drunk, vindictive. If her partner were here it would be better to split it up quickly, but I would not dare let her go off somewhere to wait for Mary Anne alone. I do not think she can take it, and is happier here with me despite the difficult and dismal situation. I put all the blame on myself naturally, and feel now that perhaps I should never start anything with the innocent again. I am not hard enough to take

it, myself, not to speak of them. I have still not had a decent time in Paris. Will I in the spring? I daresay the second Cory leaves everyone else I would like to see will leave too. I know Oliver will come but then that is not what I mean. I should love to be able to work here by myself and read and yet have a few appointments which I would look forward to with excitement. I am sorry that I went to England despite what I saw, but on the other hand I am more than pleased at the new development which will permit me to spend some time in Paris, after all. I would have been pretty mad going back to New York in March having got about two days fun out of the whole grand tour. Also I want to get much more work done before returning to the U.S.A. You mention that I shall get more work done in Tangier or New York, but it will be Tangier or Paris or both. I have no plans except to do what I want to do. If you are forced to take a boat to England we can all meet in England or in Paris. I'm sure David would love to have you and Oliver (and me too) at his house for a while. Oliver has ideas of visiting the Cliffords in Italy and wanted to take me there too. I'm sure he'd just as soon take you. Or we might all go, if there's a way to get there for me. You could eventually get to Gib. from Naples. I have a feeling Libby will be meeting you in April in Spain. She says she will either meet you then or in June after Topper's graduation on June the 12th, which she must be back for. I shall enclose the paragraph in case letters go astray. If you get a boat to London why don't you write Libby to take the Queen and we'll all meet here? I'm sure she'd enjoy a week or two in Paris or London and then we could all stick together or separate and meet later again. As usual unless a car materializes I won't want to go skipping around. I'll stick in one place and work, wherever it happens to be. Maybe Paris, maybe Tangier (if I have any work by then that I can call my own). Oliver wants to go back on a French Line, by the way, because he thinks he can get us passage at a very reduced rate. He advertised for them in the . . .
[rest of letter missing, except for P.S.]

P.S. I would be perfectly happy to [go to] England again. I just felt that I went at a wrong moment—though now that I can stay here longer it is less wrong than it was.

Jane Bowles to Paul Bowles
[Paris]
Monday [February 13, 1950]

Dearest Bup:

I enclose Esterhazy's letter. I don't know what to write him, except that I think he should do the work while he is there (*have* it done) rather than while he is away. I am having my money sent to Tangier and the bank can send me ten thousand at a time (mandat-carte). The exchange there is three ninety- five. It will be a nuisance but certainly worth it. I am going to buy some shoes, which I need desperately, a pleated skirt, infroissable, which will go beautifully with my shirts, a gay scarf and a white blouse or two. Mine are coming to pieces, the white ones, and I need some for dressier occasions. When I have bought these few things and paid my five thousand franc dentist bill, I suppose I will have spent about thirty thousand francs at least. I shall spend as little money as possible, though I shan't stay on here very long if it's going to be *la misère*. At the moment I hope to find a cheap, or a cheaper, room here or at the Quai Voltaire, as Cory is leaving in ten days. I would like to continue with my work in peace. None of the two hundred fifty franc rooms is very livable in winter, I'm afraid, and March can be quite cold. I'll pay more for my room and less for food, I guess. I am going over to the École des Langues Étrangères or whatever the hell it's called, and look into a course in Maghrebin-Arabic. I don't think I can go much further in it alone, or with Cherifa. As for Kouch, he can do no more for me, I'm sure. I just can't accept having gotten this far in the damn language, and not getting any further. I think too that it makes my being in Morocco seem somehow more connected with my work. With me, as you know, it is always the dialogue that interests me, and not the paysages so much or the atmosphere. In any case, I cannot express these ever in writing. I feel that some day I might write *Automobile* if I ever finish *this* thing. I will write you what happens with the course. I shall be bitterly disappointed if it turns out to be hopeless.

Now that Gore is with you I suppose you are less lonely and you may even put off your return. Do let Libby know definitely what you are doing, and Esterhazy too. I know either one of us or both of us will want the house to be empty for us when we are there, whether we live in it entirely or just eat in it, work in it, etc. I think it might be a squeeze for both of us unless we're flat broke. I am sorry you have been so worried about the house. I read a letter of yours written to Gordon. Sorry, but pleased, too, that you think of it. It means that you will come home now and then to roost, and not be perpetually wandering around. I am delighted that I am not in Ceylon because of your snake letter to Gordon. In his "desk," indeed, and I spend half the day at a desk. My God!

Eventually I should like to go to Venice and to Ireland. If it were not getting even further away from Tangier I would go there this spring—to Ireland, I mean—by myself (ossir). If life becomes unbearable here and my Arabic course doesn't work out, I may just go to Tangier . . . if I can get Nora to go with me. I don't want to rush off rashly though, and then feel that I have missed my chance of enjoying Paris, forever. God knows when I'll get here again.

Having refused so many invitations to Peggy's, I finally went with Cory and Nora at eight o'clock last night. We were late, invited for six thirty, and most of the people had gone. It was disastrous. Peggy took me over to Marie-Laure de Noailles and introduced me. I kept glancing over my shoulder at Cory to see if she was all right (engaged in conversation) and she was. Madame de Noailles dragged me into a different room so that we could talk quietly. I was uneasy, but Cory was still in a group with Nora and some man when I left her. We talked mostly about Cecil and Truman, and then since we had no cigarettes, I went back into the big room to get them. I was horrified to see Cory standing quite alone, framed in the doorway. I rushed up to her: she was in a rage with Nora and me, a little drunk, too. I tried to calm her down, but alas, by the time I had, Marie-Laure had wandered back into the big room. I started running about like a maniac, looking for cigarettes. It was sort of like a Kafka. I never did get back to Marie-Laure because I was terrified of leaving Cory's side even for a minute. I am sure Madame de Noailles thinks I staged the whole thing, as I never did get back to speak to her at all, and had interrupted a conversation that was obviously unfinished just to bring back some cigarettes. It was all ridiculous, and I'm glad I haven't been out with Cory more. It's hopeless, and I told Peggy not to invite me. I don't care really. Supposedly Mme. de Noailles is an old collaborationist, but she is also Peggy's guest and she must think me nuts or rude. She liked your book immensely.

155

Perhaps you can write Esterhazy. I don't know what to tell him. Audrey Wood thinks your book *is* a movie and regrets your tie-up with Helen Strauss. Have you written Strauss about it? I imagine they automatically think of those things, don't they? I'm going to see Brion today at the Quai Voltaire. He is leaving for Italy and says he has never been so desperate in his life. The Fulbright seems to have blown up, or he has. I couldn't quite understand, but I shall know more by tonight.

I have met Dilkusha de Rohan. She is really the end, but God knows I shall probably be seen sitting with her in a few weeks. I would have shot myself, however, had I waited in Tangier for her. Mary has disappeared, according to Dil. She was last seen in La Linea. Dil. said she was supposed to be coming into another nine thousand pounds, which I suppose might explain Dil's trip there. She only saw Mary *once*, in Tangier, though they did spend three weeks together in Gib. I don't know what it's all about. Sylvia Marlowe is arriving in May. I am getting rather excited about my play again. Do you think that this time it will get on? We went to the zoo and saw a whole monkey village. They lived in little Arab houses. The younger monkeys kept yanking the tiny babies away from the mothers, and then they would run with them all over the rocks. Other young monkeys were the pursuers. Rather like a wild-west movie, except that they almost tore one of the babies apart. You would have loved it. I wish I could take one of these fat (French) cats back to Tangier.

Much love

P.S. Please be careful of the snakes and insects. And what are those elephant trips you are going to make? I am frantic too about your going eventually to the place where the plague broke out. There might be a little left even when they do allow visitors. Or will it be safe?

Keep writing me here. Probably won't move but in any case will pick up my mail.

Decided to write Esterhazy not to let anyone work on the house while he's gone.

52

Jane Bowles to Libby Holman
L'Étape, Pacy-sur-Eure, France
[June 17, 1950]

Dearest Libby,

I don't know how everything got into such a mess or what Paul has written you.[42] I should have written you myself but did not dream that you would still want to come over to Spain even if Paul were going to Westport with me — or shortly afterwards.

Since he is coming anyway to do the music, we thought the earlier the better. He has been wonderful since his return from Ceylon and is even willing to risk his fare over, which Oliver won't pay him in case the Westport production never comes off.[43] If it does he'll get his fare out of it one way. I myself am terrified of the whole thing and want him with me very much to help on decisions. I know more or less what you think of this production but I can't possibly decide from here to call it off. Once there the responsibility of deciding such a thing without Paul would be ghastly if it did come to that, and if not there will be a million other things to decide. Paul should be a perfect balance for Oliver and me. I shudder to think too that you won't be around. I had hoped that you would work with Paul at Treetops and that he would be there for me to consult as well. I wouldn't dream of pitching my needs against yours if they were equal but I think in this case they are not. The play has been banging around for five years, no director seems to be willing to do it except this Garson Kanin. If he is a yenti and awful then a decision to give the whole thing up may be the *only* solution. I mean give it up forever because I don't feel that this play can go trailing around any longer — Oliver will be worn out. To decide all this by myself will be a terrific responsibility. Also without the music the play would not have a fair tryout and Paul wants to do it. I naturally am delighted he does. I don't know what Spanish arrangements you've made. Even if he waits to meet you he can only see you for a short while — a few days — and then he'll have to leave. I think that your European plans

---

[42] Paul was in Tangier.

[43] There was no Westport production of *In the Summer House*.

are wonderful, but I don't feel that it is wildly essential for you to sop up Spanish atmosphere in July and August. Is it? Couldn't you stay at Treetops and spend that time with Paul and learning from records? You'll not only be helping me, but Paul will get much more work done on the opera that way. Have you a Spanish trip worked out with some other people—or what? I realize that if you do, you might want to meet Paul just for a few days in Spain, as you would, if he sails on the 8th, miss him en route. I have understood that you arrive on the 15th.

Changing his passage is going to be difficult, and his being in Connecticut without you will be grim—for him and for me.

I feel the Spanish trip would be a pleasure for both of you, though not an actual *necessity*. There are records that you can listen to and I think Paul could leave after the Westport production is over (August 28th) so you could go to Spain then. I was with Bud [Williams][44] and so I know that your Paris concert should not take place before October or November. You may naturally have some plan about Spain that I know nothing about, but please, if you *don't*, consider staying behind just for another six or seven weeks. It would make all the difference in the world to me.

It is not easy for me to take the responsibility of dragging Paul back and I have even suggested his allowing someone else to do the music. He wouldn't dream of it and I think I would have been mortally wounded if he had accepted the suggestion. I know how much he longs to remain over here and have even written him in answer to a wire he sent yesterday about you and Spain, namely "Libby *insists* I be in Spain for her arrival," that I *suspected* him of writing you a letter that would spur you on to come to Spain rather than the reverse, to give him an automatic excuse for remaining an extra week or ten days. I could not imagine your being so insistent otherwise. He would have do so *unconsciously* of course, and perhaps he didn't. You may have, as I said, some new project worked out in Spain that makes going there and speaking to Paul even if only for a few days absolutely essential. If it is, and this really is a terribly important moment in your career, as important as it is in mine to be in America—even if only to *drop* the play—then *forgive* me for even writing this letter. It will only cause you anguish and it is not meant for this—the letter. I am writing it only because I am not at all certain that the picture has been presented to you clearly, that you even know how much it

[44] Libby's manager.

means to me that you be there, which of course is quite beside the point if your Spanish visit has become more than a useful and pleasant project and is now essential and even *if* essential is it essential that you be there right *now* and for the major part of your visit without Bubble? I am writing in the dark of course and now I wish that we had kept in closer touch with each other. I did not gather from Bud Williams (whom I love) that you had any other project except to travel through Spain with Paul and listen to music? Naturally if he *can* get a later boat which will nonetheless bring him back on time to do the music I would wire him if the whole thing blew up and thus save him his fare (he can't get over for under $500). There is an advantage in this but Oliver does not seem to think it is going to blow up at all. The difficult question is this: if I am there and you and Paul are here (in Spain) and I am 90 percent sure that the Westport production *musn't* go on (I don't *think* that they will do it there unless I consent to let it go on in New York too), then won't I be in a frenzy without Paul there to back me up in my decision to either let it go on or stop it (there will be naturally one thousand other decisions to make but this will be the big one)? Ollie and I must necessarily be on opposite ends in this thing, not always, but it *will* happen. In fact it has already about something and Paul agrees with me. I don't of course know whether or not his arrival around the 15th (if he does sail the 8th) will save *much*. I can be certain however that if he arrives just in time to do the music all will be set. If he comes over sooner as planned he might be a great help, but then he might miss you and also the opportunity of canceling his passage if it does fizzle out within a week or ten days of my arrival in Connecticut.

This whole problem is driving me quite mad, and the fact that Paul won't be living at Treetops and working with you and with me has changed everything. I am sure he can stay with the Kanins or Wilson once the rehearsals start in August but will he like that? I *know* he's okay with you, but if he's nervous and unhappy he's going to drive me crazy and it would be better not to have him there at all, but he wouldn't think of letting anyone else do the score and I am deeply happy about that of course. I know that you probably don't *want* to be around because you don't like the set-up, but why leave me then to face it all alone? No one we like will do the damn thing anyway.

Please reconsider your decision about Spain. I know you'll be fair and if it means a great deal more to you than I can imagine, *wire me at once* that you're coming. I shall have to tend to changing

Paul's passage from here. I am about one hour and a half out of Paris and shall not move from this Inn until I hear from you, except to go to Paris for the day, but I will even try to delay that so that if your wire says that he should try and change his passage I can attend to it in person rather than on this telephone which has to be *cranked* on with a handle. Don't let me get on that now for another ten pages. The operator is usually in a different town having a glass of wine.

I hope to God you will put off the Spanish extravaganza for just a while longer. You *have* before this for lesser reasons (*hélas*). If you do, do you think I ought to try and get Paul a sailing a week or ten days later than his present one? In any case that would give him the extra margin he might need if the show blew up. I will be able to tell so much more about it when I get there (ossir). I suggest this because I feel that you perhaps have some grapevine on it and might not think that the project is nearly as certain as Oliver makes it out. In that case you could advise us quite *apart* from your own plans. You could then wait in Connecticut for that extra week or ten days and if in the interim the whole thing *was* called off you could join him in Spain. If not you would stay in Connecticut and go to Spain later? I could run the same risk that way, of having to sign everything without his presence, or call it off, etc., but if you think that would be the wisest I'll take the chance. Oliver sounds very certain of everything but now he is in Rome, I am here, and Paul is in Tangier if he hasn't fled to the desert by now.

I wish to hell all this had come up while Paul was in Paris. I begged him *daily* to cable you and I'm rather furious that I have to cope with telegrams now and the horror of letters such as these. I really feel terribly discouraged and sad about it. I wouldn't write you this if I didn't feel you could get as much out of being with Paul at Treetops as you could being (with whom?) in Spain. It would naturally make a tremendous difference to me and I have felt foolishly certain and calm about his return because it didn't even occur to me that you would consider Spain if he could not be with you there for any serious length of time. When I received his wire yesterday I was terribly shocked—horrified really. Now I am wondering what it is all about. I feel somehow that something is being kept from me. By Oliver? By Paul? By Bud? By you? What is it? Will you wire me at once here at the Inn? The address is: L'Étape, Pacy-sur-Eure, France. You should say whether or not your Spanish trip still stands and whether I should try therefore to change Paul's passage for a later boat — which may easily be impossible (it would have to be within a week or so of your arrival anyway, if not less).

If not — if you do see your way to staying there without feeling that you have given up a main chance — then please wire me whether or not you think he should even so try to get a slightly later passage which would give you the opportunity of meeting him in Spain a *little* later should it all blow up. I am going under the assumption that you *may* know more about the plans for Westport than I do. Knowing me *too* you may feel sure that I myself will stop them from doing it, and that it would be far better for me to decide this by myself and save Paul $500 and his trip through Spain with you rather than to get him over there. The responsibility of course is enormous and I don't really *expect* you to advise me, unless you want to. I mean, you needn't decide anything except about what concerns you directly, which is utterly impossible since you are in love with me.

Please, please wire me immediately for God's sake. I am wiring Africa that I'm waiting here for your answer before seeing the travel man. The boats will be wildly difficult as you know. If he leaves on the 8th he should be back the 15th or 16th.

I could say much more but I think thus far my letter has been a fair one and not like a beggar's letter or even wily. I am in a wonderful garden so don't feel sorry for me.

Much love, as ever

J.

P.S. Please advise me what to bring Claudia and Johnny, and is Willie-May there and Scotty. I won't get anything for the boys. Isn't this hell?

The Westport date is August 28th by the way, so you see that there is very little time. Naturally I would be more than delighted if they could put it off. You might have spies who could telephone Jack Wilson and sniff what's going on.

161

53

Jane Bowles to Libby Holman
L'Étape, Pacy-sur-Eure, France
[June 26, 1950]

Dearest Libby,

I am surprised and worried that you have not answered my wires—either one of them. I am of course worried about this mess from every point of view. I hope my wire, the last one, did not confuse you: it was meant to help your plans. Ever since I received a letter from Paul with yours enclosed about your Spanish plans and Oliver's statement concerning Paul and the music being sent from Spain, my feelings have become much more definite. I couldn't believe that you would come all the way over here to see Paul only for a week or so unless you had other plans for Spain, but now that I know it is still the *same* plan I really think you'd be a fool to come now. I wouldn't dare to influence you if I did not sincerely believe that the Lorca opera would benefit more by Paul's return, where he would be near a piano, than by a flash meeting in Spain. Also though you have bookings in the fall and winter, I'm certain that there must be some space between these, and considering that Paris is only four hours from Madrid, a meeting later could surely be arranged. I keep thinking of Ira Bellin's flower shop in Tangier. The flowers came three times a week from Holland by plane, all dead. Does this prove my point? In any case distances are short here and I feel that Paul can come back more easily, *probably* after the Westport opening (if there is one) when things will be all set. Naturally he can't write the music in Spain when he hasn't even spoken to the director yet. I am *appalled* at Oliver's muddled thinking and I am really furious that he gave neither of us an inkling of what he'd said to you. Because of this when I meet him in Paris on the 29th I shall *assure* him that unless I am guaranteed that Paul's music will be used in Westport with the minimum number of pieces required I shall refuse to allow the show to go on. I shall insist on this in writing the very day of my arrival there so that there will be no misunderstandings. I was referring to this in my wire to you so that in case you have been thinking all along that there would be some hitch in the music arrangement which would leave you and Paul free to spend a month or more in Spain you would not any longer count on it. I would not blame you in the least for suspecting this hitch knowing the theater as you do, etc. However, I have a chance of avoiding it because I think they are too far in to want to get out entirely just because of the extra money involved in using music and I will refuse to sign anything before Paul is signed up. Paul is coming over for nothing except his passage *one way*. If it doesn't go on even in Westport I believe he's out both passages though I could not swear to this. Oliver was probably *sure* that he wouldn't come on such bad terms, not until New York. (But I don't think the play should be shown without music anywhere.) Probably Oliver by the time we discussed all this in Paris had either forgotten his remarks to you or was too frightened to mention them. I kept saying, "How can Libby send such a *definite* wire to Paul when she knows he's returning, or *might* be?" and Oliver simply said he didn't know—that he had told you Paul might be coming over.

It gives a smack on the head with a rolling pin when he comes back from Rome. I am really angry with you and I have taken the brunt, I with these agonizing letters and wires. It has been a real headache and has ruined these last weeks entirely. As for your plans, what a mess, and so easily avoidable. You should always keep in touch with me because I am the only one besides yourself who has a sense of responsibilty. I can see nothing ahead that will change my plans or Paul's unless he didn't *do* the music. I mean whether he takes the next boat or not I think you'd both gain more by meeting there. Without you he's less likely to work—I suppose. Anyway you have things to discuss but that is all up to you. I can only state the plans *clearly*. Oy! I don't know how possible the next boat is. The travel agent told me to wire Paul to try to change his tickets in Tangier. The next boat I could see leaving from Gib was as expensive as the one he's on and utterly unknown. Also I think it would be too late. It would give you eight days together, two of which would be spent on traveling (travel in Spain is slow and he must get up and down to Gib). I don't expect him to be busy on my show the *whole* time he's in America— naturally—and it will be over the end of August. After that you could work together if not in Spain somewhere near—Cuba? Anyway, you figure it out. My last letter must have sounded like a loony's letter, but knowing you I was much more careful, at least I thought I was. I didn't want you to sacrifice yourself if you had some concrete Spanish plan other than to meet Paul and that letter was about seeing him or not for a week. Now however it seems crazy if you wanted to go to Spain only to be with him, as I knew you did originally. I shall leave Paris July 7th and sail that day on the Queen Mary. Please don't meet my boat, I loathe it, but you might wire me to tell me what's up. I can't understand why you haven't so far. I know you think it is best to speak to Paul or Oliver. Someday you'll learn that it ain't. I begged Paul daily to answer your wire in Paris but he was waiting for the letter. It would have saved all this three-way tsouris.

Love as ever,

J.

P.S.   I hope my letters haven't sounded awful. Naturally I *want* you there, but even without that I now feel *honestly*, and I am honest even when greedy, that you must remain.

My address through Saturday the 30th of June will be Hotel de L'Université.

54

Jane Bowles to Mike Kahn
[New York City]
[January, 1951]

Dear Mikey,

Oliver wants my agent to send you a regular contract giving you permission to use the play in repertory for two years etc. She is in Chicago but you will get it by next week. Anyway he says it's O.K. The contract will state as well that the Chekov theatre (I mean Hedgerow) has no rights on the play if it should be given anywhere else. I don't think Oliver believes for a minute that Jasper Deeter would claim rights but I guess he's used to doing everything in a formal businesslike way.[45] This will give you the legal right to use

---

[45] Jasper Deeter was director at the Hedgerow Theater, where *In the Summer House* was produced in 1951. Mike Kahn, Libby Holman's nephew, was then working at the Hedgerow Theater.

*"Aunt" Jen Green, a friend of the Bowles family;
Paul Bowles' mother, Marion Chase; Paul and
Jane Bowles, 1938.*

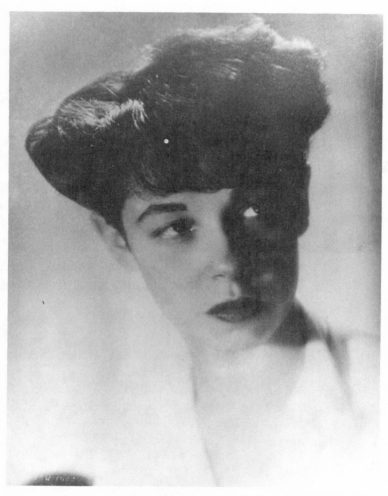

Jane Bowles, 1940s. (Courtesy Marcus Bleckman and Hedgerow Theatre Collection)

Jane Bowles, Mexico, early 1940s.

Jane Bowles, Fortin, Mexico, 1941. (Courtesy Paul Bowles)

Jane and Paul Bowles, New York City, 1944.

P.S. forgot to write you that Paul is all for my allowing Audrey Wood to represent me on "Summer House" — he thinking it will help both me & Olive — and that I'd be a fool not to. Olive twice said me that she thought the new 2nd act wonderful and that he had [but then thinks] JB he is now very happy with keeping up my morale. audrey wood (wrote me said when — probably prompted by Paul —)

Dearest Libby — love to Loutie —).

I was horrified to read in your letter to Paul that you had not heard from me — I've written twice now with old answers from you — & have been waiting & waiting on a reply. My last letter gave you an address for Paris & London — tho I was not sure you would reach me in Tangier. I shall repeat that I am spending the winter in Paris — which is now arranged with Jody — who has probably called you up about my coat — by now. Paul — (I wrote you this too) is well better on going to Ceylon — I think it would be fatal if he hung around until February — for Spain — It is the wrong time — and he doesn't have any place he wants to be — in winter — except the Sahara where there really is no piano — he can surely find me in Ceylon — He wants to meet you in spring — Either in the U.S. if you can't leave there or Spain & Tangier — Surely unless you have a tour you can forfeit the tour. Spring — just once — I am speaking entirely against myself. Actually I shall probably return for the early spring (late as March) — & then come back to the old world just as fast in I can get out of the new one — late spring — It would be ideal of course — May & June — in Spain — for you & Paul — & we could come back together, but wouldn't that be too late for you? I mean wouldn't April suit you — it better though it wouldn't me. or course I don't know what mid-april plans you have in the new world — but if its the tulips or Easter I shall be curious. If you so come over — early spring — I am terribly confused I shall then probably wait for you — I dear, let me know you as to where I live — Libby — it scares me just as little to think of it — so I don't think of it. If you would only move the entire she Bang to Tangier I'd be happy Paris was beautiful and depressing — and despite a really wonderful reception in England — & her in north Wales — I am eager to get back to the "soupe hotel" in Paris. I stayed there

Jane Bowles and Cecil Beaton, Tangier, 1949.

Jane Bowles, Tangier, ca. 1951.

Cherifa, early 1950s.

Jane Bowles, 1956.

Dearest Paul,

    I have been trying to write you for days but unsuccessfully. The fact is that I have been having the same trouble with my work that I had in Ceylon and before I left for Ceylon. I don't know whether to keep writing through the block or to get out of here now or in a month or two before I come to the end of my money. I know I can get passage back from somebody but there is always the question of leaving a little behind for Cherifa. I hope that I will come out of this alright. The fight against depression again is serious since failure follows me into my dreams, and I have been awake for many nights, as I was in Ceylon. But there is no heat thank God . If I left I would borrow from Libby and pay her back out my months checks there. I would give the money to Cherifa that I would be saving by living at Libby's. I don't really want to do this though it might be the nicest thing I can do. C. doesn't want me too either and she is very happy to have the house and says that I must not worry . She even said that with the rent she gets for the house she can live with her family and contribute her bag of flour a month and so you have done that much for my peace of mind, at least. Naturally she has gotten used to more than a bag of flour a month and I wonder if I shouldn't whip myself out of here no matter how much I dread doing it. The longer I wait the less I will have to give her unless I asked Libby for an outright gift of couple of hundred dollars. Actually before I left Libby said to me, that I shouldn't worry about money and that if I needed any to let her know. Then there are the little cats whom I adore, And C. herself whom I can't bear to leave, and you too who will be returning and I would not like to miss you though I am sure that you would probably not want to see me if I don't have a play done, and it would be a sad encounter to the say the least. Actually I cannot picture any of this happening. I cannot picture leaving, or nor can I picture your return and my having nothing to show for it. you after all this time . I hate to think of it and I get into a kind of terrible panic when I do. Still, if for some reason I did have to leave I would naturally pay the rent here untill June or whenever the contract is up and lock the door. But I would not leave the cats, naturally. They would have to come along. Ira read my fortune and said that someones death was going to oblige me to travel across water, and that as a result of this death I would inherit a little money. I don't believe of course but it did occur to me that I should tell you that in case of any emergency or even if I suddenly became a lunatic and felt a compulsion to go just because I didn't want to, that I would put all of the things into the apartment here and lock the door, leaving the key with Christopher or Ira. The person who was going to die was a woman but I can't of anyone but my mother who might leave me a few hundred dollars, but I do not really believe in cards.

    I filled a notebook with my plans and suggestions for my play and even started writing the dialogue. But now today for the first time in a week, I had a flash of an idea and so I will see if does not help. It is impossible to write a play in the dark without having some idea of where one is going. . I did get an idea but it was so definite that I couldn't go against it either. For nearly a week I have had dreams of not being able to go on with it and then my head got into such a bad knot that I took a lot of equanil and knocked off work. Today my head feels better..less knotted. I wrote you a long beginning of a letter but it was so confusing I thought I would tear it up, and I did tear it up, but at least I have been writing something. And then after I had written you the first really sad page of the letter I tore up, I made some lentils and I got and idea about cutting out one of the characters in my play. In fact two of them. One was a girl and the other a dead man. Like Gertrudes father in summer house who became such a bore to all of this. I think the girl was cut out because of a dream I had, her and her girl friend. I dreamed they hated me and that they could never be in the play. I must write it. But am I being am I fooling myself by insisting that I will . And by myself robbing C. of the last money that I can call my own.? I am

Feeling

P.S Please write . often - I love to hear about Ceylon.

Jane Bowles Letter, #61.

Cherifa, Jane Bowles, Paul Bowles, unidentified, ca. 1956.

Jane Bowles, Tangier, early 1960s.

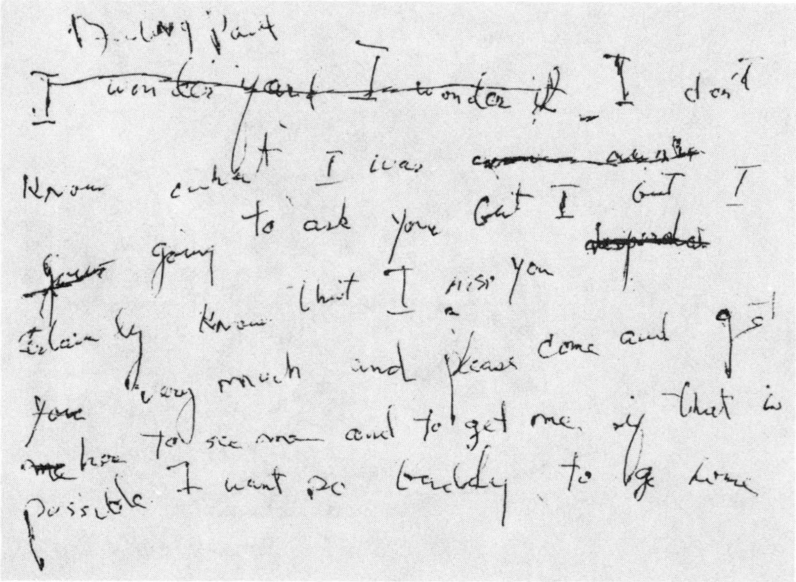

Jane Bowles, Letter #132.

the play in case I go to a lunatic asylum in which case a letter from me might have been invalid.

Please give my best love to Shirley and for yourself keep a great deal.

Your friend out of another century

Jane Bowles

55

Jane Bowles to Carl Van Vechten
[Postcard]
[New York City]
[February 8, 1951]

Dear Carlo —

How about Wednesday night after the ballet at Oliver's? He's going to the ballet too, the 14th. Let us KNOW.

Love —

Jane —

P.S.   You could bring whoever you're with.

Jane Bowles to Carl Van Vechten
[Postcard]
[New York City]
[February 12, 1951]

Dear Carlo —

Certainly bring Fania Marinoff and Saul Mauriber. I hope you have not understood that it is a party however — I wish it was! I like them. Maybe two or three other friends will come too but it won't be a real and big party. Unless you happen to run into Oliver at the ballet why don't you just come on down? 28 west 10th St. Ring the bell.

56

Jane Bowles to Libby Holman
[New York City]
[February 12, 1951]

Dearest Libby,

I was appalled to receive this letter from my mother today and I have a terrible cold too. I guess it is best to send it on to you. I do not mean to make you feel sad, but it does explain the business situation rather concisely and it's easier for me to send the letter than it is for me to explain the whole thing.[46]

I feel that in any case you will either lend me the money if you have it and you won't if you don't. I did not think from Mother's last letter that it would all happen so quickly but I guess the letter of warning was just sent to prepare me for this letter which she knew she was going to send for a few days. It's all just too awful, for her I mean, and naturally a hideous worry for me. I won't really start worrying however until I hear that you are broke, or at least incapable of laying your hands on any money right now.

I have been otherwise happy and peaceful this week. Marty[47] is wonderful. It all works out she will be a resident—next year in Switzerland—near enough to Paris for weekends. But it is a dead secret so tear this letter up. I hope you write soon.

All love as ever,

J.

---

[46] Jane's mother and stepfather owned a jewelry store in Dayton, Ohio, and apparently they were having financial difficulties.

[47] A new lover.

57

Jane Bowles to Libby Holman
[New York City]
[February 18, 1951]

Dearest Libby,

Marty has given me a little Hermes Rocket typewriter for my birthday and I am very happy about it. She is wonderful to me and I think really loves me devotedly. I know it. It is extraordinary that I should have found at last someone so sweet and trusting and gay and brave and beautiful. She has moments of being extraordinarily beautiful. Particularly in black evening dresses cut low and with long sleeves. She looks not only beautiful but distinguished and as if she could not even possibly have ever met me. Her friend Priscilla is so much more brilliant than I am and she is better looking too and quite rich so I just cannot understand my good fortune. As I have told you there is a great amount of pain in this situation, mostly because of Paul, but it is not insoluble and something will work out eventually. I have been having mild flu which makes me hang around the house, but I do that anyway. I suppose I'll only get out of my room to go to Fire Island or Africa or Europe. I heard from Heber who is making slip covers and curtains for Ollie that you were going to sing in Italy in the spring, though I wish you were working on *Yerma* with Paul. I am glad that you are getting out of that house at least. I don't have a good feeling about it. Also I have been worrying about sending you the end of mother's letter and exposing you to this Valentine remark of hers. Though I really love her it is the kind of thing that makes me shudder and it is like that more or less in all of her letters, but I had not intended to expose you to it. I meant to tear it off and then hurriedly mailed it all at the last minute. I have been worrying about it ever since naturally, though I am not thank God upset about the money thing, as far as you and I are concerned. If you have written that you can't send any I shall try to think up something. If you can suggest anything, write, but I don't see how you could really. I shall try to get to work tomorrow, Monday, before the whole thing crashes on my head. The director of *Come Back Little Sheba* wants to do my play I think but I will know more about it in two weeks. He is coming down to confer with me because he wants certain changes made in the script. I am afraid

these changes are big ones and that perhaps he just doesn't understand the play at all. He seemed puzzled by the Spanish servants
for instance, at least so he said at lunch. I am hoping that actually
he has forgotten the play and only pretended to have reread it
because he was supposed to have done so before this luncheon
arranged by Audrey Wood. I don't see how he would have had time
to reread it when he has been working so hard on Tennessee's *Rose
Tattoo*, which is a huge success. Most of the people I speak to seem
to be against his directing my play and I am once again in a most
monstrous quandary. Probably no one is right for it, except, as
Priscilla says, Charlie Chaplin. Anyway I hope the play is coming
along down at Hedgerow. I have not heard lately from Mikey and
wonder what is going on. Touche has gone down to see his mother
in Virginia. Actually I think he is spending twenty minutes with
his mother and going on to someone else's "room" also down in
Virginia. He telephones in to Alice [Astor] Bouverie and she gives
me the news. His last remark was that he did not intend to come
back ever. I don't know whether or not his flight is a sincere effort
to get down to work and stop drinking or a rendezvous with a friend
of his who goes to college in the South. He has been drinking like
a tank lately, emptying bottle after bottle all through the night.
You've seen him do it; I think that his situation with Alice has
been a strain. I think she would like to marry him and he is
probably tempted though ashamed because of her wealth and
position. Also there is his other love life who would be crushed
by the marriage, so Touche thinks. None of this really exists to
me but I repeat it to you because you are interested in Touche.
I like Alice more and more though she is tedious beyond belief.
It is just so very hard to listen to her. She talks and talks and one
is conscious only of the strain. Margaret McKean is in and out of
town all of the time and has finally understood I think that I don't
want to see her. Aside from being totally uninterested in her
romantically I can't bear her wit or the delivery of it. I find her
presence really intolerable. There is no doubt that her wit is keener
than anyone's in New York but it is frightening more than it is
amusing because it seems to operate only as a kind of smokescreen
for an endless plot which she herself ignores. She called me up
today and whispered to me that she was telephoning from the
Algonquin as if she was revealing the formula for the hydrogen
bomb. The poor woman is just hunted and haunted all of the time.
She is of course drinking like a fish, gallons of cider in public and
alone in the bathroom, gin out of her purse, I'm convinced.

Naturally she is disturbing because of her disembodied talent. Maureen Stapleton was overwhelmed by her. Do you think there is something wrong with me that I am able to turn so on someone I once liked as much as I did Margaret? In those days of course she was selfish as hell and a fat tyrant but now she is just humble and could be slavish if she had the energy or sobriety to run errands and she is fatter than ever. The terrible thing is that while all along I thought she liked my feeling for *her* but never *me*, I now feel that perhaps I was wrong because she seems dead set on me, though she behaves in a most distinguished manner and never makes me feel either guilty or uncomfortable. I think maybe she just likes my looks. Small and dark. Peter [Lindamood] gave a party last night and Ollie and I just sat here without being able to get up enough energy to cross the street. We kept calling Peter up and asking for his guest list. Ollie got sore because Peter had used some of *his* guest list, Ollie claimed, and he scolded him over the telephone. Ollie never drags himself out of the apartment either and the whole thing I suppose is terribly unhealthy. We reinfect each other with our colds and I am in a bathrobe for life. Somewhere deep inside my heart is a tiny picture of Tangier in color. I miss it desperately and it will be for a while at least impossible to really live there. If Marty gets away next year because of her work she will be centered in Switzerland, which will be near enough to Italy and France but not terribly near Africa. However I shall certainly get down there to spend some time with Paul. I look forward to a day when Marty would have some part time work which would allow her to spend half her time in Morocco. I think this work she may do in Europe (the only hope I have of ever living with her) is very likely to be only for part of the year. I hope so. It is silly of course to plan anything. Some days I am in misery because I seem to feel two equally strong destinies and one of them is to be with Paul. I miss him of course terribly. My life would have been simpler if I had never returned here but having known Marty I will not die still searching and feeling cheated. I don't know what I write you about, but you asked me to write, so I do—when it is not too impossible.

Much love always,

J.

169

In the Summer House *was performed in Ann Arbor, Michigan, in May 1953. It opened on Broadway in December and closed the following February. Soon after, Jane returned to Tangier, accompainied by Katharine Hamill and Natasha von Hoershelman. The three of them toured Morocco and then Katharine and Natasha returned to the U.S.*

From *Out in the World*
(Andrew's story)

. . . the heavy wave of peace and exaltation . . . Andrew felt resulted not from the stuff of the tale he was hearing but from the increasing certainty that he was hearing secrets. Everything Tommy told him he saw immersed in the magical light that enchants certain secrets, secrets unannounced as such . . .

As he listened to the dreary account he felt increasingly exultant. His own silence always so oppressive that it burned his throat like sand now seemed to evade him; freer now than himself it seemed to mix with the dark evening . . . This silence of his which until then had been a manifestation of misery became a reflection of his own intuition and of his own purity so that what had always been an ugly cage was transformed at that moment into a wonderful church.

58

**Jane Bowles to Natasha von Hoershelman
  and Katharine Hamill**
[Tangier, Morocco]
[June, 1954]

Darling Natasha and Katharine,

I never stop thinking about you but too much happened. Please forgive me if this is not an amusing letter. I tried last night to write you in detail but I had filled two pages just with Ellie[48] and some clothes that the ladies and babies were wearing down in M'sallah, the day you left. I think I had better simply write you a gross factual résumé of what has happened. Then if I have any sense I shall keep notes. Because what is happening is interesting and funny in itself. I am a fool to have lost two whole months of it. I have no memory—only a subconscious memory which I am afraid translates everything into something else, and so I shall have to take notes. I have a very pretty leather book for that purpose.

The day you left I was terribly terribly sad. I still miss you—in the sense that I keep thinking through it all that you should be here and how sorry I am that you left before I could truly take you into some of the life that I love. I turned sour on Ellie about half way up the pier. I could still see the boat. I worried about having exposed Katharine to all those tedious stories—touching in a way but tedious. Ice cream, herring, and the Chico Tax scandal with the brother. Of course it could only happen here on a trip for *Fortune.* I went down that long street, way down in, and landed in a room filled with eighteen women and a dozen or two little babies wearing knitted capes and hoods. One lady had on a peach satin evening dress and over it the jacket of a man's business suit. (A Spanish business suit.) I had been searching for Cherifa, and having been to about three houses all belonging to her family, I finally landed there. I thought I was in a bordello. The room was very plush, filled with hideous blue and white chenille cushions made in Manchester, England. Cherifa wore a pale blue sateen skirt down to the ground and a grayish Spanish sweater, a kind of school sweater but not sporty. She seemed to be constantly flirting with a woman in a pale blue kaftan (our hostess), and finally she sat next to her and encircled her waist. C. looked like a child. The woman weighed about 160 pounds and was loaded with rouge and eye makeup. Now I know her. An alcoholic named Fat Zohra, and one of two wives. She is married to a kind of criminal who I believe knifed his own brother over a card game and spent five years in jail. The other wife lives in a different house and does all the child bearing. Fat Zohra is barren. There was one pale-looking girl (very light green), who I thought was surely the richest and the most distinguished of the lot. She wore a wonderful embroidered kaftan, a rich spinach green with a leaf design. Her face was rather sour: thin compressed lips and a long mean-looking nose. I was sad while

[48] Pseudonym.

171

they played drums and did their lewd belly dances because I thought: My God if you had only stayed a day longer. But of course if you had, perhaps they wouldn't have asked you in (Cherifa I mean); they are so leery of strangers. In any case at the end of the afternoon (and part of my sadness was an aching jealousy of the woman in the blue kaftan), Cherifa took me to the doorway and into the blue courtyard where two boring pigeons were squatting, and asked me whether or not I was going to live in my house. The drums were still beating and I had sticky cakes in my hand—those I couldn't eat. (I stuffed down as many as I could. I loathe them.) But I was really too jealous and also sad because you had left to get down very many. I said I would of course but not before I found a maid. She told me to wait and a minute later came out with the distinguished pale green one. "Here's your maid," she said. "A very poor girl."

Anyway, a month and a half later she became my maid. I call her Sour Pickle, and she has stolen roughly about one thousand four hundred pesetas from me. I told C. about it who advised me not to keep any money in the house. She is a wonderful maid, an excellent cook, and sleeps with me here. I will go on about this later but I cannot remotely begin to get everything into this letter. You will want to know what happened about Paul, Ellie, Xauen.

Paul went to Xauen for one night, having sworn that he would not spend more than one or two nights at the Massilia. He came back disgusted with Xauen and then started a hopeless series of plans—plans for three of us in one house, and, as I wrote Lyn, I even planned to live in the bottom half of a policeman's house in Tangier Balia (the place with the corrugated tin roofs) while Paul and Ahmed lived in the little house in the Casbah. I felt Cherifa was a hopeless proposition, and had no particular desire to be in my house unless there was some hope of luring her into it. (Maid or no maid.) In the hotel I did try to work a little. But it is always impossible the first month and the wind and the rain continued. The rooms were very damp and cold and one could scarcely sit down in them. I became very attached to the French family who ran the hotel. We stayed on and on in an unsettled way. In the beginning Ellie would come by every day with her loud insensitive battering on the door, and her poor breezy efficient manner and I would try desperately not to smack her. I felt I could not simply drop her and so would make some half-hearted date with her always before lunch so that we could go to Georgette's. Ellie filled me with such a feeling of revulsion that I almost fell in love with Georgette.

172

I never allowed Ellie within a foot of my bed from the moment you stepped on the boat. I have never in my life had such an experience. Nor will I quite understand what possessed me. Some devil but not my usual one. Someone else's devil. In any case she started taking trips. The first time she came back, when I heard the rapping, I said, "Who?" and she said, "The family!" That was it. From then on I could barely stand to be in the same room with her and I hated myself for it. All this revulsion and violence was on a far greater scale than the incident deserved but it must have touched something inside me—something in my childhood. I have never been quite such a horror. Some of it showed outwardly but thank God only a bit of what I was really feeling. She always asked after you. Every time I saw her, "Any letter today?" Also madly irritating for some reason. Finally she got the message and in any case she was away so much that I managed to sneak up here into the Casbah—and I don't believe she knows where I live, though surely she could find out. I hope by now that she is off on a new adventure. Sonie (a pal who takes in the cash at a whorehouse behind the Socco Chico), sees her occasionally and reported that she had left Chico Tax and was driving her own car.

Paul had typhoid in the hotel and that was a frightening mess for two weeks. We were both about to move into our houses. He had found one on a street called Sidi Bouknadel (overlooking the sea) and I was coming here. Then he had typhoid, and then Tennessee came for two whole weeks. I moved in here while Paul was still in the hotel. For a while Ahmed and I were living together while Paul lingered on at the hotel in a weakish state. He is all right now. Ahmed stayed here during the whole month of Ramadan (the month when they eat at night) and I was with him during the last two weeks. Not very interesting except that every night I woke up choking with charcoal smoke, and then he would insist that I eat with him. Liver or steak or whatever the hell it was. At first I minded terribly. Then I began to expect it, and one night he didn't buy really enough for the two of us, and I was grieved. Meanwhile in the daytime I was in the hotel preparing special food for Paul, to bring his appetite back. There were always four or five of us cooking at once in the long narrow hotel kitchen, the only room that looked out on the sea. Meeting Tennessee for dinner and Frankie (they were at the Rembrandt) was complicated too. Synchronizing took up most of the time. We were all in different places.

I have kept out of the David life very successfully except on occasion. I could not possibly manage from here nor do I want to very much though I love him and would hate never to see him. I couldn't go it. The ex-Marchioness of Bath is here for the moment (married her lover, Mister Fielding, a charming man). I went to a dinner party for her in slacks — a thing that I did not do on purpose. They gave a party on the beach which I wiggled out of but Tuesday I must go to a big ball. However if one only turns up once every two weeks or so it's nice. Or occasionally one goes out twice in a row. They are all constantly at it. David suggested a pool of money so that I might have a telephone. Only Jaime seemed to understand that I didn't want one. The Fieldings are enchanting people and are off to write about pirates in the old days. They have some kind of little car they are going to live in. They will be gone six or eight months. By then Enid Bagnold should be back. Her play was the end or wasn't it? Please write me what you think, now that some time has passed. I scarcely ever go to the Parade. Too depressing. Then came the ghastly Indo-China Oppenheimer period which dovetailed with Tennessee's last days here and also a pitch black boy called George Broadfield who called himself "The New American Negro," and attached himself to me and Paul. I liked him but almost went mad because he was determined to stay in Tangier, and thought nothing of talking for seven or eight hours in a row. I told him he should go and live where there were other artists because there were so few of them here. (He himself is a young writer, or is going to be??) He said that Paul and I were enough for him and I was horrified. It was all my fault. The night I got *Vogue* in the mail, which quoted the remark you might have since seen about writing for one's five hundred goony friends etc., I went out and got drunk. I was terribly upset about it. Though I knew what I had meant I had certainly not made the remark expecting it to be quoted or I would have elaborated. I hate being interviewed and something wrong always does pop out, everytime. I meant "intellectual" which Walter Kerr in the Trib seems to have understood, but at the time I was worried about my friends — the real supporters of the play and the contributors to whatever chance it had financial and otherwise. Anyway I was sick at my stomach. I did go to the Parade and did get very drunk. This pitch black boy seemed charming so I latched on to him as one does occasionally. He was a kind of God-sent antidote to the quotation which I was ashamed of. Paul tried to console me saying that nobody much read *Vogue* and that it would be forgotten. Of course later Walter Kerr devoted a column to it in New York and it appeared in Paris as well where there is no other paper for Americans, so if anyone

174

missed it in New York they have seen it in Paris or Rome. I now think of it as a kind of joke. Every letter I receive has the article (Kerr's article) enclosed, with its title "Writing Plays for Goons." They come in from all over Europe and the United States. I keep teasing Paul about the scarcely read copy of Vogue lying on the floor of the beauty parlor. So much for that. But I did inherit George Broadfield for a while and because it was my doing had to see him constantly for a week. I was a wreck—nervously, because he talked so much. Then he shifted on to Paul, finally ran out of money and moved on to Casablanca.

One day before Ramadan and before Paul had paratyphoid, I went to the market and sat in a gloom about Indo-China and the Moroccan situation and every other thing in the world that was a situation outside my own. Soon I cheered up a little. I was in the part where Tetum sits in among the coal and the mules and the chickens. Two little boy musicians came by. I gave them some money and Tetum ordered songs. Soon we had a big crowd around us, one of those Marrakech circles. Everybody stopped working (working?) and we had one half hour of music, myself and everybody else, in that part of the market (you know). And people gathered from round about. Just like Tiflis. Tetum was in good spirits. She told me that Cherifa had a girl friend who was fat and white. I recognized Fat Zohra, though I shall never know whether I put the fat white picture in her mind or not. I might have said "Is she fat and white?" I don't know. Then she asked me if I wouldn't drive her out to Sidi Menari, one of the sacred groves around here where Sidi Menari (a saint) is buried. They like to visit as many saints as possible, of course, because it gives them extra gold stars for heaven. I thought: "Natasha and Katharine will be angry. They told me to stick to Cherifa but then, they didn't know about fat Zohra." After saying this in my head I felt free to offer Tetum a trip to the grove without making you angry.

Of course it turned out that she wanted to take not only one, but two neighbors and their children. We were to leave at eight thirty A.M., she insisted. The next day when I got to Tetum's house on the Marshan with Temsamany (nearly an hour late) Tetum came to the door in a grey bathrobe. I was very surprised. Underneath she was dressed in a long Zigdoun and under that she wore other things. I can't describe a Zigdoun but it is quite enough to wear without adding on a bathrobe. But when they wear our night clothes they wear them over or under their own (which are simply the underpeelings or first three layers of their day clothes.

Like in Tiflis). She yanked me into her house, tickled my palm, shouted to her neighbor (asleep on the other side of a thin curtain) and in general pranced about the room. She dressed me up in a hideous half-Arab, half-Spanish cotton dress which came to my ankles and had no shape at all. Just a little round neck. She belted it and said "Now go back to the hotel and show your husband how pretty you look." I said I would some other day, and what about our trip to the saint's tomb. She said yes, yes, but she had to go and fetch the other two women who both lived in a different part of the town. I said would they be ready, and she said something like: "Bacai shouay." Which means just nothing. Finally I arranged to come back for her at three. Rather infuriated because I had gotten Temsamany up at the crack. But I was not surprised, nor was he. Tetum took me to her gate. "If you are not here at three," she said in sudden anger, "I shall walk to the grove myself on my own legs." (Five hours, roughly.) We went back at three and the laundry bags were ready, and the children, and Tetum.

"We are going to two saints," Tetum said. "First Sidi Menari and then we'll stop at the other saint's on the way back. He's buried on the edge of town and we've got to take the children to him and cut their throats because they have whooping cough." She poked one of the laundry bundles, who showed me a knife. I was getting rather nervous because Paul of course was expecting us back roughly around seven, and I know how long those things can take. We drove along the awful road (the one that frightened you) toward the grove, only we went on and on, much further out, and the road began to bother me a little after a while. You would have hated it. The knife of course served for the symbolic cutting of the children's throat, though at first I had thought they were going to draw some blood, if not a great deal. I didn't think they were actually going to kill the children or I wouldn't have taken them on the ride.

We reached the sacred grove which is not far from the lighthouse one can see coming into the harbor. Unfortunately they have built some ugly restaurants around and about the lighthouse, and not far from the sacred grove so that sedans are now constantly passing on the highway. The grove itself is very beautiful, and if one goes far enough inside it, far away from the road, one does not see the cars passing. We didn't penetrate very far into the grove because being a Christian (Oy!) I can't sit within the vicinity of the saint's tomb. Temsamany spread the tarpaulin on the ground and the endless tea equipment they had brought with them, and they were off to the saint's leaving Temsamany and myself behind. He said: "I shall make a fire, and then when they come back the water will be boiling." They came back. God knows when. The water was boiling. We had used up a lot of dead olive branches. They sat down and lowered their veils so that they hung under their chins like ugly bibs. They had bought an excellent sponge cake. As usual something sweet. I thought: "Romance here is impossible." Tetum's neighbors were ugly. One in particular. "Like a turtle," Temsamany said. She kept looking down into her lap. Tetum, the captain of the group, said to the turtle: "Look at the world, look at the world." "I am looking at the world," the other woman said, but she kept looking down into her lap. They cut up all the sponge cake. I said: "Stop! Leave it. We'll never eat it all." Temsamany said: "I'm going to roller skate." He went off and we could see him through the trees. After a while the conversation stopped. Even Tetum was at a loss. There was a little excitement when they spotted the woman who runs the toilets under the grain market, seated not far off with a group, somewhat larger than ours but nothing else happened.

I went to look for Temsamany on the highway. He had roller skated out of sight. I felt that all my pursuits here were hopeless. I looked back over my shoulder into the grove. Tetum was swinging upside down from an olive tree her knees hooked over a branch, and she is, after all, forty-five and veiled and a miser.

There is more to this day but I see now that I have done exactly what I did not want to do. I have gone into great detail about one incident, which is probably of no interest.

But as a result of that day Cherifa and I have been much closer. In fact she spends two or three nights here a week in dungarees and Haymaker shirts. She asked for five thousand pesetas (about one hundred and fifteen dollars) so that she could fill her grain stall to the brim. I have given her, so far, fifteen hundred pesetas. She sleeps in dungarees and several things underneath. I shall have to write you a whole other letter about this. In fact I waited and waited before writing because foolishly I hoped that I could write you: "I have or have not—Cherifa." The awful thing is that I don't even know. I don't know what they do. I don't know how much they feel. Sometimes I think that I am just up against that awful hard to get virgin block. Sometimes I think they just don't know. I—it is difficult to explain. So hard to know what is clever manoeuvering on her part, what is a lack of passion, and what is fear—just plain fear of losing all her marketable value and that I won't care once I've had her. She is terribly affectionate at times and kissing is heaven. However I don't know quite how soon or if I should clamp down. I simply don't know. All the rules for the playing the game are given me by Paul or else Temsamany. Both are men. T. says if you don't get them the first two times you never will. A frightening thought. But then he is a man. I told Paul one couldn't buy desire, and he said desire can come but only with habit. And never does it mean what it means to us — rather less than holding hands supposedly. Everything is very preliminary and pleasant like the beginning of a love affair between a virgin and her boy friend in some automobile. Then when we are finally in bed she says: "Now sleep." Then comes either "Goodbye" or a little Arabic blessing which I repeat after her. There we lie like two logs — one log with open eyes. I take sleeping pill after sleeping pill. Yet I'm afraid to strike the bargain. "If you do this, I will give you all of the money, if not —" It is very difficult for me. Particularly as her affection and tenderness seem so terribly real. I'm not even sure that this isn't the most romantic experience in a sense that I have ever had — and it is all so miraculous compared to what little went on before. I hesitate to rush it, to be brutal in my own eyes, even if she would understand it perfectly. I think love and *sex*, that is tenderness and sex, beyond kissing and les caresses, may be forever separate in their minds, so that one might be going toward something less rather than more than what one had in the beginning. According to the few people I have spoken to — among them P.M. (the Englishman who wrote the book) — I hate mentioning names — they have absolutely no aftermath. Lying back, relaxing, all that which is more pleasant than the thing itself, if one is in love (and only then) is non-existent. Just quickly "O.K. Now we sleep," or a rush for six water bowls to wash the sin away. I'm not even sure I haven't in a way slept with C. Because I did get "Safi-naasu." ("O.K. Now we sleep.") But it does not mean always the same thing. I am up too many trees and cannot write you all obviously. Since I cannot seem to bring myself to the point of striking a verbal bargain (cowardice? delicacy? love?) I don't know — but I simply can't — not yet. I shall have to wait until I find the situation more impossible than pleasant, until my nerves are shot and I am screaming with exasperation. It will come. But I don't believe I can say anything before I feel that way. It would only sound fake. My hunch is she would go away saying "Never." Then eventually come back. At the moment, no matter what, I am so much happier than I was. She seems to be getting a habit of the house. Last night she said, "It's strange that I can't eat eggs in my own house. But here I eat them. " Later she said that her bed at home was not as good as mine. Mine by the way is *something*. Lumpy with no springs. Just on straw. A thin wool mattress, on straw. At home she sleeps in a room with her great aunt. The great aunt on the floor, Cherifa on the bed, natch. She's that kind. I find her completely beautiful. A little smaller than myself but with strong shoulders, strong legs with a good deal of hair on them. At the same time soft soft skin—and twenty-eight years old. Last night we went up on the topmost terrace and looked at all of Tangier. The boats and the stars and the long curved line of lights along the beach. There was a cold wind blowing and Cherifa was shivering. I kissed her just a little. Later downstairs she said the roof was very beautiful, and she wondered whether or not God had seen us. I wonder. I could go on about this, dear Katharine and Natasha, and I will some other time. I wish to Christ you were here. I can talk to Paul and he is interested but not that interested because we are all women. We see each other almost daily. His house is not far from here. And it is a lovely walk. Outside the walls of the Casbah, overlooking the beach and the ocean. Most of my time is taken up with him or Cherifa or the house and now work. I am beginning again to work. Before she came I was such a nervous wreck I couldn't do anything. Also I was in despair about all the world news and as I told you Paul's illness. Everything was a mess. Now I am in a panic about money and though I will write a play, I must write other things too for immediate cash. Not that I don't have any for a while but I must not use it all up before I have completed at least enough of a play for an advance. Thank God I am in a house and not in a hotel. Although the house has cost me a good deal until now, it won't henceforth because I've bought most everything I needed except a new bed for upstairs. I shall fill the house with beds—traps for a virgin. I feel happier now that I've written you. All the time I have been saying: I should write about *this* to N. and K. But it seemed impossible, utterly impossible to make a résumé of all that happened before. And as you see, it was impossible. I have not even found it possible to write in this letter why Tetum swinging from an olive tree in her cloak and hood should have precipitated all this but it did. I think Cherifa got worried about losing me to Tetum. She was so worried she asked me for a kaftan right off. Then started a conversation, a bargaining conversation, which resulted in her coming here after Ramadan to spend the night. But I can't go into that now. I always let Fatima (Sour Pickle) decide what we are to eat. It is all so terribly

179

simple – all in one dish. Either lamb with olives or with raisins, and onions, or chicken with the same or ground meat on skewers or beef or lamb on skewers. (You remember how wonderful they taste). Or a fried potato omelet with onions, or boiled noodles with butter or eggs fried in oil, and always lots of black bread and wine at five pesetas a quart (excellent). I've had guests once, Tennessee in fact. White beans in oil and with salt pork like the ones I cooked for you. Lots of salad: cucumber, tomato and onion, all chopped up, almost daily. Fresh figs, bananas, cherries. Whatever fruit is in season. Wonderful bowls of Turkish coffee in the morning which are brought to our bed (when she is here as she happens to be now for a kind of weekend) or to me alone and piles of toast soaked in butter. At noon we eat very little. Usually, if Cherifa isn't here (she supposedly comes twice a week but that can include two afternoons) I go over to Paul's for lunch. Except that he never eats until three thirty – sometimes four. I get up at seven and by then I am so hungry I don't even care. But I like seeing him. We eat soup and bread and butter and cheese and tuna fish. For me tuna fish is the main diet.

I love this life and I'm terrified of the day when my money runs out. The sex thing aside, it is as if I had dreamed this life before I was born. Perhaps I will work hard to keep it. I cannot keep Cherifa without money, or even myself, after all. Paul told Cherifa that without working I would never have any money so she is constantly sending me up into my little work room. A good thing. Naturally I think of her in terms of a long long time. How one can do this and at the same time fully realize the fact that money is of paramount importance to one's friend and etc., etc. – that if there is to be much sleeping it will most likely be against their will or something they will do to please one, I simply don't know. Possibly, if it came to that, I might lose interest in the sleeping part, possibly why I keep putting off the bargaining – but the money I know is paramount. Yet they are not like we are. Someone behaving in the same way who was not an Arab I couldn't bear. All this will have to wait for some other letter. Perhaps it is all a bore; if so tell me. But I thought since you have seen her and Tangier that it would interest you. Please do me a great favor and save this letter. I cannot write more than one letter on this subject. If you think Lyn would be interested in bits and snatches of the letter read them to her because I can't, as I said write about it more than once. Not having seen Tangier or Cherifa, perhaps it would mean nothing to her. But we are on an intimate enough basis –

she and Polly and myself — and they went through Marty with me a bit. I shall simply write her about my work and my health and I will tell her that you have a letter about "more stuff," if she wants to see it. And I shall tell her to call you, at the office. Perhaps you can meet some day for a drink if you all want to. I long to know Oliver's address. Lyn wrote me that he was in Calif. That's all. No address. Please write. I shall worry now about this messy letter.

All my love, always,

J. Bowles.

P.S. This letter I shall now correct. I am sure it is unreadable but I'll do the best I can. Received your copy of "Confessions of an Honest Playwright" today. Thank you. In Paris it has the other title, "Writing Plays for Goons." It's the end.

In December 1954 Jane went with Paul and Ahmed Yacoubi and the Bowles's driver, Temsamany, to Taprobane, a minute island off the shore of Weligama, Ceylon. Paul had purchased Taprobane in 1952. Upon the island was an ornate octagonal house, without water or electricity, and a botanical garden. Each night the island and the house were invaded by bats.

At Taprobane Paul was working on his novel The Spider's House. *Jane, who had hoped to write a play, could not work at all. Her hair began to fall out in great hanks and she became terrified that she was becoming bald. She suffered from alternate periods of depression and hysteria, even as she continued to consume large quantities of gin.*

In early March she left Ceylon for Tangier, accompanied by Temsamany.

59[49]

Jane Bowles to Paul Bowles
[Tangier, Morocco]
[April/May, 1955]

Dearest Bupple:

It has been very difficult for me to write you. I have covered sheet after sheet, but now I am less troubled in my head for some reason. Maybe because I hit bottom, I think. And now I feel that the weight is lifting. I am not going back in that wild despairing way over my departure from Ceylon, my missing the end of your novel, the temple of Madura, that terrible trip back alone (a nightmare to the end because it was the twin of the other trip I might have made with you). It was better toward the end, but I hit bottom again in Tangier. The house reeked of medicine and there was the smell of other people's stale soup in the velvet *haeti* and even in the blue wall. I put my nose on the wall. It was cold and I could smell soup. The first day I was in the house the whole Casbah reeked of some sweet and horrible chemical smell which doubled its intensity with each new gust of the east wind. The Arabs were holding their noses, but I didn't know that. On the first day I thought I alone could smell it, and it was like the madness I had been living in. A nightmare smell coming up from the port, and a special punishment for me, for my return. I really felt very bad. I can't even remember whether or not Cherifa came to me here that first night in the house. Truly, I can't. On the second day the barber came over to me in his white and black hood and asked me to go to the Administration about the smell. He was holding his nose. "There are microbes in the air. We will all perish," he said. As he spends his entire time in the mosque and is one of the few old-fashioned Arabs left in the quarter, I was amused. The smell is gone now. The sewer pipes had broken, and they were dumping some chemical into the sea while they were mending them. And from that day on I felt better. And the house smells better—at least, to me. Fathma said: "Naturally. Filthy Nazarene cooking. Everything made of pork. Pork soup, pork bread, pork coffee, an all-pork house." But now there is kaimon, and charcoal, in the air. I feel so much better. But I am terrified of beginning to work. I don't know what I'll do if that nightmare closes in on me again. I am sorry too that you have to live through it. I won't go near you if it happens again. Actually I cannot allow it to

[49] Taken from previously published material.

happen again. But I must work. I had some shattering news when I returned . . . *le coup de grâce*. . . my taxes. Clean out of my mind from the first second that I banked the money. Somewhere way back, someone, either you or Audrey, warned me not to consider the money all mine, and I was a fool to forget. Having never paid taxes. . . . However, I suppose it is understandable. The slip of paper doesn't say much, not even what percent I am to be taxed. Perhaps all that has gone off to you. In view of the condition I was in this winter and on the boat, I should think this blow would have landed me in the hospital. In fact I went to bed and waited. But I got up again the next day alive and sane still, though my head was pounding with blood-pressure symptoms. I had to get out of that state, obviously, and I did. I tried writing you, but the letters were *magillahs*, and all about Madura and the tax and Mrs. Trimmer and Cherifa in one *tajine*. Senseless and anguished, and they weighed a ton. Not the moment to start that, if I am to "resort to airmail." Anyway, I think I have enough money in the bank to cover the tax, and if not, I have a Fabergé gold bracelet. And I have (if I must sell it, and if Oliver has made full payment on it) my beautiful Berman painting. Naturally, if I had known this was going to be waiting for me I would not have returned, because surely I should like to have discussed the thing with you. It's a terrible bore writing about it. There are so many angles to it: what exemptions I can get . . . maybe a lot . . . maybe none. Is it best to get off the double income-tax and pay direct to the government, or should I pay to you? Anyway, for God's sake don't do anything about it until you see me. I shall wait in Tangier and I shall lead my life as if it would go on. I cannot face the possibility of its not going on. Yet I would be unwilling to stay here if it meant your giving up Temsamany and the car. I consider them essentials, just as there seem to be essentials to my life here without which I might as well be somewhere else. Maybe I'll have to be, but it is best to face that when it comes, in two months or with luck, later. I have pulled every string possible in the sense of looking for a job. I can only do it through friends. There is a terrible depression in Tangier. Hotels empty, the Massilia closing, and ten people waiting for every job. Most people think I am mad, and that I should write or live on you, or both. It is not easy to make friends take my plight seriously. Not easy at all, unless I were to say that I was starving to death, which would be shameful and untrue. I spent just a little too much in every direction. The top floor expenses in New York which I took over for a few months, taxis, restaurants, coming over travelling with Natasha and Katharine, the Rembrandt, the Massilia, extravagances with C., I suppose more dinner parties than I need have given, doctors here for myself and Fathma. I don't know . . . it went in every direction. But each thing separately is a drop in the bucket. It is just everything put together in the end. I suppose I've been bad, but not so bad. Please don't scold; I am miserable enough about the whole thing and would have pinched every penny as I am doing now, had I been less confident. Well, that is over the bridge and down the drain, like the money for Ceylon. But although Ceylon was wasted and I did not see the temples, or even Kandy, it has changed my life here to a degree that is scarcely believable. I very swiftly reduced expenses to a scale so much lower than anything C. has ever expected of me when I was here that she is at the moment back in the grain market. I think it is a healthy thing for C. to go to the market in any case, even if the funds were more adequate. Ramadan she will be going there a lot.

I am now exhausted. Ramadan would be an ideal time for me to escape to New York, I suppose, but I don't want to, until I know that I can come back here or that I can't, at least, not for a while — that is, if we are both too broke. I'll face that later too. If I go downhill again then I suppose I would go home. Finding it impossible to work again is the only thing I fear . . . the hell with Ramadan. I am rather grateful that C. does want to go to the market during that time. Because she can't come here in a straw hat, but must keep going back to the bottom of M'sallah to change into a veil and white gloves, it will be difficult for her to come regularly. And what with fasting, etc. She's been fasting now for two weeks. Hopscotch off and on, making up time. It's almost worse than real Ramadan. I am thinking of investing in a room I heard of, on the top floor of the Hotel Cuba. I will count it outside my budget, since it is not a permanent thing, but something I would like to try, just so I can get started working. Naturally when I first got back and realized about my taxes I was too accablée to do any work . . . too harassed, and still in that funny state. I think the room is a good idea, if it is still there. I have not seen it yet. But I will look at it. I can ask Mother to give it to me as a special present, or if it works out I shall simply keep it on as an outlet for as long as it does work out. Because that would mean I was working. As for C. and all that, I shouldn't even bother writing you about her since it is such a fluctuating uncertain quantity. At the same time I feel this terrible compulsion to write you about the geographical location of the grain market in relation to M'sallah and my house, and the awful amount of travelling she would have to do if she went often to the market during Ramadan, just to get in and out of her straw hat. I doubt that she will go often once the *Aïd* is over, but we'll see. I certainly do not wish to interfere with her work, ever (!). I have no right to, since my own position here is so precarious, and in any case I shouldn't. She has now expressed a desire to travel and to play tennis. Now I do have an upper hand that I never had when I spent more money. What is it? I suppose one must close one's fist, and allow them just the right amount of money to make it worthwhile and not shameful in the eyes of the neighbors. I understand many more of the family problems than I did. It was difficult before to find one's way in the maze. But for "the moment," I know that is over. Will explain when I see you, maybe, if I don't forget to. I'm sure you can't wait. I remember the glazed look you always got when I mentioned her before. I think however if that nonsense began again I would give up. If I could only work now I would feel quite peaceful.

Tangier looks worse. The Socco in the afternoon is mostly filled with old clothes. A veritable flea-market that I'm trying to preserve. I've been booming away at Phyllis about it, because she knows the new Administrator. I also asked her about my hair. She has me down on a list. It says: Janie, Grand Socco, hair. Which is just about it, isn't it? The same obsessions, over and over. When I am sure about my hair I will write. But I think the news is good. You will never know what that nightmare was like. I know you thought it was in my mind. I am going on with Bépanthène Roche. On the days I buy it I try to eat more cheaply, so that I can keep, as much as I can, within a budget. Phyllis gave me a blue bead for luck and to ward off the evil eye. Brion's restaurant is the only thing that does business in town. John Goodwin invited me to go to Spain any time during the Feria and Holy Week. He has an apartment for a month. But I'm not sure that the trip alone wouldn't come to a thousand pesetas or more. Also I never go anywhere, so why should I suddenly get to the Feria, since I didn't get to Madura. I would like to hear some Gypsies, but not with those tourists there. I do not think I will go. And certainly not if I'm working.

My terrace smells of male pipi. I suppose it will forever. Eric Gifford brought his male cat with him, Hassan, whom he never mentioned to me. Or else I wasn't paying attention. The worst of the bad weather is over, although the first two weeks at the Massilia were hell. Temsamany scared me so on the boat, about people being able to stay in one's house forever, that I offered them

185

two weeks' grace in the house. I wrote you that I cheered up on the boat when I thought of Jorge Jantus, and sure enough having him as a neighbor has made a lot of difference to me. I rather like their little group, and they are so near I can pop in there. He is bringing me some kif today. I had a cigarette of kif last night before supper and rather liked the effect. I had some drinks too, so I don't suppose I can judge, but it changed the effect of the drink noticeably.

I had dinner with Fathma, who is staying on for three hundred a month instead of five hundred, full-time as before. They have both been cooperative about buying cheap food, and C. of course is in her element. But then, that was before she decided to go back to the market.

The baqals announced a three-day close-down in commemoration of the upset here two or three years ago, and they were closed one. *Plus ça change.* Now my left hand is tired. Please write, and especially about your book, and don't above all scold me or put me in a panic. We'll talk about it all when you come, if you ever do. I wonder if instead you'll go to England? Anyway, Bubble, I think the trip has done some good. Much love. I hope you are well and that it got really hot. Write everything.

Jane

60

Jane Bowles to Libby Holman
[Tangier, Morocco]
[January 16, 1957]

Dearest Libby,

Yesterday I mailed you one of those horrible air letters, but I slipped it into something that looked like a fire plug, so I don't know whether or not it will ever reach you. Normally I mail letters from the B.P.O. As you may remember there are three post offices here, Spanish, American and French (substitute British for American, please), and all these post offices have their mailing boxes scattered about here and there. I stopped in front of one and hesitated trying to read what it said, and an Arab came up to me in rags and asked me what I wanted. I said I wanted a post box, and he said, "This is one." And I said, "Well I know that it is one but is it French, British, or Spanish? I want to mail a letter with a British stamp." "They are all alike," he said. "Put it in, they all go from here." I had to put it in because he stood there watching me and then he went off in his rags. Then the postman came along, a small boy with a pouch, and I said, "Does all mail leave from here?" He said, "Yes, yes, this is the Spanish post office box." I said "Well, I just mailed a letter from here with a British stamp." He shook his head and said, "This is for Spanish mail." I asked him what to do and he said I should wait until eight-thirty that night and then tell the postman to give me my letter when he came to collect the mail. I said, "I can't stand here, I will be too cold." It was then five-thirty. "At best," he said, "they will decide to mail it, but who knows?"

At best, perhaps they have, but if I don't write you immediately I will never know whether or not it has reached you and I shall worry. So please write me either way. I want to know how you are—I hope to God better, but I don't want to repeat myself because, at best, my other letter has arrived.

In the other letter I wrote a little about my play and in it I said that I hope that if I finished it, it would have a chance of running for a while because I needed to make a living and that I was afraid you might not like it and that it wasn't going to be very poetic. Actually I thought this over and decided that I could not really write very differently whether or not I needed money because I do not know how to write a commercial line, nor could I write *Waiting for Godot* if I was sitting with a million dollars in my pocket. I mention that because you like it so much. Paul thought it was very well written, in fact he said he was sure it was, but said he had never been so bored in his life by any script and couldn't finish it. Anyway, sometimes I am in despair about this play like today and sometimes I am not, like always.

ABOVE ALL please write me and tell me whether or not you received my other letter, and let me know how you are. Not that it was such an important letter but it was more important than this one because it had more things in it. The letter I wrote to my mother in Chicago, I sent care of Paul in Ceylon. I have trouble with letters, even when it comes to mailing them. But I will send this one from the B.P.O. direct. And if the one I sent didn't come, I'll try to remember the things that were in it and write it

187

again. I hope you are well enough to write yourself but if you are not have Rose [Rose Minor, Libby's Secretary] or whoever is with you write me immediately. I am worried. That was in the other letter.

Much love, Libby, as always

Jane

61

Jane Bowles to Paul Bowles
[Tangier, Morocco]
[February 1, 1957][50]

Dearest Paul,

I have been trying to write you for days but unsuccessfully. The fact is that I have been having the same trouble with my work that I had in Ceylon and before I left for Ceylon. I don't know whether to keep writing through the block or to get out of here now or in a month or two before I come to the end of my money. I know I can get passage back from somebody but there is always the question of leaving a little behind for Cherifa. I hope that I will come out of this all right. The fight against depression again is serious, since failure follows me into my dreams, and I have been awake for many nights, as I was in Ceylon. But there is no heat, thank God. If I left I would borrow from Libby and pay her back out of my month's checks there. I would give the money to Cherifa that I would be saving by living at Libby's. I don't really want to do this though it might be the nicest thing I can do. C. doesn't want me to either and she is very happy to have the house and says that I must not worry. She even said that with the rent she gets for the house she can live with her family and contribute her bag of flour a month and so you have done that much for my peace of mind, at least. Naturally she has gotten used to more than a bag of flour a month and I wonder if I shouldn't whip myself out of here no matter how much I dread doing it. The longer I wait the less I will

[50] Jane had dated this February 1, 1956—this is obviously an error.

188

have to give her, unless I asked Libby for an outright gift of a couple of hundred dollars. Actually, before I left Libby said to me that I shouldn't worry about money and that if I needed any to let her know. Then there are the little cats whom I adore, and C. herself, whom I can't bear to leave, and you too, who will be returning and I would not like to miss you though I am sure that you would probably not want to see me if I don't have a play done, and it would be a sad encounter to say the least. Actually I cannot picture any of this happening. I cannot picture leaving, nor can I picture your return and my having nothing to show you after all this time. Maybe none of this will happen. I hate to think of it and I get into a kind of terrible panic when I do. Still, if for *some reason* I did have to leave, I would naturally pay the rent here until June or whenever the contract is up, and lock the door. But I would not leave the cats, naturally. They would have to come along. Ira read my fortune and said that someone's death was going to oblige me to travel across water, and that as a result of this death I would inherit a little money. I don't believe it, of course, but it did occur to me that I should tell you that in case of any emergency, or even if I suddenly became a lunatic and felt a compulsion to go just because I didn't want to, that I would put all of your things into the apartment here and lock the door leaving the key with Christopher [Wanklyn] or Ira. The person who was going to die was a woman, and I can't think of anyone but my mother who might leave me a few hundred dollars, but I do not really believe in cards.

I filled a notebook with my notes and suggestions for my play and even started writing the dialogue. And now today, for the first time in a week, I had a flash of an idea and so I will see if [it] does not help. It is impossible to write a play in the dark without having some idea of where one is going. I did get an idea but it was so definite that I couldn't go against it either. For nearly a week I have had dreams of not being able to go on with it and then my head got into such a bad knot that I took a lot of Equanil and knocked off work. Today my head feels better—less knotted. I wrote you a long beginning of a letter but it was so confusing I thought I would tear it up, and I did tear it up, but at least I had been writing *something*. And then after I had written you the first really sad page of the letter I tore up, I made some lentils and got an idea about cutting out one of the characters in my play. In fact two of them. One was a girl and the other a dead man. Like Gertrude's father in *Summer House*, who became such a bore to all of us.

I think the girl was cut out because of a dream I had, about her and her girl friend. I dreamed they hated me and that they could never be in the play. I must write it. But am I fooling myself by insisting that I will? And by fooling myself, robbing C. of the last money that I can call my own? I am convinced that I should not think in these terms. Well, I will go on trying really hard for another month and see how I feel after that. I am sorry to bore you with this but I must at least mention my work or you will think that I am getting along beautifully and that makes me even more nervous. I will let you know if and when I get over this hump. I gather you are working as usual and I suppose Ahmed is too.

You never did answer my letters to Capetown. I rushed them off so that you could write on the boat and tell me at once how to treat your mail. I'm perfectly willing to send it *all* but do you want to spend all that money? There are many Xmas cards and other superfluous letters and I think *you* should decide what I am to do about them. As you know, airmail to Ceylon is not cheap. In fact nothing is cheap. Meat prices have gone way up here, and other things have risen too. The Catalana[51] is booming and none of us ever mention politics anymore. One does not feel any of that atmosphere in the streets, although the Socco Chico is still not a desirable place to go, according to Jorge. Not for political reasons especially but there are still a good many thugs around. They say there really is to be a casino here, and I suppose prices will rise even more. But it is so all over the world, and I think this is still the pleasantest place to be.

Dubz[52] tips over all the little round tables, walks through gravy, stands ankle deep in sinks full of water, opens all doors with his fat paw, particularly the cupboard door where the food is kept and the bathroom door. The bathroom is his toilet, especially the tub. He eats everything in sight and even chews through loaves of bread wrapped in cellophane.

I loved hearing about June and Paula. I lost my heart to June too and often thought in my madder moments of spending the rest of my life in that house, and loving it. I still think of it with nostalgia. Is the rice still like wild animal rice in the corner of a cage? Ask Ahmed to tell me because I don't trust you to know. I don't see how the rest house food could be much worse than it was, nor how

[51] A restaurant in the Medina.

[52] A cat.

190

there could be much less food in the market. I enclose Rose Minor's letter about Libby. It is too grisly to dwell on and I feel terribly sorry for her. Do write her. I wrote twice. I hadn't heard in so long that I was worried, and then this came. I hope to God that she will be better now and that she tries to eat as much as she can. According to Christopher the operation permits one to eat just about anything but care must be taken not to eat too much at a time.

Please give my love to June and Ina and Quintus and Elsie. Tell her that I have bought a bottle of pure silvikrin and that it has done my hair a lot of good. You don't say in your letter whether or not you are living at the hotel in Galle permanently. Are you? By the time you answer me I imagine most of the important mail you are expecting will have been headed off to Weligama directly. Meanwhile I will forward what I think I should forward, using my own judgement (which does not include Xmas cards). Please let me know whether or not you received my letter about the mandat and, as I said, don't let it lag too long or the money will be gone.

Do you feel that you do not want to return to Ceylon anymore? I would judge so by your letter. Two packages have arrived which I shall keep for you. One from the Fordyces, and the other from Conzett and Huber in Germany. The first, a book on African rites filled with pictures of little mud figurines (typical) and the second a calendar, framing a rather famous painting. Or perhaps it is not famous, but acts as if it were. A still life with a checkerboard in it from Conzett and Huber in Germany. *Who on earth is Harper?!* I met Edita Morris. The truth is that I hated her but liked her husband Ira. Please bury this letter if they should come down. I can just see it lying around on the alcove terrace—effect on one of the chairs painted silver.

Much love, as ever,

J.B.

P.S. Please write often—I love to hear about Ceylon.

62[53]

Jane Bowles to Paul Bowles
Tangier, Morocco
[February 24, 1957]

Dear Paul:

I have just had my fortieth birthday the day before yesterday, and that is always, however long one has prepared for it, a shock. The day was not as bad as the day after it, or the following day, which was even worse. Something coming is not at all like something which has come. It makes trying to work that much more difficult (or could it possibly be more difficult?), because the full horror of having no serious work behind me at this age (or successful work, in any sense) is now like an official fact rather than something in my imagination, something to be feared, but not yet realized. Well, I don't suppose you can understand this, since when you reached forty you had already quite enough stacked up behind you.

I realized about your birthday, but I don't think I mentioned it in my letters, or thought of it at the time I wrote you. Anyway, it is over. I did not tell anyone about mine except Cherifa, and I celebrated with her on the night of the twenty-first because on the twenty-second an old man from Xauen, an uncle or grandfather, was expected at her house. However, Christopher heard about it from George and called me on the twenty-second to ask if it were true, and then I did have a busy day. I sound like your mother about to say that Ulla came over and that they took a drive and later popped corn in the grate. In spite of hating it to be forty (Anne Harbach toasted me and said: "Life begins . . ." which was the last straw), I am still determined to write my play, and have no intention of going back to New York until my money runs out. I have somehow, thus far, staved off the terrible depression that was coming over me when I wrote you last — staved it off perhaps simply because I cannot ever again be the way I was in Ceylon. I mean that I will do everything in my power to pretend that I am not, even if I am. It was too horrible. And so I knocked off work entirely for a week and then went back to trying to write the play. My mind is not a total blank, which is more than I can say of the way it was before. Whether it will get beyond that, I don't know.

[53] Taken from previously published material.

I am sure you will come out all right because you always have.

Seth[54] said his first word yesterday. "Dubz." He said it clearly three times, and again this morning. I daresay it is because Seth sits in the bathroom a lot and I am always lunging in after Dubz to stop him from using the tub, and of course calling out: "Dubz!" at the top of my lungs. I hope that he will keep saying it so you will hear him when you get back.

Mr. Rothschild has been here for three days and I like him. He is giving me a subscription to the Sunday Times for a year, and it will be delivered to me from New York by boat of course, so it will always be two weeks late. It is for Berred[55] and Dubz, for their pans.

Radiant sunshine, balmy weather and scarcely any rain. The beaches are crowded. I had lunch with Mr. Mallan at the Catalana last week. The Mar Chica is booming again. Whether or not there are many Arabs in it I don't know. Apparently there is more drink than ever in their world, only not as openly. There seems to be not much fear about. Ramadan is in less than forty days, and I dread it as usual. Seth is so terribly noisy that I have to put him out on the terrace in order to do any work. I am furious that you are living in Colombo and have an oscillating standing fan. I would have loved that. If you like Weligama so much why don't you keep it . . . or aren't you prepared to live alone there? Actually I don't think you would like that for long. But maybe you won't be able to sell it. Your life in Colombo doesn't sound too expensive thank God so I imagine you'll stay there until you sell the house. Seth is driving me mad.

Dubz just fell into the toilet up to his waist and I had to help him to dry off. Mr. Mallan after beating around the bush for fifteen minutes finally asked me what color eyes Phyllis De la Faille has. He is utterly ridiculous. Please write me about him. Cherifa bought Seth a length of strong wire which she has fastened around his cup and the bars of his cage so that he can no longer dump his seeds on the floor. It is to be a great saving in money and I am glad. He just said "Dubz" again. I try to say it over and over again to him so that he won't forget.

Much love,

J.

---

[54] The parrot.

[55] Another cat.

63

Jane Bowles to Libby Holman
[Tangier, Morocco]
[April 10, 1957]

Libby dear,

It was too much—the clipping they sent me.⁵⁶ From Celebrity
Service via a friend who works there. In fact the man who came
over with me on the Andrea Doria, which has now sunk. If you
get as little news as I do you are probably unaware of this. I know
it through friends. I was so frantic I had to cable you and hear that
night; that is why I gave Jay's address. The post closes early and
I was not in my own "home," but up on the mountain taking care
of a girl who had been through a complicated horrid abortion. The
cable came early thank God but I was afraid to open it right off.
Anyway I was so overwhelmed with joy to hear that he had not
died. The clipping said critical and I was dreading the cable. This
will not be a long letter because I don't know yet what the consequences of the accident are and am waiting anxiously for a letter
from you or Rose. I can't be too gay until I know.

I hope the shock has not set you back. I was *so happy* about your
letter from Jamaica. It was in a way the first real letter that I have
had from you in many years and I have been missing that very
much.

I did not answer right away for more than the usual reasons. Not
really, but I had been working which was unusual and then it all
collapsed—stopped—dried up—but this was only unusual because
for the first time in years I thought I was going along well. It was
a terrible block but I managed to work myself out of it with more
effort than gift I suppose, but that doesn't matter. I was on the point
of writing you a despairing letter about giving up, but then I did
start again and was about to write more cheerfully when the letter
came from the Andrea Doria man, with whom the Moroccan
leather man (and scholar) is staying. (Charles Gallagher.) Because
of this week which has been sheer hell (because of this girl's
abortion), I have not done any work. I am terrified of getting back
to it and finding that the spark has died. It was a fatal moment
because I was functioning well for the first time in many a long

⁵⁶ Jane is referring to Montgomery Clift's car accident.

year but I could not let her go to the hospital alone really and it turned out to be very painful and frightening. The doctor swore at her throughout the operation and scolded her for having an upside down womb and of course I might have had one myself with the baby in it for all I was able to detach myself from the girl whom I now *hate*.

She has been sheer hell for a solid week and I have stayed with her up on the mountain because there was no one else who would. Christopher Wanklyn and I stayed (he has a car), and we worried that she might hemmorage [sic] and be stuck without one. She was a bloody bore about getting up too soon and thus started something going which laid her back in bed for two days (and imprisoned us too), though I had begged her to lie still. We had fish and squashed spinach the whole time and once just spinach and potatoes, but when her clandestine lover came (who has no chin and trains horses), she gave him soufflé and chicken and gave us the afternoon off. I thought it was very ungracious. Also she scolded me and commanded me the entire week and was so cross the whole time with me and her poor servant that we both were frightened and Christopher was very disgusted, though not frightened. I was stuck however and could not answer her back because she would have ordered me out of the house (as she did once out of the hospital), and then she would have perhaps had a hemmorage. How does one spell that? I left Cherifa for a week and came back to find that she has taken up playing cards with two women both of whom, she says, look like Pekingese. I cannot believe they do—not both of them—and think she says this to please me. They are black and their husbands are dead white and work in movie houses. I believe it's really only one woman. How could they be so identical? She is either lying deliberately or her imagination is running wild. The poor thing has a dropped stomach and that is why she has been eating less and less and getting thinner all the time. I was going to write you about this, I was so worried. Now she has a strange truss-like corset with a rubber pump and feels much better. She ate a pound of bananas all at once last night like a monkey. It is Ramadan and I get up at two-thirty in the morning to prepare the three o'clock meal. At least I did last night when I returned from the mountain. We had a big fight and then made up. The fights are never serious. I do not yet make my own bread but I suppose I will. Dear Libby do you know of any shot that will put *weight* on people? Not for anemia or weakness, but something—the best thing for stimulating appetite and adding on fat. Apparently

195

dropped stomachs need the support of fat, at least the "twenty-five cents a visit" doctor said so. Don't frighten me about the dropped stomach. I get hysterical about Cherifa the way one does about a child. But if you know of the best thing for putting on fat tell me. Perhaps you know because of Tim. Please let me hear the latest news fast. My love to darling Rose and Betty, George, Alice and Gerry—also Skipper—and thank her for the Fat Boy's Book—and love to Ross [Evans] and Monty [Clift]—and to you always,

J.

64⁵⁷

Jane Bowles to Paul Bowles
[Tangier, Morocco]
[Mid-April, 1957]

Dearest Bup,

I am forwarding this letter from Villiers. I thought it might be an invitation and so opened it, but no luck. It occurred to me that since you are spending the ridiculous extra money to go all the way to England, you might at least benefit by a visit somewhere to some capital. Ahmed certainly enjoys that even if you don't. How could you have missed up on his visa? Doesn't the Spanish Consulate exist in Ceylon? I suppose not. Boats are going through the Canal too, by the way, but maybe you didn't know that.

Berred has eczema. A famous mystery-story writer told me that it was probably from nerves. I think both cats are at a disadvantage together because neither one can get the attention he wants and demands. They are in a state all day worrying about their food and guarding their dishes against each other. At night poor Dubz gets shut in the outer room because Berred insists on sleeping with me. Sleeping is a bad word, since she has the habit now of making constant trips to the terrace and back to make sure that Dubz isn't lurking outside the window somewhere.

Seth almost broke his bars with rage because I went into the bathroom with a hat on, and he thought I was someone else. (Some

---

⁵⁷ Taken from previously published material.

196

man, since he seems to hate them most.) I don't think he should be with the green parrot until he learns to talk more, because it is obvious that when birds are together they don't learn anything. At least, they should not be in a small place where they can talk back and forth in their own language.

Ramadan is on, and Cherifa and I almost came to blows the other night. I insist that she joke at three in the morning if we are to get up then (and we do), but she refuses to treat the meal as a gay occasion. I have threatened to send her home for the month, and she in turn has threatened to stay there. I can't decide which is worse, to be alone or to go through it. I hate making appointments except with Christopher, and it gets lonely up on the ninth floor. Particularly since I am a virtual prisoner here because of the lift, and only go down with my maid, or else with the baqal boys when they deliver something from downstairs. I wrote you that there was a baqal in the building.

A boy has come here from New York, called Allen Ginsberg. He was given a letter to us through Leo Lerman. I have his book of poems, called *HOWL, and Other Poems*, with an introduction by William Carlos W. I suppose I must see him, but he is much more up your alley than mine. I will probably not be able to go on with my play if I do see him.

On the telephone he said: "Do you know Philip Lamantia?" I said: "No." He said: "He's this hep poet, been writing since he was thirteen, and he just had a vision in Mexico on *peyote*. (Peyoti, I gather.) I said: "Oy weh." Then he said: "Honest, it was a real vision, and now he's a Catholic." I said: "*Oy weh!*"

Then he named twenty-five men, none of whom I'd ever heard of, and I told him I'd been away a long time, and was too old anyway, and that I wasn't interested in peyote or visions. He said: "Do you know Charles Ford?" and I said: "Yes, because he's old." And he said: "Well, don't you take majoun day and night?" and I said: "I hate all that, and I'm sure you shouldn't see me." And he said: "Well, what about Zen?"

Anyway, he's here and he is a friend of Bill Burroughs, who appears constantly in his poems, together with references to TANGIERS (sic), and he is part of a group. The Zen Buddhist-Bebop-Jesus Christ-Peyote group. Carl Solomon is a Dadaist Bronx poet. The first *Howl* is dedicated to him. I think he is in Rockland State Hospital. Philip Lamantia, if that is his name, (I forget) used to write for *View*. Ginsberg asked me on the telephone whether or not I believed in God. I cannot decide whether or not he is up your alley.

I am referring to Allen Ginsberg. With it all he sounds like a very sweet person. I imagine he shares Bill's habits.

I am not going to forward any more mail to Cape Town. None of it looks important, except a great thick ominous letter from Heger. But it is entirely too thick. Please write me when you get to England if you decide to go somewhere on the continent.

I have not worked on my play for a week because I've been on the Mountain. Patricia was ill and I had to take care of her. I'll tell you about that when you return. If I cannot get back to work I think I'll kill myself, for I have only a few months of grace left.

I am excited that you are getting nearer. I'll do my best with "My name is Seth."[58] Give my love to Ahmed. The lemur sounded *adorable*. I'm *furious* not to have it. But I suppose it is best.

Much love, and congratulations on *Harper's Bazaar*.

Jane.

Toward the end of April 1957, one evening during the month of Ramadan, after a fight with Cherifa, Jane suffered a stroke. She was at the time forty years old.

Gordon Sager cabled Paul, who was en route from Ceylon, and wrote to Libby Holman about Jane's condition. In response Libby offered to help Jane financially and at Jane's request agreed to send her one hundred and seventy-five dollars a month.

It soon became apparent that Jane had suffered permanent damage from the stroke, including the impairment of the functioning of her hand, a residual aphasia, and a homonymous hemianopia of the right side (from either eye she could not see the right side of the visual field).

Note: The letters from this point forward reproduce all inaccuracies of spelling and punctuation, since these errors were of great concern to Jane.

[58] A phrase Paul had suggested Jane teach the parrot. "[It] sounds," he wrote, "like an autobiographical novel's title . . . something awful by Robert Graves on Biblical times."

65

Jane Bowles to Libby Holman
[Tangier, Morocco]
[Summer, 1957]

Dearest Libby

Twice I have tried to write this letter and each day I bog down
on it. I can read a little better than I could before which makes
it more difficult than it was the first day I wrote to you and now
I a am filled with missgivings and depresion about the doctors.
since Resneck [Resnick, Libby's doctor] wa not abole to understand
very much of had happened. It may be a quesion of French and
I am going to go to Doctor Spreit again and give him a tranlation
of what Resneck wrote to see if it throws any light on it and thence
to England or simultaneously. I am waiting for Paul to go and look
up the name of the english doctor[59] and which can probably be
found at the english legation. I am writing this half automotically
that is I can check back a little better than I could and make out
what I have written if there is a clue to it. The french doctor sais
that it will come back but it is slow. I am very low Libby and you
know how hard it is to talk about these things and so I better not.
I tried actually several days to write this not just two and there
was so much to say and so many details and loosends and plans
that I can't cope with, at least the writing about them is too dificult
and so I've been swnowed under. Berreds wrist, or was it my own
wrist, yes it was my own wrist, held me up for a week at least and
is now already. It was really a question of weekness and having
tried to hard to cut her meet and so I sprained the writs because
I was weak. Meanwhile time past and and I was not clear and what
I had written and explained to you and aparently according to Paul
even my last letter, that is the wire about Polly [Polikoff, Libby's
lawyer], doesn't explain that I did receive the letter about the
money.

now I have lost my place and I must go up to Pauls, to find it.
But I see more and so I am hopeful but it is taking a long time.
Libby I will simply go on as faras I can without checking with Paul
and forgive me if I am repeating. I sent the wire to you without

[59] Dr. Resnick had suggested that Jane go to England to consult with a
British neurologist, Dr. John McMichael.

consulting Paul and he says that I still havn't answerd your question about the money you sent to me for the doctor. I thought I had when I wrote about hurting myself myself on Berreds wrist and then althogh I sealed that letter op I mean Paul seeded it He didn't read it but simply mailed it and in the interrum I might have tesecoped two letters into one, the one in my head and the one on the page. Anyway something was didn't exist since you didn't get my letter thanking you etc. (explaining I understood the arrangements and was so happy that it was taken care of). One explanation for

Dear Libby:

Jane has gotten into a state about writing this letter and has come up to me to ask me to finish it for her, because she is very eager to post it as soon as possible. I read what she had written aloud to her, and she thinks I should explain that she wants to translate Resnick's letter into French and give it to her doctor here, to find out if he thinks the consultation with a specialist is something which must be done soon — if "time is of the essence," as she keeps saying. Also, she wants me to say that she has not yet paid Spriet's bill because he has not presented it, and the reason for that is that last week when she visited him and asked for it, he told her that at the time she fell ill Phyllis De la Faille here in Tangier had asked that Janie's bill be sent to her, and that he had complied. This news brought on a virtual brainstorm in Jane, because she never sees Phyllis and feels rather ambivalent about her, and consequently horribly guilty about the idea of her having made such a gesture. She told the doctor to write Phyllis that she could not accept the gift, and she has also informed Phyllis herself indirectly, and the doctor is now sending her the bill, but it has not yet come. She wanted to be sure that you were informed of all these things. As soon as she gets the bill she will pay it, and that will be an end of it. I think that's about all. Jane says she will write you again in a few days. She does better than she did two or three weeks ago, and I think each time she tries to write she will find it easier. Of course, the difficult part is not being able to read over what she has typed. But I think there is a definite improvement in this letter over the others.

[From Paul, unsigned]

[Addendum, handwritten by Jane]

Dearest Libby I was not abble to finish this letter—and I must let Paul send this now. I am actually reading this which I can do in blotches. More about Berred later! I will write again as soon as possible.

Much love

J.

66

Jane Bowles to Libby Holman
[Tangier, Morocco]
[Summer, 1957]

Dearest Libby

I am getting very nervous now naturally because everything seems endlessly complicated so much so that I seem not to be able to write down all the loose ends. I will write what I canand if I leave out half of it please forgive me but it is a gonza magella if there ever was one. Especially since I can't read it back which I am still unable to do though I would say and I pray that it is getting better slowly. I can read back snatuches if I have clues as you can see. In fact I have come a long way from just plain automatacic righting so I try to think of how bad it was and take courage. Ever since the letter from Dr. Resneck cam I have been very lost naturally because I hoped that what the doctor here was doing would turn out to be adequate and the right thing and that only time would be required to set things right. Now I have no idea what to hope for and so I have been despondent and am anxious to get going. I am very hapy—at least reassured that you are there and resnecc and that I will be I hope soon in the hands of someone competant. Paul is waiting for the answer to his letter to London which has not yet come though he wrote it as soon as he heard that he would have to go there and should not wait untill the fall when he has been envited to London in any case and would have his expenses payed except for the trip itself. He has written to this friend in Lonon who is called Pitt or Tip, and is hoping for an answer and permission to stay there while I am the dotors. It would be too much to hope for, an invetation for me as well but ut us impossible. If Paul has to pay for his own expenses a stay in London I suppose he won't be ablte to go be able go because he is very low and would have instead to wait untill the invitation is forthcoming. Meanwhile it might come any minute because these people, Pit or Tip, are not likely to stay very long away from london if they are out of london at the moment and not merely taking a little too long to answer the letter. They may in fact have another guest. Meanwhile I am frantic with all the uncertainties and it is very difficult for me to focus my thoughts and write them all down. In the beginning Dr. Sprite said that I should see a specialis and then later told me that it was not necessary but I remember he did say flying would not be advisable. Paul you know will not fly and I cannot ask him too unless it is a matter of life and death and I think I can get there either by train which is deadly between here and madrid but I think althoght exhausting would not kill me. At least I will ask the doctor. It is very bumpy and very hot but I don't imagine it woulld be dangerous only exausting. The best possibility which is by Japanese boat dirrectly from Tangier to London seems like the most possible solution but I cannot tell yet whether or not I can get on it (and Paul) untill the boat docks here. They drop pasangers off between Tokio and the Thanes and the is often room ror two passengers to London by the time. Libby I have lost my place again and it is difficult to find it. I can see passangers to London but the rest which is a simple word I can't make out. I was going to say before I left the the room it is possible to go to London from Tangier if the boat is not fully bucked. The man whom Paul spoke to at the steamsh ofice says there is a fifty fifty chance of getting on itor more. The other way is by land to through Spainwhich is to be avoided but I will find out from Spreit whether or not it would be actually dangerous for me. It is torrid until madried, with no water on the train but I guess cools off at night and I wouldn't die of it, just be tired. I don't know that my trouble has anything to do with being too hot or too cold, ; I can't go by myself because I can't see well enough or at least coordanate well enough yet to manage. Paul will or rather can pay his trip over and back. I am hoping that I won't have to stay there long naturally. I can pay the trip there maybe even back but I would rather have that in the till then count up my expenses when it is over and I have returned. I will leave money here because naturally my maid and Berred and my bills go on, but the trip over I can certainly manage with an eye to an eye to sending you the money for the trip back when I return. I am a little mixed up about what it has cos me to live a month since I am incapable of doing much and I had not been expecting to move at all. Please tell me what to do Libby and if Paul doesn't get his initation for his stay in london tell me what to do about that financialy. He can't even write about it he so counts on it because know what to do if he doesn't well, I've lost it again but I am simply incapable of writing this and Paul is much more so I'll have too. And this is why I havn't writen partly and partly because we have still no word from the doctor in London hasn't written yet.

I seem to be going into giberash because I cannot get help from anyone on this letter. Paul gets into a state and expects me to write it by myself. I am graterul that he will go with me and back naturally and pay his fair but I don't think can do much more than that — he is very low in funds though he can probably add another hundred dollars or so but as I said the whole things seems beyon him if he doesn't come up with the invetation. None the less I am playing to leave within two and one half weeks and if there is no japaneise boat I will take the train through spain if you are in occordance with this plan and tell me how to manage it finacialy. I will ad what is left of the money you gave me toward the expenses, 'n (NOT the monthley stipand) as I said toward expenses upintill the time I do leave here and the trip over. If there is money left I shall send it to you (I mean the five hundred) or kepp it if you want me too. Maybe it can pay the trip back as well, but I had better wait untill I see. I am sorry to have to write this letter at all but I may be leaving within two weeks or so, if I am lucky you had better send me some world. I am horribly deppressed because I don't seem to be seeing very much, and I worry about this more than anything naturally. But still it is more than I could see which was nothing and so I keep telling myself that. I know this is the worst letter you have had from me but it had to be written; Perhaps you will make sense out of it. I know that I must get to London. Please tell me what to do If Paul's friend doesn't turn up and if he does, you want me to about the money I'll need to start out with anyway. As I said I can manage the trip over and then I'll save how much more than that. I am too tired now to go on Libby unless you want to write me about the Villa Lobos gain which might sound like a welcome change to you after this. I wish that Gordon were here to write about these things. Maybe a letter of yours has crossed mine and clarifies everything. If anything is clarifie please send mine back so that use it again, for Villa Lobos next season. The spanish train is from eighteen forty eitght.

I hope that this will be the last of these letters.

Love,

Jane

(Later)   No letter yet from or Pauls friend—
P.s. Paul has just read this letter because I asked him too and he says that what I am trying to say because I told him what I was trying to see and it didn't seeme clear, was this;

I have enough money left out of the five hundred you sent me for trip up to London and even for the return jurney to Tangier or at least part of it.

For give this letter again. It must be as difficult for you as it is for me.

Love always,

J.

67

Jane Bowles to Libby Holman
[Tangier, Morocco]
[Summer, 1957]

Dearest Libby

If you have lived through the last letter here is another one. I have been so disturbed since the letter from Resneck that I was incapable of writing you sooner than I did—and when I finally wrote the result was what you saw. It was terrible being, in a sense without a doctor, which is what I felt was my situation when Resneck wrote that he could not tell what had happened to me—at least not exactly by reading the report Spreite sent him via Paul's letter.

Yesterday I decided to make Paul translate the principle elements in Resnec's letter—that is whether it had been a thrombosis, or a hemmoradge and I took that part of the letter over to Spreit by myself. He was surprised because he thought he had explained that thoroughly and wrote out for me that it was definitely neither a thrombosis or a hemmoradge but stopped short of that thank God. He had been as I gather waiting to see whether it would be or not but there was no sine of it—me rely what he calls a confusion or some such word; I would judge that he is a good doctor though he has not claimed to be a neurologis naturally. He is all for a first rate nurologist taking those tests but I was very much releived that there was no danger of either the thrombosis or hemorrage having taken place and that Spreit after all seems perfectly aware of what happened and compotitnt. compotint. He vetoed the trip through spain although he would not say that I would die of it he said that a trip throught spain at this time of the year would have or could have serious consequences. A plain would be dangerous if it bit a oressurized plane and according to what I here not many of the planes in Tageir are pressurized and often they break down—that is the pressurizing aparatus does (if not the rest). That leaves the boat which we had written you about in the last letter—that is if you could make any sense out of that at all. At least the frightening element seems to have been grately dimineshed by Spreits clarification of the case, and I hope and am sure that you will feel some relief too. He said there was no element of worry incase I could not get passage right away but that a thorough teste was naturally the best assurance I could find for following the right treatment over a period of time.

I enclose Dr. Spreits letter in English and in French (which Paul will write for me presently) and he inturn woulld like a little message from Resneck saying whether or not he has received the newest resume of the case which he has just clarified for us. At least in so far as there has been no Thrambossis or Hemeroadge. The names I am using, all sound like englishman. Paul will write this out properly, but I must go upstairs. Give my love to everybody. I am sorry that you have to get into this Libby because I know your capacity for shouldering the responsibly and I know that it is not good for you. I actually have faith in Spreit and feel now that I have gone there and he has put the mistake straight that you should feel better too. In case there is no boat to London this month there will be later but there is a pretty good chance of their being passage according to the steamship office. Obviously there must have been some mistake in Paul's translation of Spreits message or Spreit himself did not explain enough to make it clear to Paul. Whatever, here is his latest message and Spreit would like an answer from Resnick when possible stating that he has received it. Meanwhile I am continuing to plan to go to London although there is yet no message from McMichael. Spreit thinks I am progressing slowly but surely and I suppose you can see that yourself. The last letter was particularly bad because there was too much in it and I couldn't tie up all those loosends and ifs and buts, which alas are still pending. We have not yet heard from Pit or Tip about Paul staying there or not staying there as a guest. We are hoping for that daily just as we are hoping for passage on the Japanese frater. Coming back from England to Tangier is even more difficult as you can imagine, since the fraiter doesn't come back this way but goes on its way through the Panama Canal and we will have to find some ship that is not solidly Booked to bring us back. That is why we are counting even more heavily on finding pit or tip so that at least Paul can stay there and stay free of charge untill we do arrange some way back.

I will let you know the second there is a rift in this—a rift in what?

I considere seriously that I am right to be less worried and I do have faith in Spreit. He is one of those who does not talk but he was interested and surprised that Paul or the language had not managed to convey what he had written to Resnick. Anyway here it is again. If there is anything new in plans because of this letter naturally wire me but I will take for granted that Resnick will still think I should get there as quickly as possible unless I hear to the contrary. Please try to get him to send a note to Spreitwho wants one at this point. Above all should I go to London anyway and try some other Specialis whom Resnick would recomand or not. Suppose Dr. McMichael is away for the summer. I don't want to throw this back at you but I don't want to take any steps without Resneck either. Meanwhile enough for now, or I shall start wrighting gibberish again, because I do get tired after awhile. I have a feeling that everything will somehow work out Libby so don't get in a worse stew than you must be in already. I still can't read very much without someone elses help but Spreit says it will come back slowly, and then I am hoping to get a letter from you that isn't at the mercy of whoever can read it to me.

Meanwhile love.

J.

Dear Libby: This seems to me to be by far the best letter Jane has written since she started. It is very encouraging, I think. I haven't seen them all, but of those I have seen, it is undoubtedly the most clearly conceived. This is Doctor Spriet's diagnosis, in French and English: "Spasme cerébral avec confusion et parésie intellectualle pendant quelques jours, mais aucun signe de hemorragie cerébral ni thrombose cerébrale." "Cerebral spasm with intellectual confusion and paresis during the space of a few days, but no sign of cerebral hemorrhage or of cerebral thrombosis." I think she is much better, myself, in every way, even her vision and concentration.

Love,

Paul

In August Jane was admitted to the Radcliffe Infirmary in Oxford and then moved to St. Mary's Hospital in London. She was suffering from very high blood pressure, a condition she had had for a number of years. At St. Mary's it was decided that her brain lesion was inoperable. On the way back to Tangier with Paul she began to experience epileptiform seizures. She returned to England in September and was sent from the Radcliffe Infirmary to St. Andrew's, a psychiatric hospital in Northampton, where she was treated with electric shock.

68

Jane Bowles to Libby Holman
[Aboard the S. S. Orion, en route
from London, destination Gibraltar]
[November, 1957]

Dearest Libby,

This is a quick note that will be mailed from Naples, as we are
leaving this ship now to land in Gibraltar. My typewriter sticks
unmercifully, and I must have it cleaned, so that I can write you
a longer letter. This is impossible.

I can't remember whether I told you that I received the money
from Stamford almost at once. It was wonderful getting it all settled
and I hope to God there is no more nonsense. I have a feeling I
did write you this but such is the nature of shock treatment. I am
much better Libby, almost jolly. I dreamed about you last night
and you were not jolly. I am beginning to be able to read, with,
effort, but I am very hopeful about it. Anyway more about that
and everything, as soon as I fix my machine.

Thank you, Libby, always, and much love

Jane

> In early 1958 Jane and Paul left Tangier for Portugal
> because of concern about the general situation in
> Tangier. There were wholesale arrests of certain
> European residents by the police. (Ahmed Yacoubi
> had also been arrested.) In Portugal Jane's condition
> once again deteriorated and in April she flew from
> Lisbon to New York, where Katharine Hamill and
> Natasha von Hoershelman had offered to have her stay
> with them.

69

Jane Bowles to Paul Bowles
[New York City]
[Early May, 1958]

Dearest Paul

    I am sorry to have waited so long and I was very happy to read your letter and to know that you for the moment at least were happy set and able to eat and therefore I presume to work—or you must be by now on your way to it. I dreamed of happines and felt it in my dream as solid as gold. It was this afternoon I dreamed of it and I had the doubtful satisfaction of knowing that at last there was someting in my life that was not facke or open to doubte in any way. I have never known such misery and so I shall perhaps servive. I hope to survive because I am natural, like that wretched woman in my story. There is nothing you can do except write me that there is some hope that we may go to mexico. I could fly because that I could then go to when the time came. I have not asked the doctor yet about altitudes—what affecrt they would have on me even if only temporarly. There I could find a maid or two at least and you would be there if I could get back to work. I think of these things when I feel hopefull but when I don't see any way out of here I am desperate. Berred and Cherifa I can't bear to think about and must tretend there dead as you did Ahmed. The most important is my eyes or that field of visian—whatever it was called—not the field of visian itself because that is gone but the ability to read—there was a special word for that but I can't remember what it was we used it all the time. That is surely the tragedy if there is one unless it is simply the fact that don't like to write anyway. Libby is drumming up money from sourse and another—some from Oliver—and some John Goodwin and some from Katherine and twenty five dollars from Natasha when she has her tooth work finished. She herself has contributed the sum you're already familiar with and will continue too for life. I think this is very sweet of her and the work she is doing with my pasport and calling up these people to ask for a small sum of money from each for as long as I need it is invaluable. I will have no place to live soon and the rent will have have to be payed but according to Libby there will be enought from the various soursces. Diane [Dione Lewis] has has reappedred as if by a mirictle because I didn't know where to reach her and simply ran into her at least Natasha. She wants to take an apport with me and since there is no other place except an old lady's home or home for dissabled people scince for for various reasons nobody have me. Dionne is reatly improoved after two years of Inalisis and very warm. Mrs. Latouche [John's mother] is spending the nights with me and a nurse the dayse. It is simply because I cannot be alone I am too frigtened after the fit which took a long time coming on and I would no way to comunicate if it happened when I was alone here. Libby does not think I should be in fact she says it is out of the question and thinks there will be enough money for medisons and rent and a maid between the groupe. She is writing you all about it very soon, but she is terribly busy and I do not see her very much. It will be a good send to have Dionne because lauliness is my toupbist problemme ple the fear of being alonge because of these ghastly fits. I am staying leave on the hope that some day I will be able to write again—at least to be indepemdent. I started three days ago to have fit but I took a dillantine and it stoped it in the midle. Dyane saw it happening the palpatations and insanne pullse beating I called the doctor but the fact that it did not come to its conclusian but that I was able to stop it is hopefull. There is so much hopelessness in this situation that I did not write you. But I am not crazy and was never crazy and only fear will drive me crazy. The fit was very unpleasant and terrifying because I—I have lost my place and so cannot find it again. Surely you can make some sinse out of this letter and last enough read most of it. It is very difficult for me to write Bubby but I will certainly write again tomorow or even later tonight. Please do write my mother and sign it with an initial which I often have done to her when I did not happen to have a pen. I feel better and I take my pills three times aday it is a struggel now for survival. I don't think you should mention suiside as glibly as you have on occasion—but I don't think you would use that way out really. This may sound like a nonsequator but I am in a hurry and I reffer to a conversation we had in Portugal. You threataned suiside if you had no money or if you were trapped with me and I didn't cheer up or if you were trapped in America. Naturaly I have been in a bad state but I have to face it and not die of it. It will be wonderful if the pills really work but it will take a few monts two now won't it. It is awful writing this way not not rereading. I hope you are working and this letter reaches you wherever you are. I suppose Spaine is you nesxt stop if Portugal proves impossible for any longer. You ask me about money and I know you have any money very much but perhaps you could pay the doctor in London. The episode in Tangier has nearly broken my heart but not know I am getting cold and forget when I can. I am not actually but I preffer to pretend it is something that the didn't happen. Please for God's sake don't send me any masages saying that Cherifa is waiting for my return or expecting. I will only go back if you go back because the government has changed. Libby is still expecting to have a production in the near future so do not go too farway. I cannot write you too much because it brings the whole tangier horror back and I am utterly lost here in America and without you. Portugal was a ball compared to this, but people have been wonderful to me and Dian is coming to live with me a sublet apartment. I cannot live with Libby and she will explain that to [you] herself. She has been sweet and making great efforts collectin the Jane Bowles fund, which I started telling you about eartlier in in the letter. Please Paul wrok or you might as well be here in an offict which I never want you to be. Katherine has just arrived and she will mail this letter toninght so I must finish it before we sit down to dinner. She promises to explain what is happening because I am incabable of explaing it except that I will live in an aportment with Dyan for the nexet few month untill I say what will do next. Perhaps Mexico will be the answer but I must have somewhere to live now since Tenessee will be returning soon. I think that I I will make it somehow and above all for you do your work and don't go too Japan because you will be hearing from Liby soon. I hope you can read enough of this to understand and don't let it frighten you. There is no time for corections. It is like being naked and I hate it. I feel better then I did when I hit the "lows" as Libby calls them. My blood pressure was down today and I lost or rather gained five pouns. The readin is the saame. I hate to send you a letter like the is but it is better then a—nothing isn't it. But I was very sad and couldn't. Please wright me above all—and the less about Tangier the better unless the morrocon Government wants to make you president. I will write again and so will Katharine. Please pay money i owe in England. The rest is being taken care by friends— Katharine will explane.

Much Love—as ever—

J.

70

Jane Bowles to Paul Bowles
New York City
[Late May/early June, 1958]

Dear Paul,

I personaly—Jane Bowles I mean—cannot write you today. It is imposible. There is no point untill you do come over if and when you do and you are once more joined together with your clothes. It is a time for me when silence is the best for both. I am thinking of going to a place where they correct speach (therefore reading) a type of therapy that is new and has had good resolts supposedly. I consulted a nuroligist to see if there was anything I could do with this terrifying life of mine and he said speache therapy. (i.e. reading) They go together and it is better to work at something anyway even if it turns out to be of no avail. They don't us this in england I suppose because they are as usual far behing America in sience— at any rate. This doctor said that just reading and writing by myself of course could take a much longer time. He did not want to put a time limit on this anymore than the english did, but they are all quite aware of it here) . . what I have is called efasia. I cannot spell but that is what they say. I do not put much home in it but I must try anyway if I have the courage and if I think it will do me any good and if I can get the money. Naturally there is no limited time as usual but I suppose I could tell whether it was having any results or not. I will know more when I have been to the speeche center at Lenox Hill Hospital in a week and have consulted with the therapict there. I will know what it costs and if I can get any money for it which I am very worried about. I am not sure in fact I am pretty sure damned sure theat Libby doesn't want to spend any more on me—atleast that she can't afford two for the moment while she is gurding he loins for Yerma. It will take a pretty sumn and know of it tax deductuble. Aft about reading just by myself this doctor who is the head of lenox Hill said that I would need help. I am determined to get it if I feel it realy help me because I cannot go on this way—just sitting. I simply cannot. Please please don't think that I mean that you should pay for this I don't. I know you couldn't afford it. It won't be any fun I know but anything to hasten this waiting if it is at all possible. I am desperate because I am know fascing heavy time in a way that I didn't even when we were together in Portugal. It is not possible that it got worse. But it dead. My health is alright. I did not want to write you because I didn't want you to think me miserable but I am sure you are used to that. This seems to me the darkest time but perhaps something will break and I will be cleare cleare like I was in the air going to America. I love being in the sky and I did love being as close to the ground as possible. I loved Tangier very much. More than I knew even with all that talking but it is my sight my friedem that I want again.

It is terrible to have to be taken care of. I cannot get around her at all. But I did go out in Tangier. I went out to market and came back and spent nightss sleeping alone and not being afraid. Dione of course has to go out a lot and I have seen a few friends. John has diligently taken me out on the average of once a week. I have the same horror of stirring that I did have in Portugal, but I have to stir now and then to go to the doctors. Once night Sally[60] and a friend of hers took me to a dyke night club, It was like going there after I died. A girl started talking to me and wanted only to talk about north africa. She was an econimest and believe in evolution as the for the trouble between arab and french, inevitable evolution, if I had met her in Morocco I would have decided that she was a communist but here it is differant. She hated your book more than any book she ever read, (Sheltering sky) so I felt very flatered and famous. Please don't feel gulilty which I know is your way about any present mess I was in before or am in now was entirey of my own making and not yours. I am heart broken about my life with c. but it is not that nearly so musch as the preasant which frightens me. I shall write you more about that but it is not important. I simply want to send her some word that I am not coming back so that she can plan accordingly. I cannot send her money either. [*portion missing?*] but to keep going to the bank untill it is all used up. The only other suggestion I have is that you send her the equivalent of one thousand pesetas a month and that she keep goint to the bank to untill the end of her life. I don't ask you to do this because we have so little money and if you are going possible to live in Mexico and I too in the end it will mean a great deal of defferand to us. Yes one can still live in Mexico and there is a small town even not far from Mexico city, but lower down. a friend of ours told me that we could live for nearly nothing. I suddenly remember that I did not tell the doctor that I could nor

60 Pseudonym.

read—he tested me on writing. Naybe they were right in england. I will see what they say in the speach centar. Please Paul forgive this letter I am doing the best I can and it is very deppressing not to know the words much better know than I did when I was in Tangier. I must stop now and I am hoping to see you above all. Please make up something for my mother, based on this . She is fine.[61] Julian wants to go on eith the farse at least untill she is stronger then I'll probably have to see he. I don't know. Like yourself Julian says that one must not try to think more than a day ahead. I can't go on. I am suddenly so deppressed by the fact that I forget to mention to the doctor that I could write to a certain extant but not read that I am appaled. I can only hope the speach threapist who deals with all of those things will understand whether or not this has any bearing on the matter, or if is not more hopeless if one cannot read and less possible to cure.

I must stop this and enclose mothers letter. Despite the confusian. I know you hate not to hear at all. I am elive. Maybe in Mexico where people didn't read and write anyway—but that was only possible in Morroco. The Indian life is impossible for me and there would be no cherifas but it would be better than hear. I havn't much hope for this therapy but I must try it if it seems at all likely. I will know in a few days. Give my love to Maurice.

much love, as ever

Jane.

Jane

Dear Paul, I just saw Libby who expects to come over here in a few weeks. It is very important and you will live at Libbys with Ross Evans and Libbys nephue. She said that she was all for the retraining in reading and writing and that Doctor Eran Belle [Aaron Bell] who is the doctor I spoke to was recomended by Resnick as the best doctor in the country. (Unockn to me) Dyonnes friend actually recomented him but Dyone checked with Libby who check with Resnec. I hope there is really hope in this, because I cannot possibly go on this way forever or or for years. I don't know how you'll get over here or if there will be time before Mourice gets your stuff but it seems very important to Libby whom I know

---

[61] Jane's mother was recovering from a cancer operation.

214

has a New york production in mind after she tries the play out and sees what she has in Denver firtst. She has just now got the theatre in Denver. I hope to God you havn't gone somewhere else. Meanwhile right one more letter to my mother and I will have to spill the beans too her when you are both in the same country. Please don't worry about that. It will be very hard but I will have to. Meanwhile just keep writing.

Love

Jane

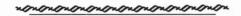

From *Out in the World*
(Andrew's story)

. . . he was walking along the road to his grandmother's house. It was in the summertime and he had not been to visit his grandmother for a year. The stone wall at his left was high enough to prevent his seeing over it. It was warm near the wall and the air was still, though across the road a cool wind was making the grass wave. He would reach out frequently as he always had to touch the warm stone. He was barely conscious of his surroundings when he reached for the wall and felt the wind blowing through his fingers. Automatically he turned and looked at his hand. There was a breach in the wall. He could see fields and blossoming orchards that he had never known existed. In the distance there were cows standing in the pastures and blue oats curving in the breeze. Some of the cows were in the shadows and others flamed red in the sun. The fields of oats and the pasture land too flashed in brightness and then darkened as he watched. Only the blossoms close to him remained brightly in the light of the sun. He stood still: The breach had not existed the year before.

Jane was admitted to the psychiatric clinic of New York Hospital–Cornell Medical Center in White Plains on October 1, 1958. By mid-December her condition had improved sufficiently for her to return to Tangier with Paul. There she moved back into her apartment with Cherifa. She was also attended by a companion, Angèle, and a cook, Aicha.

71[62]

Jane Bowles to Libby Holman
[Tangier, Morocco]
[1960]

Dearest Libby:

I am very sad not to have written you. It is too much of a task evaluating the whole situation and then writing what is important and what isn't. I can write down all my worries, and there are roughly about eleven major ones, including a very faint worry— not a worry actually, but an *awareness* that this is after all earthquake country, although we are not on the Agadir fault. That was such a nightmare. The reports on Agadir came here daily, and to top it off we had a tremor here. The people were so hysterical that they slept in the bullring all night. The Jews especially. I didn't know about it until the next morning. It is not fair to mention only the other worries since that one obsessed me for a good two months. Anyway, most of them will hold until I see you. But when will I see you? You write as if Paul and I were likely to go back to America together, or as if he would go back at all. He announced last night that he would have to see his parents eventually (I suppose within the next five years), which surprised me. So perhaps he will go back. I did not think that he would ever set foot in the United States unless it was to work. There don't seem to be any jobs for him any more now that he has so cut himself off from the market place in New York. He is more and more forgotten (even by Tennessee) unless it is simply that incidental music is too

---

[62] This letter, written after Jane's stroke, is taken from published material, not from the original, and therefore does not show Jane's spelling errors or idiosyncratic punctuation. (See editor's introduction.)

expensive and hardly worth importing someone to the States for, because of the fare. He would probably get more jobs if he lived in some accessible place, but naturally he wouldn't. And besides, his living expenses would be more, although they have trebled here in the last two and a half years. Many things are more expensive than they are in New York. Things have changed considerably, but I don't think there will be a revolution this year (according to my spies) and maybe not for many more years, depending on what happens in the rest of the world, naturally. I shall ask your permission not to mention politics. I don't like them any more.

The doctor does not want me to stay alone because of the danger that I might have a fit in the street or fall down and hit my head. I have a Spanish woman because she can keep accounts. My most solemn worry is about my work, and above all, do I really have any? Can I ever have any again? I will try to settle it this summer and next fall. (Within the next six or eight months.) For myself, anyway, because it has nothing to do with anyone else. Also there is nothing new except that I don't always know which is the stroke and which is the writer's block. I know some things have definitely to do with the stroke, and others I'm not sure of. The sheep festival is about to begin, in a month, and they are all buying their sheep now for the slaughter. I think that I will not be able to buy a sheep this year. They are too expensive for me, and Cherifa is having four teeth pulled, and later, a bridge made.

I have trouble with names, numbers, and above all the ability to add and subtract. I know perfectly well the general outlines. Two hundred dollars is less than three hundred dollars, and ten plus ten equals twenty, but the complicated divisions and subtractions and additions—! Adding more than two figures is impossible for me. That can be relearned, but I really need someone with me in this country, or they would all cheat me because I could not correct their own sums which are *always wrong*. So Angèle does that. I suppose that is the least of my worries, but I'm sure that none of this is psychosomatic, because I have no mental block about numbers, and they are worse than the rest. I don't think it would take more than six months to relearn the whole multiplication table. It is very funny but not bad, because I know what I need to know, and then can have someone else do the work. Some women are bad at computing even without strokes, and they are not as charming as I am. Don't ask Dr. Resnick anything. He might have discouraging news, and above all I must for once in my life keep my hopes up. Paul says that he spoke to the doctors and they said that nobody knew how much one could improve or how long it would take. The doctor in New York who sent me to that ghastly young man at Lenox Hill—I forget his name—said the hemianopsia was permanent, but not the aphasia, which has proved to be correct. I now know the meaning of all words. They register again on my brain, but I am slow because there is a tiny paralyzed spot in each eye which I apparently have to circumvent when I'm reading. One side is very bad, worse than the other, but on the whole I'm getting much more used to it. Don't say anything to Resnick because he can't possibly predict anything, and anyway he is apt to be frank, and maybe he would say something depressing. Undoubtedly. I have an awful feeling that I've written this whole thing before. I will send the blood pressure readings and ask if there are any new drugs besides serpasil. My own doctor is pleased with me.

Libby, there is so much talk about myself in this letter that I think I must stop. I have left half the things out that I wanted to tell you about. At least there are no politics in this one. I was fairly poetic in the old days.

Much love,

J.

72

Jane Bowles to Libby Holman
[Tangier, Morocco]
[November 15, 1960]

Darling Libby,

I was just writing my third draft of a letter to you that has been in my mind for weeks. First of all there was my original draft which I did not quite approve of because in it I announced that I could no longer write because I simply had to see you and it made me sad to write because there were too many things we could say in a few minutes that could never be said on paper. I went on and on in this draft of a letter trying to explain everything and finally nothing satisfied me so I kept tearing up draft after draft of this letter which was supposed to be a thorough report on the progress of my rehabilitation, on my efforts to write again and on the state of Morrocco in general, and of Cherifas family in particular (nin children) above all I wanted to tell you about the struggles of trying to work again because it concerns me the most and unless I can give the true picture I feel that my letter to you is a false letter. I suppose I will be content when I again reach that state of despair due only to my "neurosis" (lack of talent I think) which is familiar to me. I am working hard to achieve that state, but it means writing every day however badly. (I write so that my brain will make knew tracks and compensate for whatever damage was made by the stroke.) Numbers I will have to relearn completely as I have written you and I should I'm sure go ahead and do it right away because it is a good exercise for the brain and so I May enter school again, next semester. I have gained waight too much but I am watching it. I am much calmer with this layer of fat but I am in despair about my looks; Paul is frightened of my being thin and thinks I am ugly when I am.

Libby I was just writing the third draft of the letter to you when yours came for Paul and naturaly I was very thrilled that you might be coming and I did stop trying to write you because it seemed so much simpler to wait. I am now prepared for you to come but terrified that you won't. However if you don't I shall have to go there anyway unless my mother should decide to come over here instead. I don't think she would unless I urge her too which I naturally would not do. Please Libby you do believe me that I write these terrible dra[f]ts all the time. They are mixtures of ameteur neuroligical reports—political predictions and attempts at little portraits of the eleven members of Cherifas immediate familly. For a while they were all living on a taxi number because the taxi had collapsed completely but the number was still intact so the familly was living on that. The brotherinlaw (cherifas sister's husband) had rented the taxi number to some other man for two years. Then came the government order forbiding all taxi numbers to be rented out—in other words each taxi number had to have a genuine flesh and blood taxi to go with it. This saga goes on for a long time and it used to get me down as much as the neurological birds I view that I felt obliged to give you with each new draft no matter how I tried to keep it out of the letter. I am reading much better Libby but I think I won't go on about this unless you are not coming over in which case I shall this year come over there. I hope to God you are coming because I can't wait and please let me know definnitely (can one ever be deffinite these days) if you are coming, Ahmed said he had a letter from you saying you were coming—a more recent one than Pauls.

I cut off the part of this letter because it got too messy and put it in the trash basket with other drafts for letters that I'd written you this month.

Libby thank you for the little owles. Was it my copy of Catcher in the Rey Rie? Rye?, or was it your copy and my owl picture. Do you remmember the long tale of the elf owles? Did you send it to me because you did remember or because you thought they were so adorable. I was so happy to see them again. I always talk about them and describe them to people and now I can show them to people which is much better than going on about them.

Wouldn't you like to have some? I hope that your husband [Louis Schanker] likes them. Have I ever met him? Congratualations. I am not going to correct this letter because it takes too long. Please write me again and let me know how your plans are proggressing for the trip here. Are you going to England or to Italy. Please forgive me for not answering your letter and I hope you understand. I have been very upset thinking about it this week—but when you read this one you will realize how difficult it is for me to express anything at all complicated without messing the paper up and making lots of drafts. I have made three for this one since yester-day and I am going to send it now. If you don't come I shall have to wait and see you in the spring or summer. Please give my love to Rose and forgive this awful mess of a letter. It is unintelligable with all these corrections. I will talk to you personally when I see you anyway. Maybe it is intelligable an unintressting which is worse but don't tell me about it.

I shall send this now because Old man Beden has just arrived. She lives in the apartment next door and wears little collars and ties. She is about seventy and has changed her friend for a new one, this year.

I shall reread only this last bit and then send this on no matter how bad it is.

all my love, always

Jane

220

73

Jane Bowles to Libby Holman
[Tangier, Morocco]
[April 16, 1961]

Dearest Libby,

This will be my last attempt at writing what I consider an impossible letter. It seems inordinately difficult to me and yet it shouldn't be.

Six months ago or even farther back Gordon Sager came through here on his way to Greece with a Merril Grant for three thousand dollars on which he was going to live for a while and write a book. He told me that John Meyers had suggested to him that I apply for the same kind of grant and he came here delighted with such news but I *wasn't*. It created a terrible promblem in my mind. I couldn't possibly apply for it and risk your hearing about it from the grape vine and I couldn't tell you I wanted more money without saying I needed more money which sounded awful. Things have doubled and trippled since our original estimate of what I needed and so we are always just on the edge of being short. Naturally Paul pays up the differance but I do think that insofar as I can help by getting this grant I *should* apply for it, and I wrote to them last week. I hope something will come of it. Because I got into one of my magillas over what in hell to write you, Paul who thought I was crazy said that maybe he would apply for it instead but Gordon thought he was too successful. Of course Paul *is* very well known without making much money or barely enough and so he gets the worst of both worlds. I suppose I get the best, as a kind of failure, and can therefore apply for a grant. The money can be used for anything as long as long as you are sincerely intending to work on something. Gordon describes it as a kind of "reward." He used his to visit his father in St. Louis, part of it in any case. But he did finish his book and he lived on it while he was finishing it. If I get it I shall add to the three hundred a little each month and maybe spread it out over a period of several years or months. I don't know what it would come to, in francs, or I might finance a trip to America for a physical check up and seeing my mother which I *must do*. Naturally I would see you too as I don't really think I could ever get you over here. Anyway I have decided to apply and probably I won't get it after all this in which case I shall go on as I am and thank God for what you give me because without that we couldn't make it at all. Naturally it is always nice to have more and I think Paul considers me crazy not to have applied for it before this; I know that it is right that I should pick up as much money as I can whenever I can to take some of the onus off of you and Paul. I am glad to have writen this letter because it seemed impossible to write and I hope the grant still exists I have taken so long to get around to asking for it.

I hope that I am able to write another play as I think a novel at this point would be impossible. My vocabulary is getting richer each day and I am remembering more and more words as I am able to read more but I think a novel would be a gargantuan task. Soon I should be back to my normal rate of one novel every eighteen month—but not for a while yet. Libby I know you won't get here somehow but Lilla Von Saher[63] *will*! Do you remember her. The woman Tennessee called a big fat cow. She came to visit me in the nut house when I was there. By the way I hope I am not known as a "muschugana" now—*if I am* keep it away from me. I have become sensitive about it—like the others of course.

Mary Jane Ward made a fortune out of her experience (the snake pit, it was), but all I can remember about mine are the menues. Nothing has changed much. Like my play, but the food was differant. Potatoes instead of rice, and not enough cranbery sauce on Thanks Giving. I can joke about it now a little. I will be coming back but I am going to try and get something done first. John advised me to get something done or part of something at least before I returned and I aggree with him. I think it is going to be calm here—comparatively—at least it is expected to be a quit spell. Rumors and threats of revolution have been the atmosphere for too long now and I think it will be alright for a little while (famous last words)—but I am determined to ignore it if I can, even if there are more rumors. David is still here and Jay, but many people have left. Rose was telling me about Mexico and how cheap it was a few years ago (Cuerna Vaca). Is it? (In case we did eventually have to move somewhere else?) I have heard otherwise from some people who left here to live down there. I shall mail this before I get into another GonzaMagella. This one is called the "application for the

[63] A Hungarian ex-movie starlet who had attached herself to Tennessee.

Grant." I have about four more of them coming (letters like this but on other subjects). I shall also write a plain letter soon. I think of you and wonder about your friend in the glass house.

Much love,

Jane

74

Jane Bowles to Lilla Von Saher
[Tangier, Morocco]
[1961]

Dearest Lilla

Just a note to tell you that your letters are here waiting for Paul and perhaps by the time you get this letter he will already be back writing you. He was coming back two days ago but then wired that he decided to stay on a little longer but surely not very long because neither he nor christopher have much money with them. Otherwise he would not be back for a long time — who knows. He has rented half a little house in Marrachesh — in the medina — just like a play house not a serious house — where they can go down and spend a few days or weeks paying less than if they always went to a hotel. Even though they go to very cheap hotels — or they did but now the only descent cheap one that they liked is closed or too noisy. Forget. Anyway your letters are here and he is sure to be back within a week or even less. I am afraid if I forward them they will get lost forever because he would be back here meanwhile or have gone somewhere else enroute before he came back. Be patient and you will here soon.

Much love, when will I see you

Jane

75

Jane Bowles to Libby Holman
[Tangier, Morocco]
[April 26, 1962]

Darling Libby,

I am sorry I have not written you and even sorrier that you did not come when I thought you were going to come. I was very dissappointed, naturally and so I did not even write to you.

I am coming over to see you—if you don't come here. My mother offered to come and see me if I did not feel up to coming over but I did say to her that I would make the trip if you didn't come here because I do want to see you and so I am coming but I don't know when. Paul is going to see his parents in Florida and so we will make the trip together coming and going.

I will have to spend half the time at least with my mother in New York but Paul will want to spend some time with his parents in Florida and also in New York or Wherever you are if you can put him up. We both want to do that—stay where you are most of all and so please write us when you will be *there* and when you would like us to come—between *now* and October. At least tell us if you are leaving for Europe at any point because we don't want to come then. Paul does not want to stay in a hotel at any point naturally because it is so expensive and even if you will lend him your apartment as you have done before we both want to come to America when you are there and free to see us. This should be a simple letter but I find it very difficult to write.

Since my operation I have a crooked stomach and I am thinking of having it made straight with an operation before I come. Do you think I should. I have a fat stomach on one side because my plastic plaque didn't come fare enough around, it was put on orriginally because of a hernia. I think it's the surgeon's fault and so I should be able to get it done for almost nothing, but who knows. I don't know what to do because a woman of depth should not think about her stomach after fourty-five. Do you agree with that. Please Libby darling tell us when to plan our trip unless it makes no defferance. At least write if there is any really *bad* time. Pasage is almost impossible both ways but we can't even start trying to get it untill we hear from you so do write a note quickly. We may have to come after the summer people have returned to america or before they start coming here.

Much love as ever,

J.

76

Jane Bowles to Libby Holman
[Tangier, Morocco]
[August, 1962]

Darling Libby

I am almost too tired to write this letter but I must because I will not have time to hear from you if I don't.

I had a third operation three weeks ago and I have been too tired to write. Then I did a lot of shopping for a ball because I haven't done any in many years. I am too tired to give you the details. It was the Hernia again which he fixed up with a larger nylon plaque—and God knows whether or not it will come apart again this time. At any rate my stomach is a sight when I'm undressed so I am not going to undress. It really needs plastic surgery at this point but naturally I am not writing you about that but to make plans.

Paul wrote you but I don't think he was very explicit about our plans. I would have written but there was this operation which of course my mother *doesn't know about—again*.

Libby, as Paul probably told you, we are leaving around the six of September so I suppose we should be there around the twelfth. I can go straight to my mother's with Paul the first night if you like, and then go up to your house with Paul if you would like us to. I think Julian, my step-father, could take us to Greenwich or near Greenwich in his car if you are there and if it is a good time for you.

Paul would like to come to you as soon as possible after arriving in New York and then later go down to Florida to his mother's, at which point I would spend my time with my mother. We will

225

have to find our own ways of getting back and forth at this period if you want us to visit you then. That can be worked out later. I don't know where you are and I realize it's much harder to commute from West Hampton where I imagine you are now than it would be from Greenwich. All this is pointless until I know whether you are anywhere at all where we can visit you, beginning I don't know what date—but the Independence leaves from Algeciras on the six which Rose can figure out for you herself.

If we can come straight to you, should we spend the night in my mother's hotel and then get out to where you are or not? Mother is agreeable to anything. Please write, she—or at least someone in the family—has a car as I understand—but we can manage anyway. Just let me know where you'll be and the telephone number and if you can have us.

Much love,

J.

77

Jane Bowles to Libby Holman
[Tangier, Morocco]
[August 13, 1962]

Darling Libby

this should probably be a letter to Rose, a note rather because it is a businness letter. That is the sort of word I cannot spell since my stroke. And others of course that I am not aware of. I hope that you have *not* told Polly to hold my money in New York, untill I get home. I naturally will need it here to pay bills that can't be settled before I leave and which I will have to pay by post dated check before I get onto the boat. Your check does not get here until the fourth sometimes or even the fifth and I don't want a mess after I leave, on the 3rd or forth—for Gib.

So unless you have said anything to Polly which I doubt on your own huck (hook?) (another word which I know must be wrong) don't say anything at all or tell him to leave things as they are. I think you had better wire me if the money isn't going to come here for next month (September) but I hope you can fix it up if it isn't. I hate to leave debts behind me naturally—anyway enough of this.

Let Rose handle it and give her my love. I hope I hear from you in answer to my last letter. Judging from mothers last letter I don't think she does have a car but but I'm not absolutely sure.

Love, as ever

Jane

78

Jane Bowles to Libby Holman
[Tangier, Morocco]
[November/December, 1962]

Libby dear,

I am sending some presents back with Charles Gallagher the friend I love best in Tangier. Apparently you have met and so I don't have to introduce or explain. He is an expert on Morrocco but also laughs and jokes. He was an expert on Japan (oriental cultures) when you first met but this may have slipped your sieve-like mind, which is like my own. Everyday Charles tells me what he's doing here and I read all his resumes and articles but sometimes I forget anyway. Now he he is going to deliver a series of lectures at Universities all over the country and he will be in New York for a month before he begins. He is also going to some kind of convention held by college proffessors and "other experts." In any case I hope that you will find time to have a drink together, (his schedule is heavy too), so that he can deliver these gifts and give you news of myself and Paul. I have wondered about assigning the bags, and he suggests that I do. So the blue one (or peacock blue) is to go to Alice, the red to Jesse May and the brown to Betty. The little bright red wallet is for Rose Minor and the dark marroon wallet (man's size) is for George. If they are peeved with the colors I have assigned them tell them to settle it among themselves. I did not want to get them all alike naturally.

I am sorry to have taken so long about this. But I was not happy with the selection of gifts I found around the medina. They wanted

227

bags and they wanted them to be Morrocan, naturally, they wanted shoulder straps—but alas there are none with shoulder straps except some truly hedious cow hide bags with desert scenes and sheeted women tooled into the leather. I don't think they would have liked those do you?

These bags may be useless, the straps are too short except for dwarfs and I am sad about that. But they could put spools into them. Just a lot of odd spools and hang them up in their rooms. I mean each person could hang his bag on a nail, and look at it. It is too bad about the shoulder straps. The old arab who sold them said these straps were the fashion today. I love you and miss you very much and will write a letter to you and to Rose. Meanwhile dear Libby I wish that you would send me just a note to tell me how you are and give them all a kiss for me. I was very happy with them there and want to come back. Thank Betty and Alice and Jesse and George for making my stay so pleasant and tell them I miss them and will come back.

always,

Jane

79

Jane Bowles to Rena Bowles
[Tangier, Morocco]
[December?, 1962]

Dear Mother B.

I wanted to get this letter to you by Xmas but now I suppose I'll be lucky if I reach you by the New Year. As you know I'm terribly lazy about writing and added to that I have this trouble with spelling since the stroke, which means that I have to get hold of someone if a word looks wrong to me. It is very annoying but need not stop me from writing a play or a book. That is simple laziness I suppose, though for several years I was unable even to read, all of which Paul must have written you about. I am so sorry about not being in the day you called me—or that I was going to call you or did I call you and get no answer? It is all so far away now that I can't remember what happened or even whether or not I haven't already written you on the same subject. If I have, forgive me. Paul had a spell of the Grippe and though he did not go to bed he was miserable and without any appetite, but now thank God he is well again. He's passed it on to me naturally which I did not mind because colds are not my particular weakness. I get over them quickly and they don't knock me out the way they do Paul. Arteries are my trouble, blood pressure etc. Two night ago we were up until one A.M. looking for the cat around the neighborhood of our apartment but she was nowhere and finally we started to bed very unhappily when we heard a far away meow . . . so we rushed onto the terrace where we had searched for her and called for her over and over again . . . and there she was hopping out of a huge arab pot inside of which she had been curled up the entire time. She finds all kinds of ways to torment us, and always has. She must be about sixteen years old and is kept alive by shots mostly because for years she has had bladder trouble. I wish you the best naturally for the New Year, and I'll try to write more often—

Love to you Both—

Jane

80

Jane Bowles to Ruth Fainlight[64]
[Tangier, Morocco]
[March/April, 1963]

Dearest Ruth

This is just to let you know that I think of you all the time and wonder whether or not you will come back. I gave the letter to Fatima's[65] husband, in fact I read it to him in Arabic and he was very pleased indeed. He was glad to have the picture she sent him and I told him she was sending more. You said this in your letter. I am glad to write about Fatima and her husband because I don't want to get onto myself. Things are going badly for me. My work

[64] British poet who had been living in Tangier with her husband, Alan Sillitoe, and their baby, David.

[65] Fatima was an Arab woman who had gone to London with the Sillitoes to work for them.

has come to a standstill although I tried again this morning to start off on a new tack (spelling?). I did not scrap everything I had written but typed up the first eighteen pages of which I showed Paul ten. Paul was pleased and said that it sounded like myself and not someone else but he would have liked to see more. I would like to see more myself but I seem to have come to a dead end. I liked this letter best [when] I was writing about Fatima and her husband. Anyway I seem to get more and more discouraged and therefore it is difficult for me to write. I am afraid to have many mispellings which I think I warned you about in the past. In case you have forgotten, most of them are due to the odd affects the stroke had on my spelling but not all of them. There is no doubt that I spell better than I did before. (five years ago) It really is high time I got back to Fatima and her husband. This letter is going very badly.

About Fatima and her husband, I wish to tell you that Paul has forgotten how much money she gets a month but I haven't! She gets fifteen thousand francs a month and that is what I shall tell Paul to give Fatima's husband. As I remember He was to get fifteen thousand more at Sheep time but I am not as sure of this sum as I am of the other. Perhaps it was ten thousand! It is about time for the sheep money more or less so please write me what we're to give him.

Paul, whom I have just seen, told me that he was given money that was to be used each month for Fatima's husbands support but that no sheep had been mentioned. (He found a note on which everything was written out) Had you intended to send another check for that or is the sheep to come out of the check that Alan gave Paul for Fatima's husband. This is truly the kind of letter I love. The more I write it the better I love it. I hope you enjoy it as much as I do. Please study the wording of your reply so that I am sure to know exactly what to do about the sheep. The festival is still a month away but the longer Fatima's husband waits, the more expensive the sheep will get. He really should have bought it two years ago when it was a baby.

Ruth I miss you so very much I do not dare to think that you might possibly not return. By now Yvonne Gerofie [Gerofi] has probably told you about Noel [Noëlle Mitchell] and I imagine you are seeing her and Mira. Terrible about Noel but I hope that at least the cancer has not had time to spread, yet.

How strange it must seem to you—having Yvonne and Mira there. I have only David occasionaly, (spelling), and Ira Cohn and Isabelle [Gerofi] and every now and then as a great sexy treat—

Mrs. [Marguerite] McBey. I went to a fashion show at the Hotel Rif with Mrs. McBey and Veronica. One of the boys belonging to the cuban couple—Irving—loathes me. I have a feeling that I am going to be more and more hated as the years go by. I am thinking of leaving, but not yet. Please give my love to Tamara and Mira and Yvonne and of course Noel if you are allowed to see her. Is Sonia Orwell in London. Of course she is married to someone else now but I don't remember his name although I know him. Please write about the sheep. Tell me how you feel about London now, after your sad return because of your friend.[66] Are you still going out a lot—is Alan gone?

Write me please—Love

Jane

Yvonne's address: Cumberland Hotel
                     Marble Arch, London W1.

81

Jane Bowles to Ruth Fainlight
[Tangier, Morocco]
[May?, 1963]

Dearest Ruth

I haven't written anything in so long, that I am afraid that I will forget how to use the typewrite, if this keeps up. I have not read anything either. I haven't the energy to read since it's always a bit difficult for me because of the hemynopia trouble resulting from the stroke which you know about and which, although it is a thousand times improved, slows down my reading so much that I fall asleep with the light on. I managed to stay awake for one week reading a book called, "Plain Girl", a book for children with large print. It was about a little Amish girl who wore a little apron to school, in fact a complete Amish costume—very quaint—you must have seen pictures of the Amish in America. The Amish don't wear

---

[66] Sylvia Plath.

231

any buttons on their shoes nor do they ride in automobiles, nor do they use machinery of any kind. Their fields are plowed by hand. In rereading this I see that I say Buttons on their shoes. I seem to be more and more incapable of expressing anything. Anyway I managed to finish Plain GIRL after a week but after that I picked up a book called "Cybernetique et Société."! I bogged down after spending days on the preface which was purely tecnical and which required a working knowledge of physics. What is a working knowledge? On top of all this my bed seems to slant down instead of up which I would preffer and this too prevents me from reading anything because I am so exasperated all night. I wake up during the night and I realize that my bed is slanting down the very second I become conscious. I hope that some day this will all stop and that I will work a little because there is nothing else for me to do. I went to Sonia's [Kamalakar] yesterday and saw The Santscrit student who gave me news of the whole Lysergic acid set, headed of course by Sonia! I had not seen Sonia or anyone else (nor the Gerofies) for ten days because Libby Holman was here with her abstract Painter fisherman husband and she did not want to meet anyone nor go anywhere — so we stayed closeted for ten days. I did not write either letters or plays of course as you know. Her departure left me feeling sadder even than I had felt when she came and I am still trying to recover.

During the time that Libby was here I managed naturally to give Fatimas husband the money for the sheep and today he came for his monthly money which Paul gave him. He said he needed an extra five thousand francs which I gave him out of my own money although Paul refused to give him any because he wanted to follow Alan's instructions. Fatima's husband told me Fatima would give it back to me out of her salary. It is true that they always need more money for the children during the holidays and anyway he was very touching so I felt it was worth the risk though Paul thought you might dissaprove. I loved your letter. It was nice and fat and long and excuse me for writing you such a bad letter in return but it is better than no letter. I suppose that I shall go on excusing myself for my bad letters like a thirteen year old girl. There is to be a whole new invasion of beatnicks this summer coming to settle. Paul has taken a house in Arcila by the month — very expensive but worth it because he can no longer work at all in his studio. The woman above him hammers brass trays all night untill her croupier husband comes home from the casino at six, and the Yeshivabooka's who had moved into this building before

232

you left, start cooking at seven in the morning. The kitchen's wall is against his bed so he never gets any peace at all. I have not yet written Frances [name changed]. Please tell Fatima about her husband and write me *when* you return. Noël wrote that you had been busy every second since Alans' depparture—good. I wonder if you still want to return—or if you are only coming back because of Fatima! The GAZEBO has been rented and a bathroom added plus other improvements. Give my love to Noël and Mira if you see them and tell them I will write another note to them.

Much love Ruth—I still miss you terribly—

Jane

P.S. Love to David of course and Alan if he's back. We received 2 postal cards from him—It sounds to me as if you might be going *there instead* of coming here. I hope not—give Alan my love and thank him for sending *two* cards instead of one joint card.

82

Jane Bowles to Libby Holman
[Tangier, Morocco]
[May 27, 1963]

Darling Libby,

I have written and destroyed many letters since you left and now I cannot go on this way or you will think that I have forgotten you and that I was not happy with you and Louie. I was so happy with both of you that I have not yet recovered. I was so bereft after you left that it might have been better had Louie been a little mean while he was here. I was very happy with both of you, and give him my love. This letter is for him to. Jay raved about how you looked and he thought you had a new sweetness added to the way you looked which he attributes to Louie whom he loved. Louie is a favorite with Nancy and Sis [Eugenia Bankhead] as you know already but naturally you can see them in America if you want to. As for Alice I just refuse to mention her she gave me such pleasure. Please thank Rosie for her letter and tell her how happy I am that she liked the ashtray which troubled me so much, the decision troubled me in Tetuan.

I have bogged down really and not written you because so many complex and unintresting things have happened. They will bore you but I feel because of my german blood that I must give you a short but accurate account of what happened after you left. After you left the Tyznteshka [*Tizi 'n Tichka, the highest pass over the Grand Atlas*] Atlas mountains magilla complicated itself to such a degree that however much I try I don't think I *can* give you a german factual account of what happened. I don't know exactly at what point you left although I do think you were here when I would have had to add one hundred dollars to the rental of the car if they went by car, from here, at all. So then it was a question of going by train as far as Marrakesh and after that hiring a car. At that point I might have gone with Isabelle or not but suddenly Yvonne decided that she might leave with Isabelle and Isabelle's daughter herself which would have left no room for me in the car that was hired from Marrakesh onward. That meant that I would have to write Christopher Wynklin and propose that he drive his own car and me in a convey with the three women and a chauffeur, providing I payed for his gas and hotel rooms, food etc. As you know I think you do anyway, Paul by this time was out of the picture. This was complicated enough but Yvonne refused to decide whether or not she would go untill the last minute which need not have influenced me if I had wanted to write Christopher but it did because I knew I would feel worse if they *all* went and I didn't and I *might* have gone if Yvonne had gone because she is my favorite of the two. Yvonne did not want to decided anything untill the last minute, nor would she *sopple*. I think she was waiting for mail from Noel, actually, because she did not want to go across the Atlas with Isabelle if Noel wrote that she was going to sneak telephone calls to her from London, which Noel can't do while Isabelle is home because Isabelle refuses to have Noel's name mentioned in the house. Noel has her own room and could have sneaked calls to Yvonne when Mira, her friend, was asleep. I imagine all this was being decided by mail and meanwhile I was not writing Christopher, just soppling, without you or Louie to report to. Paul refused to discuss it at all. In fact he has gone away to Arcila which is another long letter. I got so weak, trying to decide about all this that I could barely drag around my room. I don't think I can really give you an accurate lifelize picture of all the differant elements in this Magilla. The proffesor who arrived suddenly and made it possible to further complicate things by offering to take Yvonne's place at the library [Gallimard Agency in Tangier]

234

whereas never before in thirty years has it ever been possible for Yvonne to leave on a trip with Isabelle. They have lived together for thirty years but actually Isabelle is really above Yvonne. I mean by this that she is her boss. No one else would employ Yvonne because although she keeps the books very well she is too gloomy and melancholic to wait on customers. There are many elements in this story and I must close now. The next letter will be another gonza Magella about Paul but I think this is enough about Isabelle and Yvonne. I wish you had seen them. I am so sad that you are gone.

Love darling always, and to Louie.

Jane

I have lost Gordon's address which you gave me.

83

Jane Bowles to Ruth Fainlight
[Tangier, Morocco]
[Summer, 1963]

Darling Ruth,

I am sad of course that you are not coming back but I can't say that I am in the least surprised. I expected it. By the time you had written me I knew anyway and dispite my dissapointment I think it is best for you. My life has turned into a veritable farce, schlepping between Arcila and Tangier as I do, and if I did not find it humorous I would weep.

Paul wrote Alan that he would be staying at Arcila and would therefore find it difficult to keep up his arrangment about the money from there, particularly as I myself go down all of the time and in fact plan to spend a solid block of time there at some future date. Naturally we come in here to get mail but to sincronyze (spelling?) all this with Fatima's husbands pay day might have become difficult since I would not trust anyone else to give him the money. Long ago I thought it a good idea to let the Librarie des Colonne handle it because Fatima's husband had ways of getting around me as you remember. You wrote me once that you thought he had a nerve asking for five thousand extra francs shortly after you had just given him the sheep money after I had given it too him because I am soft and I was sure the Gerofies would be more bisiness like. I took the five thousand out of the money Paul had for him, by the way, as soon as I received your letter. Now with Arcila it is better that you do arrange something more satisfactory for the man because in anycase I am not going to be here all of the time. In the spring I will go to America if not sooner. as I have just written so I would have to turn the man over to somebody else.

I have just had lunch with Yvonne and the two girls at their house except that nobody ate any lunch. Noel and I drank two litres of wine between us and even Yvonne had a little whisky. It seemed to me like some earlier time in my life, which was pleasant for a change. I turned up at Charles later with a lurching walk and slurred speach and he got rid of me as fast as he could.

But at any rate at this picnic where nobody had anything to eat at all either Noel or Yvonne told me that you had already arranged with the Gerofies to take over the money etc. I was surprised because there has been no answere from Alan to Paul's letter which he mailed him quite some time ago. I can't remember what Paul's letter said because the Arcila dance had already begun, and I never get anything straightened with Paul, nor do I remember anything that isn't written down. My mind is full of food that has to be taken to Arcilla because there is nothing there to eat at all except some tomatoes and some giant sized string beans and someimes fish is cought that Paul considers edible. Otherwise everything must be taken there in great baskets and burlap bags. You can imagine the lists that have to be made which is particularly difficult because Paul can never remember what there is left in the house when he comes here so that I am almost obliged to go there myself to see. It is easy enough to take the bus out there except that the seats have to be bought a day ahead (taxi or walk to the beach) so as to be sure to get on the bus (there are two good ones a day—early morning and five ocklock) but coming back of course is far worse because the bus starts at Larache and often comes through Arcila on its way to Tangier with no seats available at all. I such a case I just go back and spend another night in Arcila. It doesn't matter. There have been other events and complications and for that reason I have not written you but I still love you and will write you more next time. If you have arranged all with Yvonne all is well but please write me because we still have 10,000 francs of yours which we'll then turn over to her.

Much love to Alan — and to you —

Jane

84

Jane Bowles to Libby Holman
[Tangier, Morocco]
[Summer, 1963]

Darling Libby,

I wrote you an account of what had happened since you left, about the Atlas mountains trip and after that I did not write you.

You did not write me either. I am not complaining because it seems to me that I had promised to write a second letter all about the Arcila house and maybe you are still waiting.

Everything is so complicated here with Paul living there for the summer, but getting his food from here once a week that my life might better be shrouded in silence.

It exhausts me to explain how I managed this by mail almost as much as it does to live this way but I will give you a detailed account of the present routine as soon as I hear whether or not you are well or even alive. I have suddenly — well not so suddenly but bit by bit I am getting worried that all might not be well with you or the children or Loie. That is only because I have never been so long without hearing from you. Is it possible that you did not ever get my letter? Or are you still waiting for the second letter which I had intended to send. Any way Libby please write me and let me know if you did get my letter and if you and the children and Louie are allright.

I am likely to begin my ganza Magella about Arcila after that except that writing about it might make me cry. I'm supposed to laugh.

I had a letter from some young film producer who wanted the rights to my play. It would not be a Hollywood film naturally but one of those low budgeted New York films like—David and Liza. I don't know who the people are but Irma Herly [Hurley] does. She is a friend of theirs so if and when you go to New York try to find out something for me. But above all write me how you are immediately.

Love to both,

Jane

85

Jane Bowles to Isabelle Gerofi
[Tangier, Morocco]
[September, 1963]

Dearest Isabelle

I wanted to write you long before to tell you that Yvonne at least could count on me after eleven ocklock or eleven thirty if she wanted me to sleep with her. She said that she would call me if she felt she needed this but she never has yet.

Hélas I have sprained my finger and up intill now it has been too painfull to use.

Of course I have started this letter backward because at first I meant to ask you how you were and not tell you about something that is almost past now, since the whole point in mentioning my arragement at all with Yvonne was to stop your worrying in the Hospital.

I certainly hope that the opperation was not too painfull afterwards and I am waiting anxiously to hear all about it when you come.

Darling Isabelle my hand is still painfull and I cannot write a very long letter although I am going to have to write several necessary letters to other friends about my novel. Paul has gone away for awhile and so I have no one to help me.

I speak to Yvonne every day and she has been too busy to want anyone with her so far. At any rate my mother is leaving Monday. This is a kind of useless letter but I hope that Yvonne wrote you that she could have had me at night (!) if she wanted me that late. By some miracle Sherifa gave her kind permission.

I do hope that in spite of going to Belgium for an operation that you have had time for une petite détante. God knows. I think that Yvonne seems better when she works all the time, naturally. That is the system used in all sanatoriums where they treat nervous depressions.

Naturellement it cannot go too far. I am ready for a real lunatic asylum myself and tell Yvonne about it on the telephone every day.

I miss you and love you,

Jane

86

Jane Bowles to Libby Holman
[Arcila, Morocco]
[October 4, 1963]

Darling Libby,

I imagine I wrote you about Paul's flight to Arcila shortly after you left. I think I told you that I was going to write you about all the complications in my next letter, in fact I know I did, and because they were so great I never wrote at all. Anyway I lived between both places all summer long running the food department from Tangier for both towns. Sometimes I would take the food out with me and sometimes the food would go back with Paul when he returned there on Friday's. He always came in once a week and if I did not go back with him bodily I would order his food for the week or however long he was going to be there. It was so complex that I shuddered everytime I started to write it to you. I know that you would have felt for me while Louie laughed but it was too much to even write, in the end. In fact I neither wrote you, nor a play nor did I write Katharine—nobody. I felt I had to explain all this, naturally, plus give you an account of how we managed without a car, and how even fitting my leg into the bus was difficult. I used to tell you all about it before I went to sleep at night and somehow I couldn't type it all. Now the summer is over and I feel that I can write you and not mention it (ossir). I am spending the week in Arcila but the whole thing will be over on the fifteenth of October or before if it starts to Rain.

However, someday I must tell you all of it. The Ice Box (fridge) which Paul bought that was dumped here at Arcila in its crate, and which turned out to be an Ice Box that would only work in Europe, and the chickens that went back and forth on busses with me or Paul all summer long because even chickens are inedible in Arcila unless they are killed when they are still in their mothers egg. As you know I like tough chickens and grissle better than sissy tended food but Paul as you remember doesn't.

Then started the Tsuris about my play. If in case of a production I did not know whether to stay put here or to go and spend the little money I might have earned on an off-broadway production, travelling back and forth on the shrimp cocktail boat, second class, which costs a fortune because it serves shrimp cocktails at most meals. Actually I was thinking of going third class. I would be usefull at the theater to my self only because I have the right of Veto *if I am present* (accepting the cast chosen by the director or not). I don't want a disgrace in New York whether the play makes money or not. Of course if Milly [Mildred Dunnock] plays it I would love to see her once more before my death. I thought she was fantastic. All this was terribly difficult to decide from here and I sent my mother back from Tangier with a letter to Audrey explaining all my worries. My mother spent a month here and returned just about when Audrey herself came back to New York from her vacation. I was curious too about the director—Herbert Berghof, about whom I knew very little except bad things from someone who turned up here, called Alfred Chester, to whom Paul is not speaking any more because they had a fight. I don't know whether or not this Alfred Chester is qualified at all to talk about directors, but he must have had some grape-vine knowledge to say anything. Anyway I was having a fit and unnable to reach anybody because it was in the dead center of August. Alfred is a write—a critic—for the times and a novelist. His novel is wonderfull according to Paul (I mean short stories, because the novel is not finished) but that does not mean he knows much about directors. In fact later he told me I should not worry so much about his opinion. I went into a real kind of death rattle fandango over the whole thing bothering everyone in Arcila—where there was nobody except Paul and Cherifa and Alfred and then, in Tangier I would talk of nothing else.

At any rate that was the summer and since then Audrey has returned and my mother and Audrey and Oliver *and* Tennessee have all spoken together on the telephone. My mother reported all my fears plus posting the letter I sent to Audrey via her, from New York, so that now I am up to date more or less on my news. Audrey and Oliver say that Berghof is a wonderfull director but he is busy on another show at the moment, and so all that soppling about him was for nothing. Now of course I am soppling about not being able to have him. I should think that Mailand, the producer, would wait for him if he's that good.

240

He admires the play very much but I am not sure which version! Audrey and I went through that argument by mail months ago and I won't describe it to you. It was wourse than the buses and chickens. Libby, I saw Mike—we spoke of you a great deal and he was going to see you when he returned to New York. I was over-joyed naturally but know I have no word from you or him about how it worked out and if the meeting took place. As you remember you were seeing each other when I was there with you last fall. I am longing to see you again and I hope it will happen in the spring or in a year from now (next fall). Sis suggested that I go with her when she visits her child in November and I was sorely tempted. Naturally I don't even know what your xmas plans are and I doubt very much that I would come then anyway.

I don't *want* to go to Maryland now that Louisa is hooked by Tamara Geva. It's your fault because you didn't take me on turky day!

It would be good to know what your plans are though, from now on because I must see you in the spring or fall unless I do go for some reason sooner. I have a bladder complaint that might drive me home sooner.

Audrey does not advise my being there for the play if it's done. Please give all my love to Alice and Rose and give my love to Louie whom I hope is well and you to. Please write

as ever—

Jane

87

Jane Bowles to Audrey Wood[67]
[Tangier, Morocco]
[March, 1964]

Dear Audrey,

I have written pages on how I felt about this lightning production and how sad I was that I did not have even the opportunity to decide whether or not I would exercise my right to be present for casting

[67] Jane's agent.

and vetoing any choices I did not agree with. Yes, I would like to have been there although I do remember either writing you or asking you personally whether or not it would be necessary to be in New York if the play was done off Broadway.

I think you wrote that it wouldn't be; in fact I'm certain you did—and I obviously decided to put off my decision until I absolutely had to make it. I did the same about the two[68] versions of the play—but when I came to a decision it was very firmly against the Ann Arbor version as you know. In this case I had decided in my mind that I would come to New York for my play and I would have had I known in time. I would have made another try with Libby to find the score with Gerald Cook—(a musician), and if that failed I would have found one of my many composer friends to choose some appropriate music, (in public domain.)

You don't mention any music in your letter and as far as I know the artistic director is in the West Indies. I know that he has done the sets—at least lent his name to them, but beyond that there seems to be no one in charge except Lyn, who is neither a set designer nor a musician.

Libby wrote me a brief letter enclosing the clipping about Summer House (accusing me of secrecy), and was so flabbergasted by Paul's answer, telling her of course that we knew nothing about the production, that she telephoned.

The last letter I received from you before the rehearsals started, was written on January 9. It said Berghof was still interested in directing and that you were very hopeful of getting a spring production. I heard nothing after that and would naturally like to know what on earth happened that made you either decide not to warn me or forget the matter completely (which I feel is very unlikely.)

Libby asked Paul if I wanted to stop the production and Paul said: no—naturally. Unfortunately I was not home at the time.

I am now miserable and want only to know what happened, from you, and also what chances you think the play will have ever again if this production is a complete fiasco.

It is very important for me to know this if you, have anything encouraging to say to me. It is important to me for work on another play—the real reason why I never wanted some off-Broadway production to cope with at this moment.

It was Paul who persuaded me to sign the contract in the

[68] There are, in fact, three versions of *In the Summer House.*

242

beginning but knowing myself, I never wanted to. I am particularly desperate about it's being done without Paul's music naturally, and am terrified that it's being done without any music.

I know that you must have done everything you could to make this production come about and that our interests are naturally the same but please write me what on earth happened and help me at a distance if you can, in case there is a fiasco. The play until now has had a good reputation: will it change that? Will a failure prevent its ever being tried again by a different group, with the music if we find it—or new music? The play was conceived with music and I would like to have written the director about this when the time came, or better still have seen him in New York—Anyway Audrey—I send you love as always—

Jane

88

Jane Bowles to Libby Holman
[Tangier, Morocco]
[Spring, 1964]

Darling Libby,

I thank you a million times for everything you have done for me. You have acted as if you were right here, as much as it was possible, and that is a deep consolation to me for the slipshod way in which the others have acted so far.

What do you think it had to do with? Did Audrey misunderstand me? I think as I wrote you that I did ask her months ago if it was necessary for me to be there and she said no, absolutely not. I let it go at that, certain that she would in any case warn me in time, in case I did want to be there.

Obviously I would have come over if there was anything for me to do, but under the circumstances I would have been too late. It was already too late when I sent her the wire, although perhaps, if she had answered it, and I had known that the music wasn't necessarily lost, I could have come over with Paul's information in my teath like a dog and given it to you. She answered my wire by mail and by then it was too late.

On top of that a friend of mine seemed to be going off his rocker, and Paul and I were very occupied with that just during those terrible days when I was waiting for the answer from my wire to Audrey.

I wrote you a long letter first explaining why I had not written and then I wrote my mother and then I wrote Audrey. The letter to Audrey never seemed to end. I kept tearing it up and beginning again untill finally I wrote her a letter that was only two pages long, if that, and very much to the point. I had to reread these miserable letters and correct them so that in the end I strained my eyes which as you know are bad because of my limited field of vision. Of course I was under terrific tension and was writing more than I had in years. The result was eye strain and a stye which I have been treating with antibiotics. It is almost cleared up now but I haven't been able to write before this because I could not use my eyes at all.

Libby, stop worying about this. It seems a shame but "it was written." I never should have accepted the clause in my contract about Audrey supervising or any one else in the event of my absence. I remember Paul was all for my not going over, in case the play finally was produced. I never really did want to have it done off-Broadway—because I felt it was the kind of play that required a more than ordinarily good cast and I always wondred if the actors could be culled from the Actors Studio or any other acting school. It always seemed to me that there had to be at least one top rate actress in the cast and I am sure I am right. I daresay the younger people could be even better than they were on Broadway which wouldn't make them good! If you remember Lionel was played by a yenty.

I would have waited for Milly to be free if she had accepted to be in the play at all.

I was not sure of course when you wrote me about that some months ago what her actual position was going to be, nor were you. She was responsible for a little scene in my play which I can't imagine anyone else playing and I wanted to wait for her—it was written for her.

I am thoroughly depressed. They are forbidden to use any version except the Broadway version, as Audrey knows. We had enough correspondence about that last year.

I am glad you think that the play is in good hands. At this point it is up to the Gods. Thank you for sticking by me as always.

I love you,

Jane

Give my love to Louie.

Jane Bowles to Libby Holman
[Tangier, Morocco]
[June 18, 1964]

Dearest Libby,

Please forgive me for not answering your letter at once. You knew how I felt and I wanted to write you sooner so that you wouldn't worry too much.

I have not got your letter near me and I am rushing off to Gibraltar at nine this morning. I hope Louies exhibition is successful and that he is pleased with the results. I had hoped to be there for it, but now I don't think I will be unless I take a flying leap.

Naturally I felt very badly about the play but it seemg to be a very great success with some bright people—such as you and the critic on the Village Voice and others (the Post) but I will not write a long letter about all this until tomorrow or the next day when I return from Gib.

I am just writing this now to tell you that Charles Gallaghar is leaving for New York, next Monday, and will call you up at Tree Tops where he will at least get Rose if not you and try to arrange some appointment with her. He wants very much to see you. He has messages for you from me and questions and also wants to see you and Louie if it is possible. I am sure you will want to see him so please warn Rose that he is calling. I will write more as I said in a day or two.

Thankyou for everything. I don't know how I would have gone through the play Gonzamagilla without you. Kiss Louie.

All my love to both of you

Jane

Jane Bowles to Libby Holman
[Tangier, Morocco]
[June 23, 1964]

Dearest Libby,

There is too much to tell. I have been harassed by one thing and another and so deppressed and worried and frightened that I simply have not written. Each day I worry about this and I think about you and Louis and Louie's exhibition. Don't think I have not thought about it. I wanted to write but I didn't. Naturally paintings are not like plays and so fortunately they can go on selling long after the show closes. Plays of course can be revived ten years later (I'm sure mine won't), nor would it be the same cast which I never saw, even if it were revived which it won't be. Darling Libby you were wonderful to me while the play was going on and I have not been very attentive, but I've been in a bad way. Now I feel better. Paul got a movie offer (to sell The Sheltering sky), I didn't think it was very good (thirty thousand dollars and no percentage in the gross) but Paul seemed very pleased. I think he would have been delighted with two hundred dollars! I know that Albie got five hundred thousand for Virginia Woolf, and I thought Paul should be more carefull about selling his most valuable property. As you know he has no income and makes money on selling articals to Holiday, mostly, which take him so long to write that he can't get out more than two a year and he is paid very badly. Any way I was very worried and at that moment Lee Shubert came to Tangier with Ira Shuberts secretary [Lawrence Stewart], a youngish man who is a friend and business manager as well and who also eats sanwiches with Ira, at three in the morning. I don't think he is even Jewish. Lee said he was a brilliant business man and so he told Paul to ask for fifty thousand, stretched out over a period of ten years, so that the taxes would be less. All this was very complex and Paul had to send many wires to his agent who had advised immediate acceptance of the original offer. Meanwhile Lawrence was drafting a letter and wire for Paul asking for more money on this ten year basis which for some reason was to make the taxes less for both Paul and the man who wanted to buy the Sheltering Sky, I understood none of this but Lawrence, who ate the sandwich with

Ira, did understand it. Anyway it was not Lee Shubert but Ira and Lee *Gershwin*. It does not matter unless you know them. This seems to have nothing to do with my not writing you or anyone else but it does. Paul with Lawrence's help, after draftingthis very complex telegram which had in it something called a "built in contract," about how the money was to be spread out over a period of ten years and how Helen Strauss could nonetheless draw her agents fee at once if she wanted to, then waited for some answer. Lee Gershwin and Lawrence flew away to Paris and we waited. There was no answer from Helen Strauss for ten days and when a letter did come there was no mention at all of the film offer, only some refference to Larby's book[69] and some other business matter—taxes, I think, but certainly nothing about the film. I felt that by being too zealous and advising Paul to ask Lee and Lawrence what to do I had possibly spoiled Paul's chances of getting even thirty thousand dollars or whatever it would have been after tax deduction. Paul tried to console me but he couldn't and everything got worse as time went by and still no answer came. Paul was very sweet but he did say that he would have accepted the original offer immediately and knowing him I'm sure he would have. He never worries about his old age at all, puts whatever money he gets in a checking account anyway and saves money by taking two or three hours a week comparing cooky prices and choosing the cheapest. He eats a lot of cookies and I think that for him they are the only reality.

I thought it was very lucky that Lee and this brilliant secretary had arrived here just when we were trying to answer Helen's wire so I naturally advised Paul to put the decision in his lap.

Finally a letter came saying that Paul's agent had put through the original deal—without a mention of whether she had even tried to get more or follow any of Paul's suggestions. Naturally I was glad not to have to go on soppling even though I did not understand any of Helen Strauss'es motives nor did Paul—nor did we know whether she had ever tried to follow Pauls advice. Paul had written her that he was being advised by Ira Gershwin's business manager who knew just how someone called Irving Paul Lazar drew up all of his contracts. He is the best agent in Hollywood and maybe Yenty Strauss was vexed and wouldn't follow any advice coming from those circles. I really felt awful during all this and so sorry that I had opened my mouth at all.

At the moment Paul is waiting for the "less good contracts" to arrive which he will sign unless there is some new hitch! (oy)

[69] Larbi Layachi's *A Life Full of Holes*.

247

Now that I have explained all this nothing to you—I have neither time nor strength for anything interesting. Meanwhile give me news of Louies exhibition. If my agent had answered my wire in time or at all, I would have been there to see it. I have much more to write you and to ask you. Paul is not going to America as he thought he was—but nothing is certain. All that will have to come in my next letter.

Naturally he would not have written you about the film Gonza Magilla because he doesn't find it interesting and takes my soppling for granted. But I know he did write you about something.

Love always and kiss Louie,

Jane

Give my love to Rose and Alice.

91

Jane Bowles to Libby Holman
[Tangier, Morocco]
[June 30, 1964]

Dearest Libby

I said this letter would be in sections—each one more boring than the other but I feel that I have to tell you all these boring details or I don't believe that I have written a real true letter. I don't think that I used to be this way but of course I do get worse with the years. David would say, "tiresome." This section will be about my mother and Paul's job in Florida which no longer exists. I don't know whether or not he wrote you about it and so I won't go into the matter like I did about "the built in clause", in his contract, because I just can't tell you everything over again if he has written it to you. He was going to America to lecture for three months at a very good salary but in the end the "Board" decided against him—although the University wanted him very badly and were very distressed when the board did not approve the choice unanimously. It was a state university and a southern one at that, and so I can think of many reasons why the answer was finally negative. I shan't go into them all and neither one of us knows the

248

exact reason for the veto. It could have to do only with the kind of books he writes, which many southern Facists could easily not want their children to read. It could have to do with his long ago affiliations[70]—who knows. I think he is greatly relieved not to have to lecture although it would have paid eight thousand dollars which he regrets naturally. He should see his mother anyway and his father and now I suppose he'll shell out the money anyway, but when? I was planning to come over with him in December, the three months of lecturing was to begin in January, and I would have gone in December to Florida when he was going to see his family. Obviously I was going to arrange to see you before or after—I didn't know, or at three differant times—in case you too came down to Florida, but now all my plans are nebulous. I *must* see you—and I'm sorry I didn't come this spring when Eugenia left on the Constitution. I preffered going with Paul because he was going to come back here with me whereas Eugenia was staying in the states for a long time. Perhaps when she comes again this summer I can catch her going over again toward Christmas and by then Paul would be ready to come too! (Osser) I am really worried about this because knowing Paul he will put off seeing his parents as long as he possibly can and I shall have to nag him. I suppose there is no hope of you're coming over—or are you thinking of it?

Did I write you that the Village Voice gave my play a wonderfull notice—a rather long review which I have lost. Then the other day, this same reviewer was written up in Time as the best one going. Except for the fact that it isn't running and that few people had the time to see it, I feel encouraged by the critical success of my play in that paper and the Post. I still think I should have been warned by Audrey that it was going on and that my *wire* should have been answered by a *wire* from Audrey and not by a letter a week later when it was obviously too late. Lyn blames the postponement of both the broadway show and my own for the fact that we got only second stringers (except for the Post), to review the play on opening night—and I do think she is right because I know that the Tribune at least, would have given me a respectable review if not a rave. That was all the fault of changing dates she said, since both plays were postponed and opened finally on the same night. But that in turn was their fault for deciding too late

[70] Paul had been a member of the Communist Party for a short period in the Thirties.

on the change in director. If I had been there I *might* have seen immediately that this original director was wrong for my play—and I might have never agreed to have him, and the opening dates might have thus been differant. Naturally it might have been worse if I had been ther but I don't think that Audrey should have kept me away. This Berghof always sounded wrong to me, for my play, and everyone I spoke to coming through here after it was too late to change anything told me he would be the kiss of death. Anyway I suppose it should be considered water under the dam but maybe it is my only play and I can't stop feeling sad about it.

Audrey has written me that some young man would like to take an option on the play for one thousand five hundred dollars and later when and if produced he would give me the finall payment (another fifteen hundred). In other words he offers three thousand *or* a percentage in the gross (or net?). I have no idea which. She herself says that in her opinion I should take the money (the fifteen hundred) and run! She goes on to say that she is sorry that he has so little experiance and that she had been waiting to see whether or not my play was a hit off broadway before telling me about him. In other words now that it was a flop, she advised me to take the money and run. I was so depressed by this that I never answered her either way and now I am about to but I wanted to write to you first before I wrote anybody. Libby the things that have been depressing me really can't go in a letter—some have to do with my personal life—others with Paul's which I can't of course write about or I suppose even talk about and some with the situation here which I certainly can't write about, either. The only thing that seems safe are contracts so I guess I'd better stick to them. My book is going to be published in England—maybe Paul wrote you about that. I really didn't want it to be and refused a year ago. The publisher at that time agreed with me—and wrote that it would be deppressing for me if it got bad reviews. Now he's written again having heard around London that it was some sort of modern classic and he had reread it since last year and *wants* to publish it. I can't imagine whom he's seen. Anyway I shall certainly *mind* when the reviews come out.

Much love,

Jane

P.S. I hope you will write soon and give me news of yourself and Louie and the whole family.

250

92

Jane Bowles to Libby Holman
[Tangier, Morocco]
[August 8, 1964]

Dearest Libby,

I promised you three dull letters and so far have sent you only two. Now I don't remember what this third letter was supposed to be about. Perhaps the fact that my book (old novel—since there is no new one) was to be published in England. I will go on about that in a minute. I have not heard from you at all since I wrote these letters nor has Paul and I am beginning to wonder if some mail has gone astray. Naturally I left you for a long time with out mail but that was because of my worry with contracts for Paul's novel—the movie contracts. It was of no interest this long letter but I really couldn't write anything else untill I told you about everything. Now I think there are new things but of course not knowing whether or not you received my old news I hesitate to write this third dull letter. No word about Louie or his show yet and so now I feel cut off as you must have felt when Larry—Ira Gershwins sandwich secretary was here and I did not write.

I have a feeling that at the end of my second letter I told you that my book was going to be published in England next year. I am filled with apprehension and have been warned by the publisher that I must not pay any attention to the critics. Last year he had been shown my book by Alan Sil[lit]oe (The Lonelines of the Long Distance Runner) who read it here and liked it very much—and as a result of this Peter Owen asked Paul whether or not I wanted it published. He published one book of Paul's in England (Their Heads Are Green), but otherwise we did not know of him. His list however is distinguished and you would like him enough because he has had two nervous brakdowns and is not in the least a comercial type. I don't want to have my book published because again I shall be torn to bits by the press naturally and if it hadn't been for the publisher's insitance, and Paul's of course, I would not have concented to it. It is very odd, the fact that he is now so enthusiastic, because when he first read it he found it a very distinguished work I guess but he had not cared terribly when I refused to have it published. In fact he wrote Paul that he understood my feeling very well because there was nothing so deppressing for an author as a book that doesn't sell. Then almost a year later he wrote again that his wife and he had reread the book and he was even more enthusiastic about it than he had been the first time which he went on to say, had always been, for him at least, the final test of any work. He said too, that he had heard from various people around London that the book was a minor classic etc. and he did wish that I would allow it to be published. I don't understand his change of attitude but Paul says that I should have it done, and it is true that it would be nice to have copies of it again to give to a few friends. Maybe some people will like it those who are not enthusiasts of the "cut up" method.

Now I am so depressed about Gold Water and the whole negro civil rights scandal that I think to write of anything else is beside the point. Tennessee is here at the moment in his terrible hell because of Frankie and I see him although I don't feel it does much good. Libby, I will write you again.

Much love to all

Jane

P.S. I received Roses note—with you're change of telephone number. Otherwise I would think you were dead. I cut out the end of this letter because it was such a mess. I have now written three times and I really wonder how you are because there is no news.

If Polly calls you about my check—don't worry—it is now all straightened out at this end. For some reason it was sent to Casa. Is Louie all right? I feel something is wrong. I must close because I am in a rush. WRITE me.

93

Jane Bowles to Ruth Fainlight
[Tangier, Morocco]
[September, 1964]

Dearest Ruth,

Thank Alan for the quote he gave Peter Owen for the book jacket, and kiss the baby whose age I ignore. I go on missing you both too much. I have never really had it so good here in Tangier except much earlier when I was still in my thirties and I lived on the mountain and later in my own little house in the Casbah.

I am still brooding about a letter you sent me months ago in which you said you were looking around for a place to stay for awhile, (outside of England of course). I thought about this for a long time wondering whether or not you would try Tangier again, but the problems here were still fresh in my mind and I could not decide whether the problems were at that time worse or better or the same. I delayed writing for so long that I finally heard through Tamara that you had gone to Mallorca. I was very sad because I thought that maybe a letter from me might have influenced your decision.

As you probably remember, the stroke I had affected my my spelling rather badly though now it is much better than it was when you were here. I am still loath to write letters, partly because of that; half the time Paul is not available or I could just call out and ask him for the right spelling. He is spending this summer on the Mountain, (two doors away from the Gazabo) and very often I bring the food up there in a taxi. It is easier than last year when I used to take Chickens over to Arcila by bus or with friends who had cars.

Paul just came down with a letter from you (for him) in which you say that you look back on youre stay here with nostalgia. It is strange that the letter should have arrived just as I had written the above, about you and Mallorca. Would you consider coming to Tangier for awhile at any time—ever again? The problems *are* the same as I wrote a few minutes ago. It is of course getting more expensive all the time but I don't know how it compares with England. There is no point in my elaborating if you have no intention of coming ever again.

I am going to America in the spring—I suppose April. Last month David, who was driving up to London for Christmas, was trying to urge me to go with him and I was considering it because I wanted to see the oculist and Peter Owen if I could be of any help on my book, and you and Alan if you were there. I more or less decided against it because I could not picture myself staying anywhere (I know your set-up), and a hotel was not exactly a solution because I knew I could never get around by myself. Then David's cousin Caroline suggested her house as a solution for the whole three weeks which David plans to spend in London with his mother. She lives in North Wales.

She is very charming—mysterious, anti-social, melancholic and grave but responsive to wit. Having tried very hard to have a child she has adopted a son. If there is still enough reason for me to go to London I will go although now it would involve passage both ways on a boat, David having given up the idea of driving which would have been cheaper for me—I suppose. If I came I would certainly want to come to London to see you, to go to the oculist and to see Peter Owen if he thought it was important that I come to England. Paul just reminded me that he had suggested that I stay with him for the publication of my book but I should think that it would be more useful for me to go now (if useful at all.)

I don't expect to earn money on my book, but anything to forestall a bad reception, I mean one so bad that I will regret deciding to have it reprinted. I doubt that anything will help that except blurbs that will keep critics in check a little anyway. Thank God for Alan's.

I could go on forever about all this, the pros and cons of going or staying here but I fear that the letter will turn into a fifteen page ganze magilla of, "if's and but's" which I shall never send and then more months will go by and I will never write; but the letter could be used as a document for some doctor who specializes in states of anxiety.

The trip *will* be expensive for me in the end so please give me your opinion (you and Alan) if you have time on what good I could accomplish by coming to England in a couple of weeks.

I shall certainly write you again now that I've started but you may come to dread these tortured letters about tiny decisions. I am famous for them or I was when I was famous, with a few friends (most of whom are dead.)

I go to New York in April for a few months. That at least is decided and surely I could find an oculist there, don't you think?

Please write me, and tell me if there is any chance of your coming here in the near future.

Much love

Jane

94

Jane Bowles to Libby Holman
[Tangier, Morocco]
[November 26, 1964]

Dearest Libby,

At least I have stopped writing those terrible letters to England and I can now write you. Perhaps you did not know about the "letters to England?" I shall tell you very briefly in case you have heard from me about them, but I very much doubt it because I tired my eyes so much writing them, that I did not have time to write you although, you have been, as always, very much on my mind. I did get your last letter to me answering my question, "Is Louis alright?" and since then I don't think I have answered any questions of your's or written at all. My "English trip" was such a gonza Magella that I couldn't even write you and I don't know why I call it my English trip when I didn't even make it. I could still take it maybe but I'm almost certain not to since I have given up my passage on the boat.

David was going to England for Christmas and suggested that I *drive* up with him. My god now I'm sure I wrote you all of this but I can't remember, exactly so I'll go on. Anyway I then started writing letters, asking for advice to my one literary friend in England (Ruth Silitoe), to my publisher, to Sonia Orwell, to Mary Louise Aswell, to Cyril Connolly, asking them all whether or not I should go to England. My publisher had asked me last summer to try and be in London when the book came out, but I said I would hate that since I expected nothing but the worse from the critics and would rather hide out—here. He did not agree with that attitude and thought that my being on the scene might help. The matter was dropped and then David started with his "English trip." I had no place to stay of course nor anyone to stay with and so I was against it feeling that even if I managed the hotel by myself I would never manage getting around London. I had decided "No," but David who was adamant found a way. His Cousin Caroline invited me to stay with her at Veynal, a house she has in North Wales where I had already spent xmas once before when Paul and I motored with David to Paris and then to London. It was at the time of the "Sheltering Sky" (when it was first published I mean). All of this is neither here nor there but the decision was difficult to make, because I had always been terribly attracted to Caroline and was leery of making any decision on those grounds. I'll tell you why when I see you. Meanwhile the publisher was in New York so I could not ask him what he advised and so I wrote Ruth Sillitoe instead.

I told her that I could not make up my mind and asked her whether she thought it would be helpfull for me (as regarded the book) to go to London with David around xmas time instead of at the time of publication which was impossible for me or David. She answered that the publisher might give me a few parties which could *possibly* help the book along but that I would have to get that advice from him. I had given up my passage by then because although I had written her quite a while ago it took practically a month for her to answer without even considering the vageries of the post.

I then wrote Peter Owen directly feeling sure or almost sure that he must have come back from New York. That was another Gonza Magella letter asking for "Advice," even though my tiket had long since been given to someone else. I suppose I mean my *passage* on the Oriana not my ticket. The awful truth is that I am still wondering what to do and yesterday David said to me, "Maybe you could *still* get passage if you wire immediately to the Orient Line." Isn't it horrible? I could not go "just for fun," and then hope that in some way it might be usefull to the book, because it is not *in me* to have *fun*, in such ways, now that I can't drink very much, although I do drink a little Vodka now which I didn't do before or did I? Vodka or Scotch, but never very much. Not enough to make a trip bearable — and certainly not delightfull. You know how I hate them. That is why I have to justify spending the money and going to England on a wild goose chase. Obviously if I were longing to go I would not really feel any need to justify myself. I don't want to go and therefore I must find a justification for going so that I can then force myself — I don't know. The symptons for the past two months — which is about when "the English trip" started, are the same old symptoms. Remember the Atlas trip that I didn't make with Yvonne and Isabelle Gerofie? I think even Louie was in on that one. It was the topic at the pool a few years ago. I don't even remember the details of that one — but there was a trip and a decision. I finally went over the Atlas mountains a year or two later.

Anyway since I began this letter (three days ago) I had an answer from Peter Owen who is in London now — just back from New York, as I thought he would be, and he says, "I gather from your letter that you hate the idea of coming to London, and in that case It would certainly not be worth the expense to come especially for the book as it it is certainly difficult to predict whether personal appearences on television (oy!!) etc. can be arranged. I thought perhaps you might be coming to London anyway and that it would suit you . . ." etc. I won't quote more but that was certainly enough for me. I decided immediately not to go to London and I felt very relieved. But then bit by bit I felt less sure particularly as Paul for some reason seemed to be all for it, even though I am coming over in the spring to see you, mostly and because Paul has decided that he must go and see his mother. Surely I have written you about all of this some time ago—at the time of the play and the Audrey Wood Crisis. Naturally if I went to England now I would certainly not go for any special reason but to prove that I could do what other people do so lightly. Paul said he would treat me to the trip which is not as I said, too expensive. Please don't write me that you think I should have gone because by that time it will be too late and you will only make me unhappy. This letter is written to explain my late silence. The next will be about my plans and yours. But I could not write any think untill I told you about the trip I did not *take* (unless I take it). Give my love to Louie and the family at Treetops.

Always—

Jane

(Sorry this letter is so long and messy.)

95

Jane Bowles to Libby Holman
[Tangier, Morocco]
[Late January/early February, 1965]

Darling Libby,

I Think I should write this letter to you and Louie because I feel particularly bad about never having answered his telegramme. In the first place I went down to the post office twice and could not

257

get anywhere near the wiket, there was such a mob, naturally; We can't telephone telegrammes from here but must go into town at certain hours. Then the "rains" came and it was impossible to move anyway. Then my fat friend Sonia died just when our relations were at their worse and I felt so bad about that I almost took to my bed. Her daughter was on her way to spend xmas with her so she came for the funeral instead. The telegramme made Paul and me laugh very much and I wanted to answer him immediately but it just wasn't possible. Between the bottle necks at the post office and the deluge and Sonia's death a few days later the time had Passed for my answer, which was of course something to make him laugh. I forget it now. But Louie I *didn't* go, but I soppled for a month and a half after xmas anyway—naturally; *I should have gone.*

I will tell you all about it when I see you but now I am wondering if I will see you ever this year. Libby, I was very upset by your plans for the spring but very happy for you that you are going on tour again, which is wonderful for you and everyone who loves to hear you sing.

After Sonia's death, Ramadan came, and I did not sleep more than a few hours a night because I cannot sleep when others are up and about eating (cherifa and Eisha[71] and the little girl). Of course in the day when Cherifa did sleep (always untill three thirty in the afternoon), Eisha and I were awake as usual. I never can sleep later than nine and I'm almost always awake by eight no matter when I go to bed as you know. During Ramadan I would not get to sleep until six or seven in the morning. It was a wretched month and I did not have the strength to write to you and Louie and explain why I had not written. After those nerves then came my "book" (oy) which made me so nervous that I couldn't ask you all the questions I wanted to ask. Anyway I guess it hasn't done too badly (prestige at least). I will quote Peter Owen's letter in a minute and let you judge for yourself. I was afraid of an English "disgrace," but it was not like that at all. The Times I did not consider good at all except that he did not deny the value of the book he simply did not like it any more than he liked Ivy Compton Bernette [Burnett], which is an excellent way to be put down. The blurb's were excellent and to quote Peter Owen, "The book is getting a big press here and is being treated as an important book as it deserves."

Actually he was very dubious about the press before he published it because he did not think many of the reviewers were up to it, so I guess he must be pleased. Now enough about the book. It is

[71] Aicha, who worked for Jane.

good that I now have more coppies of it. I don't see any point in sending you one via Peter Owen (the publisher) because it would certainly be much quicker for you to send for it yourself. Actually the service between here and England is not so bad but it would take longer than you're sending for it directly *if* you wanted it.

I am very preoccupied now by your departure. I worry that you will be gone before I arrive. Paul plans to go now in the beginning of April. When exactly do I have to arrive to catch you before you go. Or how long do I have to stay in America to catch you on you're return. Please answer this as fast as possible. If you're going to spend many months in Europe then of course I might not be able to wait. My mother has just had pneumonia. I did not hear from her for weeks and was getting more and more worried, in fact just about to wire when my uncle wrote that she had burned her hand cooking goulash. I did not believe it and so wired back asking for the truth. He wired that she was recovering from pneumonia and would write soon. I have wired her that I would come if necessary by plane; if not, by the next boat which leaves in March, and if not as I had planned with Paul in the beginning of April. I am worried that if she has no one but her nearly blind husband to help her she might exhaust herself. I naturally suggested she take some kind of maid or helper until she was well. I don't know anything. Not even whether she's in the hospital or home. If she wires me to come I will naturally go but it wouldn't help my seeing you much, would it, if I were down in Miami on my mother's couch. There are only two rooms, of course, and it is nowhere near town. God knows what I'll do. My step father is too blind to cook or drive and has gotten blinder in the last few months, so I daresay he can't help at all. I am waiting for a wire but meanwhile please write immediately telling me how much longer you'll be in America and when you are coming back. My plans were before at least if Paul agreed to go to New Mexico from Florida and then to go to TreeTops or vica versa. But at least it would give us more time in America — even time to see you after your European tour, if that's the only way it's going to work now. Is there any chance of getting you and Louie over here again? I don't feel that there is. Anyway please wire me or rather write me your dates — departure for Europe and return. This after the English trip is just too much. I am deeply sorry now that I did not go for Thanksgiving. I will send this now with a heavy heart.

Kiss all the family there — and love —

Jane

259

Jane Bowles to Lawrence Stewart
[Tangier, Morocco]
[February, 1965]

Dear Lawrence:

We are planning to go to the U. S. in late March or early April, and there is a hope that we might go to New Mexico a little later, after we have visited our respective parents, who are all in Florida. We have friends in Santa Fe whom we want to see. One of these is Mary Lou Aswell, who published most of my stories in *Harper's Bazaar* many years ago when she was Literary Editor of that magazine. According to her, Truman is supposed to be arriving there in the Spring with most of Garden City. She and Truman are great friends, of course. I should love to see both of them, but who knows whether our dates will coincide. We won't be staying with Mary Lou, but with John Goodwin, another old friend. Tell Lee. Maybe she will come to Santa Fe while we are there.

We are both eager to have your opinion on Paul's new book [*Up Above the World*]. Are Lee and Ira going to be in California at any time in the spring, and do you think there would be any possibility of Paul's spending a few days with them and seeing the three of you? Probably you will be going around the world or something like that. Or maybe Lee will be in New York. In any case, please thank them for the Christmas telegram. I wanted to write them, but a friend of mine here in Tangier died just before Christmas, and I was so depressed I didn't get around to writing to anyone.

I really want you to see the new book, because I have a feeling it can be a great success, and I'd love to have your opinion and suggestions on how to handle it. Paul does not like to discuss it.

Please give my love to Lee and tell her the dress she gave me is David Herbert's favorite.

Love

Jane

[72] This letter was not typed by Jane.

97

Jane Bowles to Libby Holman
[Tangier, Morocco]
[February, 1965]

Dearest Libby,

This time I shall try to stick to the point, although I preffer the
ramblings off the main road, the alley ways, where Ugly Eisha eats
her soup and bread at five in the morning, just before the cannon
sounds, and the fast begins. Anyway those three or four weeks
during which time I could not write because I had no energy left,
have certainly ruined everything.

Had I known early enough which I would have, I suppose, had
I written you—I could have left in winter heavy seas or not. Now
what shall I do? Mother wired last night, or rather, Julian, that she
is better and out of the hospital and back home. I have written
urging them to take a maid or helper because of his blindness, so
that she does not have a relaps. The quickest boat that I can get
to see *you* before you leave, sails from Casa Blanca on February
twenty fifth landing the fourth of March in New York. Julian
advises I come in April to see Mother with Paul. Paul does not
want me arriving half cocked in New [York] with no one meeting
me and with nothing arranged. Paul wants to see you as well
naturally but of course it means something very special to me.
What shall I do. After the English trip this is really too much for me.

Certainly you and Louie can see the problem. I am waiting for
Paul to figure out a wire explaining all the facets but I don't think
he will. I'll name them by mail now. To begin with I don't know
that I can get a passage this late. I have to get to Casa of course
and start wiring at once from here, but supposing that I *did* get
it—a single—Then would I be with you for one day or three or not
at all anyway. I have no idea when in March you leave as I
explained in my last letter. Naturally Paul tries to travel with me
because we can share a cabin and can see me through mobs at the
boat in New York and I just hang on to him. Crowds confuse me
and though I can see perfectly well straight in front of me I don't
see on the sides and keep loosing sight of people at which Point
I can get Panicky—still I have all my pills which I'd clutch and
somehow I'm sure I'd get through. At any rate I'd preffer it [to] the
claustrofobic nightmare of a plane. God knows that would be

261

simpler (that is if you could meet me at the airport) but I suppose the best would be to see you after you came back from Europe if you weren't staying too long.

I think that I would have to stay after Paul went back to Tangier if you came back after June. I might have to get a first class cabin in order to be alone coming over now, at this late date—who knows. I suppose in *either* class I could try to arrange with the ships doctor to find someone to stay with me on the dock, untill I was met. I had intended staying with you at least ten days or two weeks to make it really count because much less would not be worth it do you think. I think since Louie is so good at making my plans he can decide the whole thing for me. Paul and I are both devastated by the new turn in events although delighted that you are going on tour for youre sake as I wrote you. He says he knows you would never come *here* on a european tour, and there is no point in my thinging in those terms. I mentioned to you a possibility of our going to New Mexico which would seem to me even more possible if you are not anywhere in sight—we could wait in New Mexico ten days at Johnnie Goodwyn's "maybe." We were going there for several reasons—one of them (the most important), to see someone whom you don't know on the coast about Paul's book. I suggested he get advice from him and *if* it worked out at Johny's for a weekend I could see Mary Lou and Paul could go to Hollywood for a week end. I could never explain what all this is about and finish this letter as well. All this would be just a by product of our being in America in order to see my mother and spend some time with you and Louie. Now there remains only the duty of seeing my mother, Natacha and Katherine of course—and other by products. We cannot possibly change our plans to come untill the fall because our families are expecting us and would be very dissapointed if we didn't come. None of them are well anyway; Paul's father is in his eighties and bedridden. Obviously if I'm at my mothers which I *would* be in April I could wait there for awhile untill you came back from you're European trip which is when?

All of these things are difficult to wire but I might at least wire something. I had always thought that I would either go alone or come back alone (to Tangier), but I thought that it would be because I wanted more time in America to see you. Of course there are no possibiteas of my staying in New York at all unless at least Rose is there. There is of [course] Mother in Florida but God knows how long I could take that. I expected to stay there too or three weeks at the most, but I could stretch it a little if you were really coming home. Is there any place where Paul and I could stay, I mean, is there any room available at sixty first street for Paul. What with not knowing whether Rose is to be at Treetops or if she is to be on vacation I am really getting in a proper panic. I know too it is difficult to get back here during the high season, beginning in the middle of June or earlier, because people get passage so far in advance. If Paul is reduced to Hotels with neither you nor Ollie around he will surely go back as soon as possible, but in any case he always does anyway unless something else turns up like a job. The New Mexican situation is very nebulous.

Paul says (he is now awake at last) that he knows very well that unless I wire I will never be able to get to Casa so that I may wire at least so that I know when you are leaving Treetops and when you're coming back. Who knows the European trip might even be put off, but we must make our plans for even April almost at once.

According to what you say in you're wire I shall have to send you another wire if trying to catch the Casa boat seems plausable.

Much love to all,

Jane

98

Jane Bowles to Libby Holman
[Tangier, Morocco]
[February, 1965]

Dearest Rose, Libby, Louie, Alice,

I don't know who is there and if Rose is not than I am really sunk. I think I shall write a note to Libby saying that she can open Roses letter in case Rose is not there.

Last night I had dinner with Mary I suddenly forget her name — (this happens since I had the stroke), but it will come back. Here it comes — BANK CROFT. I will not go into it untill I see you but during dinner she told me about you, Libby, and she said that she [thought] you're house would not be available to anyone because of the insurance complications which I was not surprised at. I said I felt that it would be difficult for you to put up *even* Paul in the top room that he used to occupy off and on, and I was practically sure that there would be no place for me in Shirley's room, so none of us were counting on anything, but Tree tops at some point. Now that we know more certainly about the Insurance I think I must begin making plans for our arrival in New York otherwise Paul will collapse. Mary Bankcroft suggested that we stay with her but Paul was not with me when I met them, and I doubt that either one of us would want to impose on someone we barely know. They said they had a big apt. with two extra bedrooms on Sutton place and that it would be no trouble at all to have us. I can't picture any of it or why she should be so generous but I certainly thanked her for the offer.

She said that we should simply call up from the dock and come over." Obviously even if I knew her better there would be no guarantee that she would be in when I called nor did I dare question her about it any more closely. I thought that when I came I would go at once to a hotel with Paul and from there make my arrangements for the next few days. I will certainly call her but only after I've spoken to you Libby or Rose or Louie but that too is full of complications, even if you should advise us to call her. It seems to me that one can't possibly stay with people one doesn't know however generous and sweet the offer is. I suppose for a night or two it wouldn't matter to them—if they have servants but I don't know how the house or apartment is run. Paul knows nothing of of this but in any case do thank her for me and tell her we'll call her when we come to New York naturally. The boat arrives on the second of April in New York which seems terribly soon. If we are lucky maybe Libby will be there as well and Louie and Rose and then I can at least find out something from somebody. I arrive on Sunday the second of April so that will be deppressing enough without not knowing exactly when I will see you. Naturally the concert dates are all important so I won't know whether you'll be there when I arrive in New York or not, naturally. I will write in time to tell you what to reserve for us in the way of rooms if possible, the very second I hear from Paul.

"Later"—I now have a letter giving the name of his hotel and the address so I can easily telephone Casa, in a day or two. After that I will write you exactly what accomodations we'd like if possible. I hope Libby that as soon as you are there you will invite us to TreeTops. I have writen mother that I would not know my plans untill I know yours. If this letter turns out to be to you Rose you'll give me the news. I doubt that I have you're telephone number but I can telephone my mother in Florida who will.

Anyway someone will know my number because I will be staying at the hotel you book us into. It is a shame the boat arrives on a Sunday because otherwise it might have coincided with one of you're days in New York Libby—and then maybe I could have driven out to the country with you.

I am tired now and I don't think I have made anything clearer by this letter. I should be leaving Tangier the twenty-fourth or third, of March, so you have time to write just a short note The Boat is the "Independance."

Love to all of you—

Jane

99

Jane Bowles to Frances[73]
[New York City]
[Early April, 1965]
[Fragment]

Darling Frances

Thankyou for calling me. I wanted to call you but I had told you that I wouldn't unless you asked me to. It is an invasion of you're privacy I know and I thought it was best never to wake you up if the telephone was turned on and not to call and interrupt you in case you had friends. I wanted to call very much and finally when you didn't write me I decided that you were either against seeing me at all or ill. I worried terribly about you're being ill but still I never would have called. I am not going to New Mexico now that I have heard from you but I felt when you told me that I should go to Libby's that you might not want to see me again and I told you I was going to New Mesico. It came into my head because in the last weeks—or few days I had thought I would never see you again somehow and that New Mexico was best. Of course I could

---

[73] Pseudonym for an Englishwoman Jane had met in Tangier who became her lover.

not do that anyway because there is not that much time left. Paul came in with Libby from East Hampton on Tuesday—having spent one night in Connecticut—and then wrote that he had several dates in New York, (one with Audrey), on wednesday and Thursday—whireas Libby decided to go back almost at once so he went to the Chelsea. Then John Goodwin called both of us from Sante Fe and Libby or Rose Transferred the call to the Chelsea. Paul left for Santa Fe—and I think he was wise. He has always thought, as I have, that it might be a place to settle when Tangier proved impossible. I will surely stay here and may have to take a room somewhere because it is much to difficult either fitting my shcedule to Libby's or inconveniancing all my friends. You are quite right I shall see Libby Tuesday night for drinks at least because I do not know what her plans are with Louie.

If she is going out which she might be I'll stay home alone or try to see Katharine or Dionne unless you are free. Anyway I'll get the luggage over to Libby after one ocklock unless for some reason she is not there. I have already written that I did not know whether or not I was

100

Jane Bowles to Frances
[Florida]
[May, 1965?]
[Fragment]

Darling Frances,

I seem to have bogged down in my depression and decided, at least that you were right, "that it was useless to send you a letter about a decision which was already made and certainly now to late to change." It is a hairraising document this letter, and the prose and cons of the decision to be made so minutely gone into that it really should be solde to a library for "Psychiatric research in extreme states of of anxiety."

I shall certainly hang on to the letter but it does seem dead now and I only wish that I hadn't told you that you shouldn't call. Actually some of you're discretion *had* come off on me for a moment but of course at the wrong moment when it was entirely unnecessary. That is inevitable when one tries to please without quite understanding what one has done wrong.

I guard David's secrets—when he tells me to and I would automatically anyway when I saw fit. I think he tells certain things to me and to Margaritte only because he knows we would never betray him. Anyway I do get the picture now, a little better, than I did before when I thought your secrecy and fear of being discovered had to do with Tangier though I must say that I suspected you would not seem more free in New York. Now that I know more or less that you should never be subjected to any panics that have to do with me, I am likely to exaggerate the other way, which I'm sure you would rather I do than the contrary. It's true that it would be difficult for me to telephone you again before thursday or friday because he[74] would think me a "spend thrift," no matter who it was. Obviously if I called you every day as I long to he would think so even more and he would know how I felt about you. I don't care but my mother would mind his guessing anything and she knows me too well for me to hide much. She is quite remarkable in that way and wants me to be happy . . . however she would always hide that side my life

101

Jane Bowles to Libby Holman
[Florida]
[May 3, 1965]

Dearest Libby,

Paul has just written me that he has gone off to New Mexico. I was going to send him John Goodwin's letter and suggest that he do, just that—because John wrote me that he could not understand why Paul thought he [had] *not* invited him to Santa Fe which Paul had insisted on when I told him that he would be welcome there. We were still on the boat at the time. I had always thought of it as a possible place for us to settle when and if we leave Tangier and wanted him to judge for himself. I am afraid it costs more than *I* can afford but if Paul makes money here in there on the Coast then it would be a good plan. Even if I can't go I'm glad if he can. I was longing to go myself and Mary Lou Aswell and I had a long

[74] Julian Fuhs, Jane's stepfather.

correspondence about it (from Tangier to Santa Fe). Not so long—one letter each. However I could not really see Mother and you and some friends in the East and still go there unless I flew now—or had come here in the beginning with Paul to Florida and then seen you at the end. God knows I think I have done very well so far having the train Trip or half of it behind me and still time to see you and other friends ahead of me. Here there are the largest sandwiches in the whole world and I can smell the dill pickles from mother's corner. I am very very sad and I hope that you and Louie are very happy. I am denying myself everything—Sandwiches—(corned beef and roast beef as well), plus cheesecake and motza Ball soup and Herring with sour cream. I don't think it's good to stuff with melancholia. There is a kind of sorrowfull compulsive eating that I might give way to but I think it brings on more despair than cheerful compulsive eating—so I go to the corner which if [is] where they eat when they are not eating Chinease and I sit with them picking at a thin inferior fish while they stuff in the good things. There seems to be a pound of corned beef in every sandwich. The place is called "Pompernicks." It must seat about nine hundred people and is always crowded from four ocklock on. Not even beer is served. The lighting is so dazzling that I have to take a sedative because I am not normal. Anyway Libby I am so glad that at least Paul has gone to Sante Fe even though I couldn't. It is better that he should because it would do no good for me to go alone and like it if he didn't. I would even like New York or Connecticut. Don't frighten Louie—I mean somewhere anywhere not so far away as Tangier—because I have a feeling that I'm going to make more and more Trips because of my mother. I am terribly deppressed as I told you. I am coming back—arriving either monday or Tuesday, and I would like to get my things over to 61st street on Tuesday if the house is open as it usually is. Who Knows. Don't concern yourself with me. If you are eating in I shall probably have some drinks with you or a drink and if you are not there I will stay with Katharine or Frances. I wrote Frances a letter to which I have no answer and probably won't.

I shall probably hook up with Frances or Katharine for later so that you are free to go out if you have planned to and don't worry about me even if I've arranged nothing. I'm not much on eating at seven so don't concern yourself with any dinner plans untill I get there and make my plans with you, I can buy a sandwich anytime. I can certainly not go to a hotel the night I arrive whenever it is because they are a bit difficult I hear because of the world's fair. You must feel as free as you did when Paul was there because now having made the trip to Florida by myself I can certainly get back and forth to TreeTops when you are free and I am not busy in town. My travelling arrangements from now on are going to be very simple (osser). Please please look up Mildred Dunnoks address and telephone number, for me. I think you have it—at least the address or telephone number in Connecticut. She wrote me and the maid threw away the letter hers *and* Paul's. I am worried that it will take forever to get it from Audrey although I am writing her too.

I would call you but I am afraid that I would only be able to talk a few minutes—(three) calling from here but if you would like that I will. I would love to call you and stay on the phone longer but it is difficult—they are now being very carefull about money—We are almost always home except when we go to "Pompernicks" for dinner—back by 10 or 10:30—and anyway no one answers the phone here if we are not home. I may call you any way. I feel so sad here— but you'll understand if I don't talk long. I will write Rose.

Love to Louie—

Jane

P.S.   Don't sopple about the clean laundry I left in my room at 61st. I meant to have left it at Treetops. It is washed but not ironed—and it is not much—but it is a mistake. I will write Rose about telephoning me if you ever want the number and the hours, etc. I wish you would.

Write me when to call you.

102

Jane Bowles to Libby Holman
[New York City]
[May 14, 1965]

Darling Libby,

It was wonderful to hear you talk because even though I always do like to hear you're voice I espacially needed to. I was very sad when you were not in on Monday and got so flustered that I must

269

have confused Rose terribly. I understand now what happened I think. I meant to tell her that I was coming in on *Monday* and would go (if you were there and not somewhere else) to the "Flat" on Tuesday. but somewhere along the line Rose must have thought, or I must have said, I wanted to bring my luggage over on Monday at which point she would certain have said, "William isn't there on Monday." In fact she said it was William's day off on Monday, but as *I had understood it*, she said Tuesday. Later I pondered on this for many long hours because I knew that Tuesday *was* the day you always came in and so I couldn't understand it being Williams day off. Still I decided, if he was gone Tuesday I should not take my luggage over Tuesday. Than Frances called me, and I said I could not go over to you're house until Wednesday when William was back. I also invited her to dinner because I thought it was mean to leave her sitting there with my luggage — of course she was quite drunk on the telephone so she may not remember. who knows but if she does she will be upset if I change it, having asked her to keep me an extra night as a favor. I daresay she would like to have me there anyway, in fact she has always said so but it is so terribly difficult for both of us as you know. I cannot be with her unless I am entirely with her or at least from dinner time on because of the key situation. As you remember she was terrified to allow even the doorman or elevator boy to open the door for me nor did she want any one else to come back with me. Her fanatical secrecy about nothing at all is so irrational that I am frightened for her because of course I sniff a pschosis rather than a neurosis (sniff, indeed).

It would be nice to get the luggage to TreeTops if you leave with William before me but I have not decided where in the end my luggage should settle untill the final departure. I just don't know anything and I am more troubled than I have been in a long time. Meanwhile I had better not start trying to "explain" all the different possibilities for the luggage, which is now three different places — because this is the road straight back to White Plains, God forbid! As a matter of fact if F. and I both went there at least the luggage would be in one place, that is if I got the stuff from sixty-first and TreeTops.

Wonder if you read the Puppet Play[75] and if so do you think they should do it, I do. Please Libby try to find Mildred's address or telephone number — she sent it to me and the cleaning woman

[75] The puppet play was originally performed at Spivy's nightclub under the auspices of *View* magazine, in 1946.

got into my papers, and threw it away. Please also find out if David Jackson and Jimmie Merrill are still there. I don't see how we can see them any weekend except *this* weekend *if* you do want to go up there because the next weekend is Tony's weekend. Anyway I will talk about this when I see you on Tuesday

I thought David and Jimmie had shown the puppet play to the puppet boys ["The Little Players"] but if they haven't why *don't* you. Tell Louie I'm sorry he didn't speak to me the night I called. I took for granted he was in town with you or at the studio, and then Rose told me he was on his "way out of the kitchen." Give him my love and kiss the cats for me.

I think I can only see F. by meeting her in a bar or restaurant because of the elevator situation. Oliver mentioned wanting to see us when he got back from the coast but God knows when that will be. Anyway please bring the puppet play *in with you* and find out about Jimmie and David and Milly if you can and it's not too much trouble. Perhaps I should not use the word psychosis in regard to F. but extreme neurosis—but I am no doctor. However I don't think White Plains would refuse either one of us. This letter is really ridiculous because yincha Alla I will see you on Tuesday—but at least you'll be prepared for the "discussion." Whatever I say I love F. very much because she is a tragic—fanatical—Electra kind of figure in a "tea pot."

[unsigned]

103[76]

Jane Bowles to Cherifa
[New York City]
20 de mayo [1965]

Querida Cherifa:

Por fin ha llegado su carta y estoy muy contenta que Aicha está bien y que tu estás bien. Ayer llegué de Florida donde vive mi madre, y ya estoy otra vez en Nueva York. Hamed todavía no tiene teléfono, pero voy a mandar una carta a su dirección, para que venga

[76] Formal letter written by Paul for Jane, to be read to Cherifa in Arabic by a member of Cherifa's family.

271

a vernos en el hotel de Paul. Espero que todavía está aquí en America, y que no se ha ido a Alemania. Mil recuerdos otra vez a Aicha, la niña, tu hermana así que toda la familia.

No puedo escribir mucho porqué tengo muy poco tiempo ahora para acabar con mis cosas. Vamos a salir de aquí el día dos de junio y llegaremos, incha'Allah, a Casablanca más ó menos una semana después. Muchos recuerdos a Seth y al Berred si todavía está viva! Tengo muchas ganas de verte, y espero que estés contenta y de buena salud. Hasta muy pronto,

su amiga,

Jane Bowles

103
[Translation]

Jane Bowles to Cherifa
[New York City]
May 20 [1965]

Dear Cherifa:

Finally your letter has arrived and I'm very happy that Aicha is well and that you are well. Yesterday I arrived from Florida where my mother lives, and now I'm once again in New York. Hamed [Cherifa's nephew] still doesn't have a telephone, but I'm going to send a letter to his address, so that he'll come to see us at Paul's hotel. I hope that he is still here in America and that he has not gone to Germany. A thousand remembrances again to Aicha, the little girl, your sister as well as the whole family.

I can't write much because I have very little time now to get things done. We're going to leave here the second of June and we will arive, God willing, at Casablanca a week later, more or less. Many remembrances to Seth and Berred, if she's still alive. I have a great desire to see you and I hope you are happy and in good health. Until very soon.

Your friend,

Jane Bowles

104

Jane Bowles to Libby Holman
[Tangier, Morocco]
[August 26, 1965]

Darling Libby,

I wrote you as I remember a short and unsatisfactory not a little while ago and now I shall write you another short and equally unsatisfactory note again. I don't know what I said in the note which is going to make this note even worse than the last one? Did I tell you that I went to Casa Blanca because I didn't feel well or didn't I. Now I am back without any spectacular news from the doctor there. I am still suffering from slight dizzyness but not very much. I don't know how to spell that. Any way there is nothing new wrong with my brain so I guess it must have to do with my eyes or liver or my drugs (medicin). I never did have a thorough check up I guess I'm alright. Paul goes to Afghanastan, for Holiday Magazine at some point—I hope not too soon and certainly not if they haven't stamped out the recent Cholera epidemic, that stemmed from there, and had reached God knows where last I heard of it. Of course I don't know now whether the Cholera was heading east or west but in any case it was in Afghanastan when I heard about it. Ask Shirley. I am really in a black state and trying to keep it from Paul as much as possible—which means that I don't discuss myself and my life and my work too much (just a little). I miss you and I miss being near you and the friends I have left very badly. I am obviously as worried as I can be about what's going on in the U.S.A. and wonder about you're state of mind as I told you in my last note I think. Maybe you will write me about the boys in your next note. I am sorry Frances took up so much of my time (and my mother) when I was in America last but maybe I can come soon and arrange things differently (I can hear Louie growning).

I don't know when that will be this year or next but would like to come more frequently than I do. Obviously I am just talking in the air because I am depessed and feel isolated. Frances writes me but I don't think I could put myself through that again ever (famous last words)—but I really don't. Please write me some news and give my love to Lucia [Cristofanetti Wilcox] if I didn't send it last time and give me more news of Spivy. I should really be in East Hampton. I don't know what I'm doing here.

Libby Paul wrote the little new song to take the place of the old song [from the puppet play] that was lost (the one called the Frozen Horse). Did he or I write you about this? He has so much to do that I can never even keep track of that Frozen Horse which he was kind enough to write over again. He is never around when I write you so please if he hasn't written you, Tell the boys if you can that the new song is completed and ask them where Paul should send it. I suppose Paul might, have the address but I shall wait for you're instructions. Maybe Paul will write a more sensible letter. This letter is getting very involved so I'd better send it off.

Give Louie my love. If Rose is gone at the moment I suppose you won't write me.

Love to Alice if she's there and to Rosie if she is. I wish you'd get back into Tree Tops where you belong—so I can reach you more quickly—I suppose. How many more months are you going to be at the beach house any way? Have David and Jimmy gone away to Greece?

Much love

Jane

Please write—excuse this mess of a letter.

105

Jane Bowles to Libby Holman
Tangier [Morocco]
[December, 1965]

Darling Libby,

It has been so long now that I do not even feel sure of how to spell you're name. I write less and less of anything because I run into so many spelling blocks that I give up and put the letter aside. I don't know that I am better or worse or rather whether my spelling is better or worse and why should it matter, but it does. I was so gratefull to get you're long letter that I was certain I was going to answer it at once but I didn't, now the letter is up on Paul's floor so I won't be able to answer it accurately. I don't remember the details of that letter but you did say that you wouldn't be responsible—or accountable for what you'd do if the boys were drawn into a war. I am not quoting you very accuratly but you're sentence went something like that. I have turned into a complete slob—I sit for hours and do nothing and at the same time I am nervous and erassable. This spelling is an example of why I don't write letters. "irasable" could be spelled in many different ways except this one, and since I don't know whether or not to look it up under "e" or "i" I am discouraged. Sometimes, in fact most often I don't send the letter at all. perhaps you understand—it looks so wrong to me and yet I cannot correct it unless I look up all the possible ways of spelling it, which is also difficult and half the time impossible. There is never any one near me with whom I can check except Paul and he is half the time not available. Naturally a secretary would be ideal. I am not suggesting that you send me one. Everyone is wild about Truman's book [In Cold Blood] but I suppose I will never get through it, however I hope to be able to look at it eventually. Paul has written the "Little Players" because they never did ackowledge receiving my or rather his music for the little song Paul sent them a month or two ago. It is strange—I mailed it to them from Gib. registered so they must have received it. I told my friend Gordon Sager to ring you up He said he knew you and wanted very much to see you if you were free to see him. I'm sure you remember all about him and perhaps by now he has telephoned you. He wrote me and I never answered him but I hope to today. I have lost the letter with the concert date in it and as usual Paul has probably answered the letter and thrown it away. Gordon is staying in New York for awhile and so if he gave up trying to reach you or never did try I wish you'd call him and ask him for drink if you are not too busy. I would thus get direct news of you when he comes back or if he doesn't come back you could give me news of him. I am depressed and also very sleepy. I don't find letters satisfactory—they don't take the place of seeing the person at all and I am desperatly missing my close friends at the moment *more than ever* if possible which makes me less inclined to write less. I don't include Frances among my closest friends. She is something else of course (but I don't write her either). I suppose you saw Louisa for Thanks Giving etc. When I return I have no intention of staying with Frances though will have to stay in some hotel for a little bit of time I suppose in order to see the friends I want to see. With all you're boys and their girl friends looming in the future if not now, do you think there will ever be any room at Treetops again—for a two weak stay or whatever it was last time. I suppose this letter is premature but I might come and try to catch you before the East Hampton exodus begins and that means summer holidays—(no room for me anywhere), except in the very beginning as I remember. I don't know why I should bother you with all this now since I don't know really whether I'll come in the spring or the fall or the summer but obviously if you have any idea at this early date what you're plans are going to be I would like to know because my own always do depend on you're's to a large extent because I don't ever want to be there when and if you are certain to be away for a long spell. Please write to me and let me know at least whether you and Louie are well and whether the concert or concerts have or has take place and how everyone is in the house. I am sad to write you such a dull letter but perhaps the next one will be better.

All my love,

Jane

106

Jane Bowles to Libby Holman and
Louis Schanker
[Tangier, Morocco]
[December, 1965]
[Christmas card]

For Libby and Louie—

Won't you ever come back?
Please kiss all of my friends who are there and the children.
I have never sent a xmas card to anyone in my life but this is a very pretty one and is meant to lure you back—very sad not to be with you—

all love—

Jane

From *Out in the World*
(Emmy Moore's Story)

At the party in Andrew's house she is addressed as Mrs. Moore. All at once she feels that to be her age is her responsibility—that hidden behind all her problems was her age—waiting for its natural dress—which she has denied it. She sickens and sees all this clearly in a flash—tries helplessly to set the table. . . . Did Emmy Moore lose her age when she was little?

107

Jane Bowles to Libby Holman
[Tangier, Morocco]
[April 1, 1966]

Dearest Libby

For days or perhaps months I have been looking for a letter you wrote me which made me feel very happy. I was in a bad state and I wish that Rose would look up somewhere the date of that letter.

I had all kinds of answeres ready for that letter in my head but each time I began thinking about answerering you I would get so excited that I would stand up and walk ghri right out of the room and even run about in circles and then out of the appartment entirely—instead of ansering answering you. It was a wonderfull letter and it came at the moment when I needed to be sure that you and TreeTops existed.

I am almost sure that Jay died after that very shortly but I'm not dead sure. I have been thinking that that was why I did not answer as quickly as I should have after all my excitement of running around the appartment. I will now spend an hour looking for a letter I found which was also of great comfort to me but I do not think this letter which I am now looking for was the one I reffer to. Just a minute.

Well I can't find even the letter I don't think it was nor the letter that I do think it was. Jay died on xmas morning—in his bar on the way to have his xmas lunch alone with Jessie Greene—who is eighty seven years old and who has been in love with him for many years. She had his preasants all wrapped up for him and the turquey—a gift from an Arab, was Stuffed and in the oven and waiting for him to arrive.1 He stopped off for a minute at the bar having just left her after they had gone to Church together as they always did. A couple of hours later While Jessie was waiting for him to come and eat his turque Lillie[77] the bar woman called up and told Jessie that Jay couldn't come because he had died. It was a terrible shock to the whole town as he had been perfectly I was very unhappy Libby and spent many days with Jessie—because all of her close friends were in England for xmas and the few who were not were in Marrakesh.

Since than many things have happened and I have been looking around hoplessly for that particularly wonderull letter which maybe Rose has a record of. The one nearet to that date I found as I told you but but I don't think that is the one I mean. It was however written before Jay's death but I think too months before so I am eager to see it the one I found among my papers is the only letter or it indeed there was another one closer to the date of Jay's death but of course before and not after.

I want to get this letter off to you before the endless weekend begins. The murder of the sheep will take Place friday and their will be no mail coming or going untill next monday. Today it Thursday and I must reach the post now.

The deppression after Jay's death was bad and I did not start coming out of it for a month. For me it was the death of an eppoc—the spelling of that is driving me crazy but since Paul and I keep different hours and live on different floors I just can't correct anything. I know you wrote me that it did not matter. If I have not written I had reasons.

The confusion in my life has been fantastic and I think impossible to write about. I am not sick but I am not well or I am having change of life and the dissiness gets better and then worse. I wrote you about it a year ago—because I found an old letter about it last week. It was written nearly a year ago. Meanwhile Please write me again when you are going to go on tour—if you go Israel—I don't want to miss you and must know because I too am thinking

---

[77] Lily Wickman, the new owner of the Parade Bar.

of moving over to America for a couple of months at least so we must not cross. I don&t want you to come here with Jay dead and Paul in the orient and me in Florida so please for God's sake write me again what you just wrote me about you're possibilities. Some times I get so disscouraged by my spelling that I don't ever want to write a letter again. I thought I would improve more than I have but it does not really matter does it.

I will write Katharine that you wrote me. I am glad that she is alive since I never put pen to Paper people give me up. It's quite naturall but writing letters drive me crazy because of the spelling. I could write a book more easilly maby mabey. The word maybe is a tippical word that I can't spell. Sometimes the word comes right in the end and sometimes not. Please please write me you're plans again just for the concert and for the possible trip. I would love to see the little Players. I have much more to write you and will try to go on tomorrow and sent it Monday. I will mail this without corrections because it's time you got a letter. I have much more to tell you. I know I wrote mostly about my spelling in my last letter and I know you wrote me that you would send me Rose maybe (on a longc chain?). Anyway tell Rosie to look up the dates of you're last two letters and mine. Give my love to the familly and thank you for the book and more in my next. I shall run to catch the post.

[unsigned]

108

Jane Bowles to Libby Holman
[Tangier, Morocco]
[May 10, 1966]

Darling Libby,

My plans are at a virtual standstill. I don't know what to do. Martha[78] who was, I thought, going to go over to America with me — and come back as well is now putting off her trip untill the fall. She says she will deffinitely go back with me in the fall because

[78] Princess Martha Ruspoli de Chambrun, a resident of Tangier, whom Jane met in 1963, and who subsequently became her lover.

she needs to in order to keep up her residence in the U.S. She was going sooner because she wanted to take a stab at breaking her trust again, since the money she gets is less than ever before enough to make ends meet. However although her son and daughter finally agreed to sign certain documents necessary for the breaking of the trust, they think that she should not move until Mr. "Katz" of Cincinnati writes that there is reason for her to come over. I doubt that she will ever break her trust—that is succeed in doing so, but she swears she has to go over anyway once every two years to keep her residence, in the United States. If I go into that and who she is and why I even know her etc., I might as well ask you who is going to finish this biography after my death. Libby, my spelling worries me so much that I am afraid to come home and see what is wrong with me that wasn't wrong with me before. Maybe some premature deterioration due to the original stroke. I don't know. I don't know what is physical any longer and what is mental. I hoped always that I would get better but it does not look that way (the spelling), does it? I am frightfully depressed and I don't know how I can start off alone. Can I wait until the fall, untill Martha is sure to go? (osser) Anyway she "says" so. If there is anything wrong with me then I'm sure it's so bad that nothing will help it, and if there isn't, then I suppose it must be some reaction to all these years of drugs. I hope so. My book, *Two Serious Ladies*, I made no money at all or to be exact about four hundred dollars since publication including the advance. It is at the same time considered To be a literary success in certain circles which I never get into since I am not there, I am here. I don't know if I ever sent you the book or whether or not we decided that it was useless because you had read it. Perhaps we decided that you should have a copy in order to lend it to friends. I don't know. My memory is so bad because of my stroke and the premature senility that resulted that I keep forgetting everything. At the same time if you saw me you would notice that I am still charming and seem very very bright and even young. I am horribly worried about myself but on certain days I am less. Please ask Resnick if a neurologist is the best person to go to for possible beginings of Parkinson's Disease—after effects of a stroke, such as advanced hardening of the arteries, overdoses of drugs, but I think that poor Dr. Resnick will be unable to answer, so don't mention me. My doctor[79] told me that she was sure I did not have Parkinson's Disease but she

[79] Dr. Yvonne Marillier-Roux.

didn't *sound* sure. I might fly to England for two weeks where I can see my original stroke doctor if he is alive. Veronica Tennant is flying there and so perhaps Martha could join me from Paris and come back with me to Tangier. I cut all that part of the letter out because meanwhile Martha has decided to go to Italy and visit her dead daughter's tomb. (She has been dead for ten years but there is no room yet in the ground for her.) I don't think that I will go into this, either. Anyway, her live daughter is there and she *will* see her. I will go nowhere at the moment unless I am really in an awful state, that my woman doctor will recognize. Since I must come to America anyway and want to I shall do everything in one city that is country—although I suppose it is even more expensive than hopping across to London—and then later coming back here anyway which I must do. I just don't know. I'll think about it. Martha said she would go over with me if I needed a nurse (to London that is) in any emergency, but at my expense, of course, the way I paid that boy to go with me to Tangier several years ago. I gave him one hundred dollars to deliver me to Tangier and then he took the next boat on to Italy which had been always his final destination. I hope that I shan't have to do any of that, and can simply come alone and have someone meet me.

Several years ago I told Katharine that she must not hesitate to cut me off the list if she retired because she was worried about those twenty five dollars. I must write her and tell her not to worry because I'm sure she will be upset if I don't. Thank God for the money that you continue to send me which includes Oliver's share. Obviously I cannot write him about it but maybe when I see him this time I'll talk to him about it. The money means a lot to me. If someday it doesn't I will let you know at once so that it can be free for someone else—

I have Paul available today to correct the spelling of this letter and so I will wait until he gets down here. I have thought, as you know, about sending the letter without corrections but I think Paul would be horrified and ashamed for you to see so many mistakes, and you yourself could be depressed.

Louie's catalogue was a joy to both of us and I would love to be able to buy some of the sculptures, in fact all of them. If I could buy only one I would buy number eleven (bronze), I am crazy about it. Where is it? There is a lot more I could tell you—but I don't want to start in again. I hope to God that you have written though I deserve not to hear for awhile. I asked you questions about your present schedule and whether or not Israel was still on it. If there

281

is any chance of your coming here I shan't stir. I don't think that I will right now anyway, but please let me know what you think you're going to do as I asked you in my last letter. I don't feel I have Parckinson's Disease today at all but I must have something. Martha's mother had it and that's where it all started. Those two ladies from the library were about to start over the yenti atlas again and I almost died thinking of Louie and you and me around the pool talking about my trip. Lee Gershwin was here and gave me a very modern tiny slip for skirts that are above the knees. Naturally I could not wear a skirt above the knee with my leg but I love the the baby slip. My slips are more like slips for a concert pianist. I was upset about the Leary scandal which Paul heard about from Susan Sontag, whom you've surely met or at least heard of. Much love to the whole family and please write me.

Jane

109

Jane Bowles to Hal Vursell[80]
[Miami, Florida]
[July/August, 1966]
[Fragment]

Paul and I decided to go on to Spain if those conditions didn't clear up by the time we arrived in Casa. It was alright but I would not have liked being on the boat alone with People possibly meeting me and possibly not because of the riots—or at least threatened riots. This happens in Casa but thus far has never happened in Tangier where I would get off anyway because it is my destination. I don't see why you should take the time to read all of this but it is perhaps to justify and clarify to myself as well as to you my own impotence to make a decision in this tiny little nightmare among other nightmares. I think therefore it is wise to stick to the plan of going quickly and thus avoiding anxiety all the way over because of Casa Blanca or Algeciras. I am going to have my typewriter fixed because it sticks. I am glad that I came to America now and not later when you would have been gone. Soon

[80] Jane's editor at Farrar, Straus & Giroux, which was about to publish Jane's *Collected Works*.

I will write Libby or telephone, perhaps both—certainly both becaus Libby has to know as soon as possible, about holding the weekend for me. Obviously there is *no way of my getting there*, and back because of my peculiar incapacity—physical and psychic. Enough of that. I am getting into more and more trouble with my typewriter and must wind up quickly before it sticks forever—the train trip was fine and the duplex very livable. I don't know what I am being sent for the return but either a peculiar duplex or a bed room will do. I found out from the train conductor, (very charming), that the only thing I couldn't travel inside of was a "ROOmette". I'll see what that lady sends tomorrow or soon after. Nothing as yet. Thank Richard Holland for standing there in the station and not complaining. Actually it was one of the least depressing moments in my life and the station looked so nice. In spite of Casa and Algéciras if from your end things don't work out for my interviews unless I do stay here longer I will.

Give my love to Frank—naturally—

devotedly

Jane

110

Jane Bowles to Gordon Sager
[Miami, Florida]
[July/August, 1966]

Darling Gordon

I have talked about you a great deal with Hal—that is on the night we dined. He is both a true friend and admirer of yours. It's a bore that my typewriter has been broken since I arrived because it is very difficult for me to write long hand. The stroke affected my right hand slightly—which is not important since there are typewriters. However I can only write a little at a time so I shall say little—only eessentials—before my hand buckles under— Another system is to lie down and dream for one hour untill one can go back to the writing table. This is about all I can take right now—Goodby I am going to dream.

I am back briefly—Gordon I am worried so please write me a line. I expect to come back either on a boat that leaves on the 22nd

283

of August from here or on a boat that leaves the first of September. I shall let you know very shortly. I preffer the first date because that boat comes directly into Tangier and avoids Algecirras nerves. But I don't know if I can make it. If not I'll give you a choice of people to meet me—if *you* can't. I know you would if you aren't ill—I hope to God you're alright—much love—

Devotedly—

Jane—

111

Jane Bowles to Libby Holman
[Miami, Florida]
[August, 1966]

Dearest Libby—

It is very hard for me to write long hand since the stroke. Not very important but my hand buckles under after a very little time so I won't be able to sustain this for long.

Briefly—Frances can't drive me to Long Island. Boat leaves Monday noon August 22—and not Tuesday as Hal wrote me unless the American express people *here* are crazy. But then I doubt it because we checked twice. I would have to be in New York Sunday night even if its one in the morning and who in hell could drive me. Have late afternoon interviews Wednesday and Thursday. Naturally free after that but must be on time for boat Monday morning—I suppose around 10 or(?) 11 the latest—sailing at noon.

Looks very difficult fore you rather William or whoever would help.

Please telephone—tried tonight Tuesday—but no answer. Please telephone me any morning after ten or any evening from Friday the Fifth—onward. We stay up untill one. In the afternoon we go out.

Please call and we'll discuss it can't write any more—

Much Love

Jane

284

112

Jane Bowles to Paul Bowles
[Miami, Florida]
[August 9, 1966]

Dearest Paul,

I am delighted that you received my first letter that I wrote to the ships address. Today I had the letter written to me from "in the middle of Gatun Lake," on the fifth of August. I suppose I received it several days ago but it seemed to me like today because my typwriter has been on the blink and I had to eak out a few pain-full letters by hand, one to David and one to Gordon and one to Mme. Roux—all of them to explain why I could not write which meant that I had to go into the weak condition of my hand a result of the stroke. I hope I'm not going to begin explaining this to you. I mention it because I have been so worried that the machine would not be back in time enough to write you. I certainly needed to send you more than a few lines. Now however my hand hurts because I did make all this effort to send word to friends and the position and now typing seems strange although a million times better than writing by hand. I am sending you Peter Owens account as I said I would. Julian says that if he gets thirty percent[81] which is the final sum we settled on, as I remember, then his calculation would be about correct. I would earn about one thousand dollars according to Julian and I'm sure that you will agree with him. On publication of course I will get more.

I called up Dr. Dean, actually to have someone to hang on to while I was here because Naturally I was in a panic that I would somehow not be able to get out of here which panic still exists but I do have Dr. Dean to hang on to. He gave me any number of pills in a brown paper bag. I thought he had brought some groceries with him, (He came to see me. I did not have to go there.) untill he opened up the bag and showed me that it contained about fifty little celophane packets of pills each packet containing three tiny pills and these wrapped separatly although they are in unts of three in a packet each one isolated from the other. I fear this will turn into a "building the bridge", at "Camp Cataract". I know that you will be carefull not to hurt Peter Owens feelings about

---

[81] From the American publication.

anything. The money has not yet arrived at my bank but that may be do to the Strike which continues as you know by you're ships radio—ships wireless I'm sure. As for my health I am bewildered by the sensations I have—the same symptoms as I have always had only much worse. I am going to the M.D. today and I will "Play it by ear". He is so busy that I could not get an appointment untill today which is the ninth. I arrived here on the twenty seventh. I think Dr. Dean is writing you a letter saying Mrs. Bowles is much better than she thinks she is. I can't get a cabin to myself on the boat and there are slim chances that any will turn up at the last minute. I am returning to New York City on the 15 of August, where Hal has arranged three interviews for me. Each one in a dark bar. I am terrified and wish that I had never accepted because they will want me to talk about Morocco, and books. I won't talk about the country I live in and can remember having red only a little of Susan S. Simone Weil, and you. The interviews are over by Thursday evening at which Point Hal will put me on a train to Stamford, arranging with Rose by telephone which train she's to meet. Then I spend the evening with Rose and she will drive me out to Libby's the next morning. Then back to New York on Sunday with Rose, who will leave me there in order to go back to her house in the country or town. Who knows.

Martha is thrilled because the cat has now eaten his first grass, while he was playing in the Garden. He was kept in by himself the first week and then gradually started eating pieces of fish with the others and Martha who gives half of her meat to the dogs and cats who are always grouped around her waiting.

I think I must stop now or this letter will not reach you. It was bad luck that I have had the use of the typwriter only one day.

I am happy that Libby wanted to see me badly enough to make all these arrangements. I am going to send this without corrections because I am afraid that if I reread it I'll miss the post.

I am delighted that you have liked your boat so far. It sounds wonderfull. I'll write to Bangkok, next. Martha has written me two of her usual sweet letters and even wired once because I told her how uncertain the mails were. I pray to God I'm on that boat by the twenty second.

All my love

J.

113

Jane Bowles to Gordon Sager
[Miami, Florida]
[August, 1966]

Dearest Gordon

Thank you for your letter. I have been worrying about you and also, I have been in a frenzy about the boats. I have decided that although I can use weeks here to track down Millie and Oliver (because I am sure Oliver will be sad not to have seen me) I have nonetheless decided that I will leave here in August and arrive at Tangier on the date I will give you as soon as I have seen mother who is in the next appartment. If I should decide otherwise I shall certainly send you a cable. I shan't send you any more explanations or I would get into one of those long painfull recitals that you know so well. I am trying to remain—precise, casual as well, as if the whole business didn't terrifie me. I am leaving the day after tomorrow for the Chelsea hotel. I am so deppressed that I can barely lift up my feet and drag into the next room. I shall not ask mother to correct this letter for me. If the boat whichever one it turns out to be arrives at some ungodly hour I don't know what I'll do. Hard to choose which Port would be the worst for *me*, Tangier or the other two but I have decided to try getting off at Tangier unless they suddenly change plans. I mean the boat. If that happens I shall sit in *Algecirras* and send millions of wires before they take me off to the nut house.

I'll go and get the sailing date from my mother since I really don't foresee getting off at Algecirras. My boat leaves on the 22 and arrives yincha allah, on the twenty ninth in Tangier. That means passing La semaine de Tangier in Tangier. After that who knows. I had news from Martha three times but now I don't hear. She is probably very very occupied, in fact she wrote me that she was. Please tell David I wrote him a letter naturally and tell the Gerofies that my typewriter has at last been Fixed but I won't have time now to write. Please give them all my love—and I miss you very very much,

Love,

Jane

287

114

Jane Bowles to Paul Bowles
[Tangier, Morocco]
[September, 1966]

Dearest Bup,

I did not think I could possibly send you the letter that I wrote you yesterday because it was too full of neurological mean- derings opinions on my own, state of being, doubts about not having been to a Neurologist at all, finally, and mispelled words, etc.—that I destroyed it. I did get to Florida and back and finally here to Tangier. I came much too early as far as Martha is concerned because she is such a busy women still; It is hard for me to tell whether or not I shall ever see her as I did. She assured me that I would when she grew less busy but I see no end to it. I think she believes there is an end but I don't. There will be time when her friend Yvonne Silva leaves perhaps, unless her next visitor comes just as the present visitor leaves—which is very possible. I may go to England if things do go on this way but it is too early for me to tell. The voyage back to Tangier was a nightmare since they never knew really whether or not we could land in Tangier, untill the bitter end. It is always like that because of counter currents. Naturally I was worried all the way by the thought of having to land in Algecirras by myself and to keep my eye on seven pieces of luggage. You can image what I went through. Thank God I had Dr. Dean to call up in Miami because my terror there of landing forever in a "rest home" was grave. I got dizzier and dizzier so I fainally did call him. He said he knew a woman Neurologist but by the time I got arround to making the decision to see one, it was too late for me to see her and catch the train. I myself was of two minds about ever seeing one and I do believe that if I did, it should be a first rate one in England, if any. I think my symptoms may be neurotic but I think more likely that I am possibly suffering from the equivalent of the fits that I used to have and have no longer, at least have not had for nearly three years. I have missed Rabit [Mohammed Mrabet] but have left a message with Yvonne for next friday which is the day on which he comes. If by some miracle they take me with them to Marrakesh then I won't be here. However I will leave messages for him in anycase. He wants news of you which he has not received, so Mme. Jerofie said. Anyway I will keep my eye out for him and have him ring me up as soon as possible. Next Friday unless I have gone somewhere, but it will be soon. He comes every Friday to the book shop and is very polite. I intend to make an appointment with him or at least talk to him on the telephone. It does not look to me as if Martha would ever call me but perhaps she will again. The last two nights have been hell but you're cat is fine and very happy at Martha's. I think it was really Mario's girlfriend who did the work on him. But of course Martha would never admit that. He is happy and plays with imaginary mice in the garden. I know that he is better off here and is part of their family—much more than me. I'm sorry to tell you that Berred died.

You have a check at Yvonne Gerofies which she says has to be countre sighned, Which of course I can't do. I will go and take a look at it, from the outside and tell you who its from.

I think it's for deposit and I don't know why it has to be counter . . . signed? How would she know anyway since it is not open. Anyway I miss you terribly and I know that it was foolish of me to come this soon.

I could have stayed with Katharine. It doesn't matter. I am seeing Mrs. Dickson [Dixon, wife of the Consul General] on Thursday, she wants my book or books and would like to write some friends to look you up in Thailand. Thank God for Dr. Dean in Florida. Otherwise I might never have gotten out of there—I was so frightened of loosing my mind and not being able to cope.

Much love naturally

J.

115

Jane Bowles to Paul Bowles
[Tangier, Morocco]
[September 28, 1966]

Dictated in part to Carla Grissmann[82]

Dearest Paul,

Carla Grissmann is typing out these few addresses for you, which I've guarded with my life and found very difficult to keep track of. Charles Gallagher says that you know these men anyway. There

---

[82] A teacher at the American school in Tangier.

are: Bill Forbush, Kyoto. Also Bruce Rogers in some illegible place near Kyoto; Donald Richie, Tokyo.

Your letter was fascinating of course, but I have no news from here to give you. I'm worried about all kinds of things naturally but they don't bear writing about—and you are too far. I miss you very very much, but thank God you have landed somewhere, and I am now not Carla Grismann but myself continuing this letter. How I wish that I were with you now. I saw Bill [William Burroughs] for a few minutes, he called by to see me or I told Bryan [Brion Gysin] to let him in—rather send him in. I don't quite remember. Bryan is here Charles is leaving in a couple of days and I am anxious to get this letter off so that it will reach you on time.

Charles felt that you would certainly be able to stay on in Bangkok but got these names in case. I can't tell what is going on because I am not seeing many people. I think Carla has fixed these margins so that they are too narrow. And so I have re done mine. I hope that you will write me even though I can't seem to answer your letters and stick even the slightest bit of fun into mine. I wanted to say morcel of fun into mine. Not a very good word and I can't spell it anyway. I suppose I was trying to write, "titbit" If that is the correct spelling.

. . . . Next day. This is Carla again (I did *not* fix the margins, they *were* like that, and I've just found out how to widen them— much better, non? Janie is on her way—)

Dear Paul, I just got your second letter today, from Bangkok, of the 22nd, and I wish more than ever that I'd gone with you. I seem to be very depressed, but don't worry. There's nothing you can do about it, and I hope that you do get out of that sticky climate. No, I don't think Martha would ever come out anywhere around there with me, her life seems very much booked up at the moment—her painter arriving soon and then Italy in the spring—I suppose you didn't ever really believe that I could come or that Martha would.

The little animal sounds delightful, but I don't think it should be moved around. I had heard that there were air-cooled flats in Bangkok, but you'd still have to wander around the steamy streets even [if] you did find one.

Yes, Mrabet is here but I can never get over to see him—I can send messages through Madame Gerofie—

Thank you for writing me such a long letter—nice long letter, and give my best to Oliver Evans.

It looks to me as if you'll be gone six months at least—Gordon would like to have rented your aprtment while you were away because he has decided to get out of York Castle. He realized the complications and he shall probably leave Tangier before long if he can't find another place. The children here started making little orchestras of tin cans—they begin their jam sessions early in the morning and go on til quite late in the evening—It is very terrifying—The place has become a real *slum* but what can I do.

Anyway, the little fur animal sounds adorable. The Blackcat seems very happy at Martha's so I think it would be mean to put him back in an apartment—

What is the name of the man who collects your *taxes*—if I had that to give Jack, he could arrange something with the English agent who represents Peter Owen. *May*be. Jack asked me for his name so that I could get out of English taxes on my *book* so I wrote him to get in touch with Jane Wilson, but I also wrote that we have joint taxes so I don't know whether he can do anything about the English tax. Anyway, I don't see what you can do about it—I haven't written Peter Owen at all. The whole thing is much too complicated. Howard Moorepark is the English agent in America on my book and he is the one who asks Clareman[83] for the name of the man who collects my taxes. He seemed to think it was all easy to arrange but of course they did not know that I did not get taxed myself, just you. Much too complicated. Anyway, I hope you haven't gotten Peter's back up, which I'm sure you *haven't*. I would much rather write about the animal with the black fur face.

I suppose the names Charles gave for you aren't of much use but anyway I wanted to get them to you.

Much love,

[unsigned]

116

Jane Bowles to Hal Vursell
Tangier, Morocco
September 28, 1966

Dictated to Carla Grissmann

Dear Hal,

I know you're not back yet, but I wanted to let you know that I got here. Please send a copy of my book to

83 Jack Clareman, Libby's lawyer.

Dr. Henry L. Dean
150 East 22nd Street
Miami Beach, Florida.

I want one sent also to Libby Holman, Treetops, Merrie Brook
Lane, Stamford, Connecticut.

I'm dictating this letter, because I don't have the courage to write
it myself. Deep depression. I thought I'd get these two things done
before I got any less capable. Dr. Dean helped while I was in Florida.
I shall never forget how nice you were to me. I don't want to say
any more right now because I don't feel this is an especially private
letter. I hope to God you're alright and that everything is the way
you would want it.

All my love,

Jane

117

Jane Bowles to Paul Bowles
[Tangier, Morocco]
[September/October?, 1966]

Dictated to Carla Grissmann

Dearest Paul,

Carla Grissmann paid the patente for me, I could never have done
any of it by myself. I'm very frightened being here by myself and
never realized how complicated it would be for me. Gordon is
trying to help me, although he gets very fed up since I don't
understand very much, indeed anything, about how to handle the
money. I always have needed more than I get and now I'm terrified
of leaving things up to the last minute. I should have gone with
you no matter how hot or uncomfortable it might be. I could have
stayed in the room. It particularly worries me that you don't have
any idea of when you're coming back, although I can well under
stand it. It terrifies me to live from month to month and so I have
sent for extra money, via the bank, but even so until it comes I
will be on tenterhooks, and *will* it come? I've had to drag Gordon
to the bank manager because I can't express myself clearly. I still
have money in the bank, though Gordon will find out how much,

as I don't know where it's written. There's no point in writing about this as you can't do anything. What I want to be sure of is getting money out of my capital into my checking account, if necessary. I am not spending an extra *sous* but there always are a great many expenses beyond the $275. I naturally want to be well covered, particularly with you not here. What can I do if I suddenly have no money? You were always here to handle these things. The only friend I have here now at hand who can help me is Gordon if he will and doesn't get too irritated—he said he would on Monday. Paying your patente was an insane experience, ridiculous of course, as everything is here.

I think a stole would be best, because I never get around to having anything made. I have a red one, so pick something with greenish-blue in it?

I don't remember sending on any letter from the Swedish publisher,[84] except vaguely. It was about a photograph, and I think my mother has a good one, but it is all too complicated.

Sorry to bore you with my worries about the bank, but I decided it was best to have a reserve, and one to arrive here and not in Casablanca never to be *seen* again. Do you remember *that*? It still has not been found.

I worry about your being in so much *heat*. You don't say how long it will take you to get from Bangkok to Kyoto, so that I imagine you will be gone for years. Charles said it took a month to get from Bangkok to Japan. Would you then return the other way? Anyway I miss you very very much and please write me quickly. I really can't think of what color to have the stole in, and naturally if I were anyone else I would get a suit—too complicated. You will find a pretty color that will look nice on me. I didn't mean to tell you about my worries about the bank and money, etc., ways and means of doing these transactions, the bother I'm causing Gordon and worrying other friends but I can't free myself of this basic worry. We never did talk about money before you left, and there's nothing you can advise me about now. I'm very grateful for Carla writing this. Write me if you have any idea when on earth you'll be back. Martha is fine, but I wouldn't write her the nature of my worries if I were you.

The Siamese sound wonderful, I love those stubby tails.

Much love,

[unsigned]

[84] Of *Two Serious Ladies*.

Jane Bowles to Claire Fuhs
Tangier [Morocco]
[September 30, 1966]

Dictated to Carla Grissmann

Dearest Mother,

I'm writing from Carla Grissmann's house where I'm spending the afternoon. She's an expert typist and I felt that I had to get a letter off to you first before I had tea. She suggested that I write this at her house as she types so much quicker than I do.

I'm *haunted* by the fact that I didn't stay with you long enough, and by the fact that I did not accept Julian's suggestion that he bring over the commentator so that I could listen to what he had to say. The whole thing seems to me a nightmare and I should have arranged things differently. Tell Julian I *realize* that and to forgive me. I could at least have encouraged him to bring the man up, and I'm very sorry.

I have no news to give you, except that Veronica is very very ill and they have sent for the family, as David doesn't want to take the responsibility. It makes her very happy to have her family there, although she is suffering a good deal.

I got your letter about the bank, I don't know whether there were any other checks after the last one you mentioned. I don't think so, as I certainly didn't make any out here. I'm very worried, because as they send the statements to you do you think I'll be able to get money here when I wire for it, or rather write? It is very difficult for me to figure out what to do, and I wonder if I shouldn't put them back to sending the statements directly to me. It's a mess. I've written the bank to honor any checks that might come in, including my own, but naturally I do worry now that I'm here alone. I can't really explain to you what I'm worried about 'cause it's too complicated, just that they might get mixed up. I'm so fed up that I'm almost ready to come back but with *whom*? I couldn't go through *that* again. All this will work out so don't *you* worry about it.

I'm well, and give Julian my very best love. And all my love to you,

[unsigned]

Jane Bowles to Paul Bowles
[Tangier, Morocco]
[October 11, 1966]

Dictated to Carla Grissmann

Dearest Paul,

. . . Dear Paul, this is Carla and with sending you my best greetings I wanted to write just a few words before Janie comes to you. I am here having a chat with her and since I type so much faster she said yes that I should write a few words: she has held up sending the last letter for fear it sounded too gloomy and didn't want you to fret, but since you might be leaving any moment she did want to send it off with this note added. A few "money" points have come up since she wrote, 1) the lost May check has been more or less traced, as having been paid into your account here on June 15th. Gordon will probably go down there to check.

[Jane dictating] I'm having Gordon do as much as he can as I can't cope with these money matters, as you know. As I've said I've sent for money because I want to keep ahead of the game here and it should be arriving somewhere between 2 and 4 weeks.

Martha has been very sweet to me and I've seen a lot of her but that will cease I imagine as soon as her house guests come, the young painter, Tony, and his wife. They're coming to stay with Martha who is at this moment alone and doesn't like that very much, any more than I do. However she is rapidly finishing her book and she works on it at least four hours a day, aside from making various trips with the car and her man Ahmed to some deserted beach, from where they bring back huge rocks I forget why. I had dinner there last night with George Greaves, and Cyril Hanson. I never said a word. Neither did they, until the very end. Martha entertained us all. Poor George is not feeling very well and is unable to drink anything. I wish I could get down to writing but I can't and you know all about that and what it does to me. I am longing for you to return but I know that it can't be done very soon. I'll send this quickly so that you'll have it before you leave. My mother told me that she had a beautiful picture of me in a magazine, I suppose from years ago — that because you mentioned the Swedish publisher. Jack Clareman thinks they can't get me out of British taxes because I'm a resident of Morocco. Actually I'm *not* at the moment but I don't have the energy to go to that police place.

I have nothing but *complaints*, so I don't feel much like writing as you must know by now, but *please* don't let me down, and keep writing to *me*. This letter doesn't seem very much better than the *last* one, which I purposely withheld from you because I didn't want to upset you. I still don't. Isabelle is still attending to the money you left with her and as far as I know all goes well. I'm not awfully good at dictating letters because I've never done this before. Veronica has been desperately ill but seems to be getting a little better.

Write me more about fur animals and also when and *if* you plan to come back, if you know. I must have repeated this twenty times in my letter already. I am very *quiet* and don't find many amusing things to say or to write, that's why my mail is scarce, but I always remember that you said it's better to write a dull letter than no letter at all; so here is my dull letter, about as dull as a bank but not as useful.

[unsigned]

120

Jane Bowles to Libby Holman
[Tangier, Morocco]
[October, 1966]
[Fragment]

Dearest Libby,

My eyes are bad again—won't focus at all. I got much too nervous taking those trips and trying to fend for myself on the boat I imagine.

Anyway I am here but everything swimms before my eyes. It is a kind of "nervous breakdown," and I should never have gone. Or I should have stayed longer. It was folly to come back that quickly and I deeply regret it. I had no time to see anyone because of my obsessive terror that I would in the end not get back at all. I did not want to go on that trip with everyone to you're aunts for the weekend which you said you might invite me on if you could fit me in. I don't know whether or not you were serious about this or whether you knew I would balk at the idea of getting onto a plane. I don't know but I *would* have been better off getting on the plane than I am having come home.

Because of my eyes I can't read the zen book. It would be a great help right now. David Holman [Libby's nephew] was very sweet. I wanted him to hide from You the state I was in—and it is not a state that is so noticable except that I am very quiet. I am writing these declarative sentences so that I can get through them before they turn into Gonza Magillas. At which point I would have to abandon them.

I told David Herbert who wanted very much to meet David—I told him that I was very much frightened that if you heard anything about a nervous breakdown You would cut me off I was half joking but it was a feer. David Herbert said I was crazy, but there is no limit to what I fear even so we went on with the conversation. Than David Herbert told the story to David Holman, which made everything terrible. Worse than that I told David Holman not to repeat it to you because it does sound crazy and he said he wouldn't dream of it so I'm repeating it to you and I'm sure David Holman will tell you that I'm not crazy. Just depressed and with reason. I'm trying to Pull out of it But I realize that this little deception I was trying to get away with was not going to cease bothering me. Untill I came straight to you with it.

It was a horrible fear that came over me when I was having lunch and so I came out with it to the other David, mine who then repeated it to you're David. Anyway please Don't cut me ough because you think I'm crazy or for any other reason. I manage the accounts with another friend very reliabe and count very much on you're gift to me—obviously.

I have no friend because no sooner was I back than began brooding

[unsigned]

297

121⁸⁵

Jane Bowles to Carson McCullers
[Tangier, Morocco]
[October 31, 1966]
[Fragment]

Dictated to Carla Grissmann

Dearest Carson,

I was so happy to hear from you after all these years. I did not want to bother you, otherwise I would have given your name to my publisher and you might have written a short blurb. I can't write my letter, but am having it typed by a friend. Forgive me.

[unsigned]

122

Jane Bowles to Libby Holman
[Tangier, Morocco]
[1966]
[Postcard]

Dearest Libby

I will be writing you—

always

Jane

I hope to God you are well

85 Written in response to a letter of admiration from Carson McCullers on the publication of Jane's book.

123

Jane Bowles to Frances
Tangier [Morocco]
[November, 1966]

Darling Frances

I am in such a depression that I can't answer any of your thoughtfully arranged questions. May I ask you one myself. Can you possibly go first to Paris (France) as you say or whatever other place you are going and then come on to me. The room upstairs is a mess but I could fix it up. I suppose you can not do it that way around or you would have suggested it to me. My life is one of great pain and torment now and I don't see my way out of this trap. If I go to America there would be only the state Hospital and in England the same because I don't have the money to pay for a getter place. My deppression has gotten worse and worse and I don't know what to answer you about coming right now. I would rather not say anything today but I'm writing you know not to leave England or France without leaving me an address. I don't know yet Whether I I would rather go or stay. That's why I can't write you. I suppose its too late now and you have gone to America. If you haven't then come here. You can tell by the way I write that I am in a bad way.

Love

Jane

On the other hand come I should say if you don't have any other place you'd rather go first. I'm a little bit hard up

124

Jane Bowles to Paul Bowles
[Tangier, Morocco]
[December, 1966]
[Fragment]

Dearest Bup,

I am afraid that by now it is too late to reach you for xmas and you're birthday. I feel quite sick about it and about not having written you. I have received all of you're letters and I don't think

299

it was a good idea for me to stay here without you. The explanation of that will come later. They have been very kind about helping me but you always did that month by month more or less and now I don't seem to be able to accept any reasurance about whatever financial arrangements I make. It is hell. You're own letter sounded so sad that I had to write you although I have far less to say than you about my own my own confusion all of which Yvonne is trying to do her best to allay. I have no idea how to spell that word. Aisha to whom you sent the card is here and sends you love, or greatings as they do, and I did not tell Cherifa that the card was not for both of them, obviously. Mme. Roux may have written you by now or at least the letter may have written you about the possible opperation that I might have but I think I shan't have it and that I shall just stay as I am. Enormously fat in spots because my degestion is at a standstill. I long for you to come home but I can't really tell from you're letters how terribly long this is going to take. Naturally I was horrified by you're letter about my book but it is exactly what I expected. As you remember I did not really want it republished at all. But you say that books are written to be punlished. Tangier is humming with xmas activities and I am worried now that this letter will reach you too late for youre birthday or xmas. There have been no new terrors but theyre will be I suppose. O I am very worried about all kinds of things that I don't want to go into and can't. I did not write you for so long because I was in such a depression. Now it is something else. You're work seems very arduous and I'm sorry, almost in despair that you should be so lonely. Perhaps something will change.

[unsigned]

125

Jane Bowles to Libby Holman
[Tangier, Morocco]
[February, 1967]

Darling Libbie

I have been for six months in a nervous deppression—I will be well soon—

Love—

Jane

I think of you all the time—Love—Love—Love the interview that came out in the times was invented by the times man.

From *Out in the World*
(Andrew's story)

Looking back on those early days he realized that he must have seemed nothing like the others; he did not allow himself any close friends or companions. He was fearful that too much proximity would reveal the difference he was concealing from them with badly suppressed excitement. . . . His painstaking travesty had indeed lent to his face a look of flushed headiness that rendered him suspect to his companions though he had certainly not been aware of this: his eyes too had a dangerous sparkle. Very rapidly the lie changed until it was not his family that he was concealing any longer but a private monster whose shape was not even visible to himself. Like other odd children he was in the end simply concealing an oddness. He could not remember when the lie melted away so that he could no longer feel it. Poison ceased to drop into his heart . . . little by little the lie vanished. His breast was emptied of the bitter vial. There was a possibility, he realized, that it had not vanished but engulfed his spirit so totally that he could no longer find it anywhere. This latter possibility he sincerely believed to be the more likely one.

In mid-April 1967 Paul took Jane to Málaga, where she was admitted to a psychiatric hospital for women. There she again received shock treatment. The letters from here on are handwritten in a disordered script that is barely decipherable. From this point forward, the transcriptions include not only vagaries of spelling and punctuation but also notations of crossed-out words.

126

Jane Bowles to Libby Holman
[Málaga, Spain]
[1967]
[Fragment]

Dearest Libby—

I can write with out being ablle to sead [For   Fat   Fe *crossed out*] jet *y y y* yet. I hope that soon I can. I am very sad and also Bewildered—*you* seemed better I hope soon that you will right what happend or a little news—so that at least I will know whether or not your olcer is still alright. I cannot right you very much because I write the words with [the *crossed out*] being able to see them yet—so there isn't as much privacy [I have I as *crossed out*] as I could have if I needed no guidance. Readis is allmost out of the question but I am so much [beeter Beter *crossed out*] Better that [tope *crossed out*] I hope [I a *crossed out*] write [all *crossed out*] you to write you so y

[unsigned]

In May 1967 Paul brought Jane back to Tangier. Her condition worsened during the fall and in late December she moved out of her apartment, taking Cherifa with her, and went to stay at the Atlas, a small hotel near the Parade Bar. Sitting in the Atlas bar, she began to give away money, first cash and then checks. She gave away her clothing and all of her jewelry.

127

Jane Bowles to Paul Bowles
[Hotel Atlas]
[Tangier, Morocco]
[January 11, 1968]

Handwritten by Alfred Chester except for last line.

Darling Paul—

It will be all explained—I mean, your financial dilemma—in one half hour. I mean, by me. It's true you should have a separate

302

account. I have not spent as much money as you think. Please don't think it's your financial problem, *but mine*. We will talk it over and understand everything.

All my love

Jane

P.S.   Alfred is the secretary.
Part of the love is for Alfred—

> *Jane's condition deteriorated even further. She was in a very agitated state. Although she at first resisted returning to Málaga, she finally consented, and Paul took her back to the psychiatric hospital there.*

128

Jane Bowles to Paul Bowles
[Málaga]
[Spring, 1968]
[Fragment]

Dear Paul—

Please try to forgive me for the way I've behaved. I am longing to come back and start fresh again. I was not drinking when I went away and lived at the [Atlas *crossed out*] Atlas. I don't really know what I thought I was doing. I know that I have to fix my teeth—I had [a *crossed out*] only a temporary arrangement on them which will have to be finished now. I've forgotten the name of the man [? near] Tangier (you use him too.) But naturally I would not be instend tha gng of Malaga. I would like to live in my [home *crossed out*] house—cook etc.

Please give my love to Noelle. Please Pall don't try to figure this out but believe me I want [I *crossed out*] to go back to Roux and get going with my [den *crossed out*] Dentist. I'll try to explain to you someday [abu *crossed out*] about the Atlas [bu *crossed out*] but I don't even understand most of it myself. It is very hard to write with no machine and I wish you would explain this to Libby & my mother.

[unsigned]

129

Jane Bowles to Paul Bowles
[Málaga]
[Spring, 1968]
[Fragment]

Dearest Paul—

thank you a million times for [ceep *crossed out*] ceeping in touch.

As you know its terribly hard for me to write—with out a [machin *crossed out*] machine and I don't even know kow w hiter I still can use one its been so long. I want very much to see you & get this [word *crossed out*] way of life [over with *crossed out*] over with. I'm longing to come home and lead my li life. I don't feel like [wri *crossed out*] w riting because there is too much to dis cuss.

Actually there is nothing to discuss—except the fact that I am not home & & would like to be there [son *crossed out*] as soon as possible [word *crossed out*] I chan't [word *crossed out*] write about any thing but my dentist and ask how you are. The dentist should be in around a month if not know but it certainly must be soon. I sorry about having simply walked out and gone to the Atlas—I promise you I was not drinking. I want to go to dr I've suddenly

[unsigned]

130

Jane Bowles to Paul Bowles
[Málaga]
[Spring, 1968]
[Fragment]

Dearest Paul

[W 1 you *crossed out*] Please call for me as soon as possible tomorrow afternoon. today is Monday   I don't write a a long letter but I Is simplest [Is *crossed out*]—I [a *crossed out*] leave it this way—so that it will be finished by monday—byme that's [temam *crossed out*] tomorrow.

I [supp e *crossed out*] suppose that will leave Noel in the awqward [?] position of no bath room or me

[unsigned]

> *In June 1968 Paul took Jane out of the hospital, where she had again received shock treatment. He had arranged for her to stay in a pension run by an American expatriate in Granada. At the end of ten days, he took her back to Málaga, where she was admitted to a casa de reposo, the Clínica de los Angeles.*
>
> *The last three letters are from the Clínica, where Jane stayed until her death in 1973.*

131

Jane Bowles to Paul Bowles
[Málaga]
[1968-69?]

Dear Paul

I miss you very much and I miss not having hear from you for so long. Please come and see me and if possible to get me.

Could you come [right now? *crossed out*] here [you *crossed out*] quickly as possible [any way *crossed out*] and then we will see. E[?] Dr. says the [*word crossed out*] orders you should take me. Please [write *crossed out*] come soon

Much Love

Jane

132

Jane Bowles to Paul Bowles
[Málaga]
[1968-69]

Darling Paul

[*I wonder if and I wonder if crossed out*] I don't know what I was [*several words crossed out*] going to ask you but I but I certainly know that I miss you [desperdat *crossed out*] [you *crossed out*] very much and please come and get [me *crossed out*] here to see me and to get me if that is possible. I want so badly to go home

[unsigned]

133

Jane Bowles to Paul Bowles
[Málaga]
[1970?]
[Fragment]

Dearest Paul

Just right me another [?] note and when you have written ask here [to a wom *crossed out*] talk to a woman called "Rgennia [?]" — which is the way a mexican would spell her name but do it soon —

Lots of love

I'll finish this off [*word crossed out*]. If I wanted to spend more time [*unclear crossed out*] *time* [if *crossed out*] I would let you kow — about any

From *Out in the World*
(Emmy Moore's story)

She could not stand the overheated room a second longer. With some difficulty she raised the window, and the cold wind blew in. Some loose sheets of paper went skimming off the top of the desk and flattened themselves against the bookcase. She shut the window and they fell to the floor. The cold air had changed her mood. She looked down at the sheets of paper. They were part of the letter she had just copied. She picked them up: "I don't feel that I have clarified enough or justified enough," she read. She closed her eyes and shook her head. She had been so happy copying this letter into her journal, but now her heart was faint as she scanned its scattered pages. "I have said nothing," she muttered to herself in alarm. "I have said nothing at all. I have not clarified my reasons for being at the Hotel Henry. I have not justified myself."

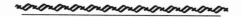

From *Out in the World*
(Andrew's story)

[He was wearing] a green sleeveless tunic that buttoned below his knees, and a yellow paper ruff that scratched his chin . . . real corn sprouted out of the cardboard hat . . . He was the only vegetable in the room. He had felt ashamed of his costume and the weight of the corn on his head; but of all the costumes in the room his was the only one that seemed sweet and natural to him. The others were alarming. He wanted to stare at each one forever and at the same time he wanted to hide his face and look away.

His arm grazed the peculiarly dry flank of a papier-maché cow. The painted eye came close to his. Through a hole in the stiff pupil he saw another eye moving: his stomach wobbled and he hurried away, embarrassed and excited, the smell of glue in his nostrils. From a distance he watched the cow. He could still feel the touch

307

of its dry powdery flank on his arm. It was the most important costume in the room. Other costumes clustered near it, one a policeman's suit with a club.

The cow moved backward and forward at the same pace. It stayed near the middle of the room. There were children inside it. He knew that. He gazed at it with a feeling of deep longing and admiration. It had a serene face, whether it walked backward or forward — and everyone was paying attention to it, talking and laughing with it and with the children inside. He longed for the cow and was dreaming a plan of how they would meet, and prayed that it would not come near him.

The cow was millions and millions of miles away from him, across the ocean, across several oceans and another ocean, where instead of land a whole new ocean began . . . When he reached the middle waters of the second ocean he would be able to see the cow's land, where it lived. But that would not be for many many weeks or months or years. When he reached the middle waters of the second ocean, the cow would tell the children that he was coming. Then the children and the cow would go to the water's edge each day and look out to sea . . . they would have a place ready for him inside the cow . . .

While he was deeply absorbed in his long dream a paper costume smashed into his face and chest. When he opened his eyes, everything was pink. He commenced to thrash at the paper but it backed away of itself. A little fat girl stood blinking at him. She was dressed as a big rose. Her face was beet red and her spectacles were gold-rimmed. She pointed her fat finger at his hat and started screaming. It was a happy scream. He watched her jump heavily from one foot to the other and listened to the faint paper crash of her petals . . .

"Corn for the cow — corn for the cow — corn for the cow —" she sang out.

They were coming toward him singing and clapping. He had seen the cow turn around slowly in the middle of the room. It was moving toward him with its serene face and its stiff painted eyes. When the cow was so near that he could smell the cardboard and the glue, he wanted to run from the room. He would have done so had not the paper hat been strapped firmly under his chin and the corn wired to its crown.

They were praising his costume, admiring the lettuce green ruff at his throat and the way the corn sprouted out of his hat. The cow's large and weightless head prodded the corn in a mild simulacrum of a cow eating.

He had his eyes shut when the corn wobbled ever so lightly on his head. He tried not to feel it. He was not ashamed of his costume, but it was not sweet and familiar to him any more. He would have run away but he stood there stiffly waiting because his costume was not his own any more. It belonged to the children inside the cow. . . .

Chronology of the Life of Jane Bowles

1917   Born February 22 in New York City, daughter of Sidney Auer and Clair Stajer Auer.

1927   Auer Family moves to Woodmere, Long Island.

1930   Sidney Auer dies. Jane and her mother return to New York City.

1931   Jane attends Stoneleigh. Falls from a horse and breaks her leg.

1932-34   Treatment for tuberculosis of the knee in a sanatorium in Leysin, Switzerland.

1934   Returns to New York City to live.

1935   Operation performed to permanently stiffen the knee joint.

1935-36   Writes *Le Phaéton Hypocrite* (manuscript lost).

1937   Meets composer Paul Bowles. Travels to Mexico with Paul and Khristians Tonny and Tonny's wife, Marie Claire.

1938   Marries Paul Bowles. Honeymoon trip to Central America and Paris. Begins work on *Two Serious Ladies*.

1940   Goes to Mexico with Paul and Robert Faulkner. Meets Helvetia Perkins in Taxco.

1941   Lives on Middagh Street in Brooklyn with Paul. Returns to Mexico with him. Finishes *Two Serious Ladies*.

1942   Returns to U.S. with Helvetia Perkins.

1943   *Two Serious Ladies* published by Knopf.

1944   "A Guatemalan Idyll" published.

1945   "A Day in the Open" published. *A Quarreling Pair*, puppet play, performed.

1946   "Plain Pleasures" published.

1947   Paul's "A Distant Episode" published. First act of *In the Summer House* published. Paul goes to Morocco. He completes "Pages from Cold Point."

1948   Jane goes to Morocco. Meets Cherifa. Paul completes *The Sheltering Sky*. Jane completes "Camp Cataract."

1949   Jane completes "A Stick of Green Candy." "Camp Cataract" published. *The Sheltering Sky* published in England. Jane in Paris with Cory, working on *Out in the World*.

1950   Paul's *The Delicate Prey and Other Stories* published.

1951   "East Side: North Africa" published. Jane returns to Tangier. *In the Summer House* produced at the Hedgerow Theater.

1952   Jane goes to New York. Paul's *Let It Come Down* published.

1953   *In the Summer House* produced in Ann Arbor, Michigan, and in New York.

1954   Jane returns to Tangier. She goes to Ceylon with Paul and Ahmed Yacoubi.

1955   Jane returns to Tangier. Paul's *The Spider's House* published.

1956   Jane transfers house to Cherifa. Cherifa moves into apartment with Jane. Paul goes to Ceylon.

1957   "A Stick of Green Candy" published. Jane suffers a stroke and goes to England for treatment.

1958   Jane and Paul go to Madeira. Jane goes to New York and is hospitalized in White Plains. She returns to Tangier with Paul.

1965   *Two Serious Ladies* published in England. Paul's *Up Above the World* published.

1966   *Plain Pleasures* published in England. *The Collected Works of Jane Bowles* published in U.S.

1967   Jane institutionalized in a psychiatric hospital in Málaga.

1968   Enters the Clínica de los Angeles in Málaga.

1969   Returns to Tangier. After four months goes back to the Clínica de los Angeles.

1973   Dies May 4 at Clínica de los Angeles.

A Note on the Institutional Locations of Sources

Letters 6, 7, 8, 9, 12, 13, 14, 15 and 16 are at the Music Library, Yale University, Virgil Thomson Archive.

Letter 10 is at the University of Georgia Libraries, Special Collection, Katherine Cowen De Baillou Collection.

Letters 18, 19, 20, 21, 22, 23, 26, 27, 28, 30, 32, 33, 49, 70, 74, 112, 114 are at the Humanities Research Center, University of Texas at Austin.

Letter 54 is from the Hedgerow Theater Collection.

Letters 55 (a and b) are at the Beinecke Rare Book Library, Yale University.

Letters 106, 111, 122 and 125 are at the Mugar Memorial Library, Boston University.

All letters to Libby Holman are printed with special permission from the Holman Estate.

Index of Persons Named in the Letters

315

Kahn, Mike, 164, 168, 241
Kamalakar, Sonia, 232, 258
Kanin, Garson, 157, 159
Kazin, Pearl, 37, 83, 85, 94, 95
Kerr, Walter, 174, 175
Knopf, Alfred, 95

Lamantia, Philip, 197
Lantzmann, Jacques, 81, 109
LaTouche, John, 18, 19, 26, 45,
  47, 51, 55, 138, 142, 168
Layachi, Larbi, 247
Lazar, Irving Paul, 247
Lerman, Leo, 68, 197
LeVoe, Spivy, 17, 273
Levy, Miriam Fligelman, 15, 18,
  19
Lewis, Bobby, 40
Lewis, Dione, 47-50, 134,
  209-11, 213, 214, 266
Lindamood, Peter, 169
Lloyd, George, 144

Marillier-Roux, Dr. Yvonne,
  284, 285, 300, 303
Marinoff, Fania, 165
Marlowe, Sylvia, 92, 156
Marty (pseudonym), 166, 167,
  169, 181
Mary Anne, 68, 77, 128-30, 138,
  152
Mauriber, Saul, 165
McBey, Marguerite, 231, 267
McBride, Miss, 134, 135
McCullers, Carson, 33, 95, 123,
  298
McKean, Margaret, 86, 168,
  169
McMichael, Dr. John. 199, 206
McMillan, George, 13
Menotti, Gian-Carlo, 50, 54
Merrill, James, 271, 274
Meyers, John B., 221

Minor, Rose, 188, 191, 194, 196,
  220, 222, 226-28, 233, 241,
  245, 247, 252, 262-64, 266,
  269, 274, 277, 279, 286
Mitchell, Noëlle, 230, 231, 233,
  234, 236, 303, 305
Morris, Edita, 191
Morris, Ira, 191
Mother. See Auer, Claire Stajer
Mrabet, Mohammed, 288, 290

Nessler, Harry, 50
Nora (pseudonym), 147-50, 155

Ober, Harold, 94
Oliver, Mary, 23, 25, 118, 121,
  126, 127, 156
Orwell, Sonia, 231, 255
Ouezzani, Mohammed, 104,
  111
Owen, Peter, 251-54, 256, 258,
  259, 285, 291

Perkins, Helvetia, 6, 26, 27, 29,
  30, 34, 36, 39-41, 43-50, 52,
  55, 58-60, 63, 65, 67, 70-72,
  77, 84, 86-88, 91, 113-115,
  119, 121, 123, 125, 126, 129,
  130, 136, 138-39
Phillips, Genevieve, 16, 17
Plath, Sylvia, 231
Polikoff, Bennet, 106, 199, 226
Price, Frank, 145, 149

Quinza, 81, 108, 127, 125, 133,
  136

Ray, Nick, 50
Reille, Peggy, 143, 147
Resnick, Dr., 199-201, 204-6,
  214, 217, 218, 280
Reynolds, Christopher, 31, 38,
  75, 76, 78, 79

317

318

Jane Bowles was born February 22, 1917, in New York City, the daughter of Sidney Auer and Claire Stajer Auer. Her father died in 1930. She attended Stoneleigh, but her education there ended when she fell from a horse and broke her leg. From 1932 to 1934 she was in a sanatorium in Leysin, Switzerland for treatment of tuberculosis of the knee.

Returning to New York, she began and completed a novel, *Le Phaéton Hypocrite*. (The manuscript has been lost.) In 1937 she met writer-composer Paul Bowles and went to Mexico with him, along with the painter Tonny and his wife. The next year she and Paul were married. They traveled to Central America and to France, then returned to the U.S. She began work on *Two Serious Ladies* in Staten Island and completed it in Mexico.

Jane returned to the U.S. in 1942. The following year *Two Serious Ladies* was published. Three short stories, "A Guatemalan Idyll," "A Day in the Open," and "Plain Pleasures," were published between 1944 and 1946. Her puppet play, *A Quarreling Pair*, was performed.

In 1948 she went to Morocco, following Paul who had gone there a year earlier. She completed her story "Camp Cataract" and "A Stick of Green Candy." She continued to work on her play *In the Summer House* and on her novel *Out in the World* in Tangier, Paris, and New York. The play was performed at the Hedgerow Theater in 1951 and was subsequently produced in Ann Arbor, Michigan and in New York. After the production she returned to Tangier.

In 1957 she suffered a stroke and went to England for treatment. She returned to New York the following year and was hospitalized in White Plains. At the end of 1958 she went back to Tangier with Paul. In 1965 *Two Serious Ladies* was published in England. In 1966 *Plain Pleasures*, her collection of stories, was published in England and her *Collected Works* was published in the U.S.

Her health declined and she was institutionalized in a psychiatric hospital in Málaga, Spain in 1967. She returned to Tangier for a short period of time but then was rehospitalized in the Clínica de los Angeles in Málaga. She died there May 4, 1973.

A native of New York City, Millicent Dillon currently lives in San Francisco. Her publications include *Baby Perpetua and Other Stories* (The Viking Press, 1971), *The One in the Back Is Medea* [a novel] (The Viking Press, 1973), and *A Little Original Sin: The Life and Work of Jane Bowles* (Holt, Rinehart and Winston, 1981). She has also published a number of short stories and essays.